Your
CHRISTIAN
Vocation

Your CHRISTIAN Vocation

Ave Maria Press AVE Notre Dame, Indiana

The Subcommittee of the Catechism, United States Conference of Catholic Bishops, has found this text, copyright 2020, to be in conformity with the *Catechism of the Catholic Church.*

Nihil Obstat: Reverend Monsignor Michael Heintz, PhD

  Censor librorum

Imprimatur: Most Reverend Kevin C. Rhoades

  Bishop of Fort Wayne–South Bend

Given at: Fort Wayne, Indiana, on 24 June 2019

The *Nihil Obstat* and *Imprimatur* are official declarations that a book or pamphlet is free of doctrinal or moral error. No implication is contained therein that those who have granted the *Nihil Obstat* or *Imprimatur* agree with its contents, opinions, or statements expressed.

Scripture texts in this work are taken from the *New American Bible, revised edition* © 2010, 1991, 1986, 1970 Confraternity of Christian Doctrine, Washington, DC, and are used by permission of the copyright owner. All Rights Reserved. No part of the *New American Bible* may be reproduced in any form without permission in writing from the copyright owner.

English translation of the *Catechism of the Catholic Church* for the United States of America copyright © 1994, United States Catholic Conference, Inc.—Libreria Editrice Vaticana. Used with permission.

Catechetical Writing Team

Sarah Kisling

Jackie Arnold

Michael Amodei

Theological Consultant

Reverend Monsignor Michael J. Heintz, PhD

Associate Professor of Systematic Theology

Mount Saint Mary's University

Pedagogical Consultant

Michael J. Boyle, PhD

Director, Andrew M. Greeley Center for Catholic Education

Loyola University Chicago

© 2020 by Ave Maria Press

www.avemariapress.com

Founded in 1865, Ave Maria Press is a ministry of the United States Province of Holy Cross.

Paperback: ISBN-13 978-1-59471-745-1

E-book: ISBN-13 978-1-59471-746-8

Cover images Getty Images.

Cover and text design by Christopher D. Tobin.

Printed and bound in the United States of America.

ENGAGING MINDS, HEARTS, AND HANDS for FAITH

An education that is complete is the one in which hands and heart are engaged as much as the mind. We want to let our students try their learning in the world and so make prayers of their education.

Bl. Basil Moreau
Founder of the Congregation of Holy Cross

In this text you will

 undertake a thorough investigation of several specific Christian states of life, including consecrated life, committed single life, marriage, and the priesthood.

 learn a prayerful discernment process that will aid you in responding to God's call for your life.

 understand that because no vocation is lived in isolation, you must interact with other people and be at their service.

CONTENTS

INTRODUCTION:
CALLING
YOU TO COMMITMENT

World YOUTH Day LEGACY

After a large number of young people turned out for a gathering for the International Year of Youth in Rome in 1985, Pope John Paul II decided to initiate a regular youth gathering now known as World Youth Day. He told the College of Cardinals that year that "the whole Church, in union with the Successor of Peter, must be more and more committed, globally, to youth, and young adults—and to their anxieties and concerns and to their openness, hopes, and expectations."[1]

World Youth Days are an important legacy of the historic papacy of St. John Paul II, who was canonized in 2014 by Pope Francis. Nevertheless, he always insisted that the origins of World Youth Day were with the energy and initiative of the young people themselves. Pope Benedict XVI and Pope Francis have continued the tradition.

At a recent World Youth Day, Pope Francis challenged the attendees:

> We can say that World Youth Day *begins today and continues tomorrow, in your homes*, since that is where Jesus wants to meet you from now on. The Lord doesn't want to remain in this beautiful city or in cherished memories alone. He wants to enter your homes, to dwell in your daily lives: in your studies, your first years of work, your friendships and affections, your hopes and dreams. How greatly he desires that you bring all this to him in prayer! (Final Homily, World Youth Day 2016)

FOCUS QUESTION

Are you **WILLING** to make a **LIFELONG COMMITMENT**?

INTRODUCTION
You Are at a Crossroads

MAIN IDEA
As you near high school graduation, it is important to formulate and ponder important life questions in consideration of making lifelong commitments.

As you are looking to finish high school soon, you have probably heard *the* question more than once: "*What's next?*" Perhaps this question excites you, maybe it frightens you, or it could even just leave you numb. Regardless, you are at a crossroads moment in your life. You might be asking yourself things such as:

Should I go onto college?

Which college should I attend?

Should I enter the workforce?

Should I join the military?

Should I take a year to do volunteer work?

Should I live at home or move away?

There is little doubt that this time in your life is one of the most anxious and exciting that you will ever experience. Whatever you decide to do after high school graduation, your life will be different than it is now. Your school days won't be governed by homeroom attendance, ringing bells or blaring horns to separate school periods, and daily assignments. Your social life will be different too. Even if you are not going away to college, some of your friends probably

NOTE TAKING

Identifying Details. Use a chart like this one to keep track of details about three main points introduced in this section.

What are some things that might change in the next year of your life?	What are some distractions you face that keep you from self-reflection?	What are some things you associate with lifelong commitment?
• Where I live	• Social media	• Marriage

are. Your relationship with your parents is likely to change as well. If you live away from them, you will communicate with them differently: primarily by talking on the phone, texting, or writing emails. And when you come home for holidays and the summer, it may take some time to reestablish yourself in the rhythm of family life.

"*What's next?*" and all of the concerns around this question are topics that you must ponder earnestly. The ancient philosopher Socrates famously said that the unexamined life is not worth living. Unfortunately, the modern world offers many distractions. You may check your phone as soon as you wake up in the morning, blast music while getting ready for school, engross yourself again in social media on the way to school, chat live with friends every free moment during your school day, incessantly sift through interesting web news and social media while doing your homework, and end your day by falling asleep while texting. Days can pass without any type of meaningful self-reflection. This is problematic because the crucial first step in deciding what to do with your life is a careful examination of your hopes, desires, fears, strengths, and weaknesses.

Considering God's Invitation

Sometimes the very thought of commitment can be intimidating. Today's world offers distractions that are not only endless but often fleeting. What caught your interest yesterday may bore you today. The news story at the beginning of this chapter recounts the massive success of World Youth Days. Pope Francis challenged the young volunteers at a World Youth Day in Rio de Janeiro:

> Today, . . . they say that it is not worth making a lifelong commitment, making a definitive decision, "forever," because we do not know what tomorrow will bring. I ask you, instead, to be revolutionaries, . . . to swim against the tide; yes, I am asking you to rebel against this culture that sees everything as temporary and that ultimately believes you are incapable of responsibility, that . . . you are incapable of true love. I have confidence in you and I pray for you. Have the courage "to swim against the tide." (Address to Volunteers, World Youth Day 2013)

Pope Francis expressed his confidence that you can indeed dedicate yourself to something bigger than yourself for your entire life, even if the culture says otherwise. And he was not referring to just any commitment.

The pope was talking about **vocation**. This course will address the meaning of vocation in depth, but to introduce a brief definition in the meantime: a vocation is an invitation from God. It comes from the Latin verb *vocare*, meaning "to call" or "to cry out." Often, the word *vocation* is used synonymously for one's **primary vocation**, or state of life; you will examine the primary vocations in Chapter 1.

As you stand at this particular intersection of your present life and your future life, those around you will very likely continue to ask you, "*What's next?*" This course offers several resources to help you examine your life in the light of a divine calling.

---

vocation The calling or destiny one has in this life and the hereafter.

primary vocation (state of life) The specific path God has for someone on his path to holiness. Primary vocations are marked by vows and/or a sacrament. The traditionally recognized primary vocations are marriage, priesthood, and the consecrated life.

FRIENDSHIP

The people with whom you chose to associate and share your life can help or hinder your choices and self-examination. The Book of Sirach gives a good insight into the gift of a good friend:

> Faithful friends are a sturdy shelter;
>   whoever finds one finds a treasure.
> Faithful friends are beyond price,
>   no amount can balance their worth.
> Faithful friends are life-saving medicine;
>   those who fear God will find them.
> Those who fear the Lord enjoy stable friendship,
>   for as they are, so will their neighbors be. (Sir 6:14–17)

A true friend is someone who can walk with you in your life and help you in your relationship with Christ. Though you are called to treat everyone with the love of Christ, true friendship differs from the relationship you might have with someone who has a similar interest or objective, such as a teammate or a person you work with. A true friend is not merely a party buddy or a person you enjoy just for social purposes. A true friend is someone with whom you mutually work for each other's good. A true friend should call you—in the words of C. S. Lewis in his book *The Last Battle*—"onward and upward" toward what is best for you: ultimately, God.

ASSIGNMENT

The friendship of King David and Jonathan, the son of Israel's first king, Saul, is well known. Read part of their story in 1 Samuel 18:1–5, 20:1–42. Using at least two Scripture references, write a one-page report that describes some of the qualities that made up their friendship.

SECTION ASSESSMENT

NOTE TAKING

Use the chart you created to help you answer the following questions.

1. How do you understand *self-reflection*?
2. What are two parts of your life that need your attention now?

VOCABULARY

3. Write a sentence using the term *vocation* as it applies to some goals and dreams you have for your own life.

APPLICATION

4. What are two important decisions you will have to make over the next year? Write some thoughts on how you will approach these decisions.

SECTION 1
The Difference between Vocations and Careers

Sometimes a person's vocation is associated with a career. But a vocation is different from a career or job. A career builds on the kinds of work you have aptitude for and like to do. Careers are different from jobs too; whereas you may have several jobs in your lifetime, you may change careers much less frequently.

Vocations come from God and carry a deeper meaning than a job or a career. The definition of *vocation* in the Glossary of the *Catechism of the Catholic Church* says that vocations are "the calling or destiny we have in this life and hereafter. God has created the human person to love and serve him; the fulfillment of this vocation is eternal happiness."

Careers, by contrast, tend to serve earthly concerns, such as making money to provide for your human needs, building up a skill set, achieving success, or serving society. One doesn't necessarily have to believe in God to have a strong professional life. In short, careers or professions have a *horizontal dimension*, in that they are connected with things of this world, whereas a vocation has a *vertical dimension*, in that it reflects your relationship with God. No matter how wonderful your job or career is, it will never completely fulfill you. Chapter 1 reminds you that only God can ultimately satisfy your deepest desires.

NOTE TAKING

Similarities and Differences. From the section material, determine the similarities and differences between career and vocation. Under "Career" and "Vocation" write characteristics of each.

Career	Vocation

The Catholic Medical Association is an organization that supports future physicians to live and promote the principles of the Catholic faith in the science and practice of medicine. Research the group if you have an interest in pursuing the field of medicine.

How Careers Serve Vocations

This is not to say that careers are unimportant. Quite the contrary. Careers can often be a way to share in Christ's work of serving and loving people. Careers offer opportunities to share your faith with others. And certainly your work can serve your vocation. Fr. James McTavish, a Scottish doctor who became a priest, wrote about how a Catholic doctor can make his or her work vocational:

> I always encourage doctors . . . telling them that they have the great privilege in their work of treating the sick, and when they touch the sick person they are touching Christ himself. In a more mystical way they can also recall the words in the institution of the Eucharist: "This is my Body." Those words are true not only in the Mass on Sunday but also in the operating [room] or clinic on Monday. ("Formation of a Catholic Physician," *Linacre Quarterly*, February 2015)

You can apply this approach of seeing Christ in others to many careers. For example, a lawyer preparing the estates of older people can view the connection of aiding this person in need as an encounter with Christ. And yet, if a doctor is asked to perform an immoral medical procedure or an accountant is pressured into illegally altering records, they must always make their choice based on their Christian vocation—in these cases by declining to engage in the immoral medical procedure or the immoral altering of records.

Or consider the man whose primary vocation is husband and father. He fosters a career and works at his job to provide for his family. Serving his family in such a manner can lead him closer to God. However, in order to better serve his primary vocation of marriage and fatherhood, he may have to decline a promotion at work if he knows that the time commitment and travel required of the new job would cause undue upheaval and discord for his family. One of the key ways to discern among choices involving career and vocation is to ask yourself: Does this choice lead me closer to or farther away from heaven?

SECTION ASSESSMENT

NOTE TAKING

Use the chart you made to help you answer the following questions.

1. How are vocations and careers similar?
2. How are they different?

COMPREHENSION

3. What are differences between a job and a career?
4. What is one of the key ways to discern among choices involving career and vocation?

CRITICAL THINKING

5. Explain the *horizontal dimension* of a career and the *vertical dimension* of a vocation. Share an example of how each of these dimensions might impact your vocation someday.

What Is Discernment?

MAIN IDEA
Discernment is the process of making decisions in light of what God wants for you.

NOTE TAKING

Summarizing Steps. List the steps of discernment introduced in this section; include in parentheses, as necessary, actions that support each step.

1. **Acknowledge that God loves and cares for you. (Do this through prayer.)**
2.
3. **Take active steps toward a decision. (For example, visit a convent or monastery.)**
4.

At this crossroads moment in your life, you will have many decisions to make. God is involved in every choice in your life, big and small. You should make sure to remember this and invite him into the choices you make through prayer. Sometimes it is easy to recognize the direction in which God is leading you. This is especially true when you have to choose between moral and immoral actions. For example, it is straightforward to know that God does not want you to cheat on an exam. It is clearly better for you to learn the information for the course than to steal your classmate's work, which is a violation of the Seventh Commandment.

However, when you are choosing between things that could all be good for you, such as different universities or college majors, the process merits **discernment**. The word *discernment* comes from the Latin roots *dis*, which means "off or away," and *cernere*, which means "to distinguish or separate." This means that discernment is distinguishing what God wants for you and separating out the rest. Your **free will** is an important component of discernment. Free will is your ability to choose with your reason, not merely instinct. It is an essential aspect of your humanity. Even though you, like all humans, have free will, not every choice you make leads to your greater freedom. Choosing what is God's will for you will always lead to greater personal freedom. This freedom is sometimes referred to as "freedom for excellence"—when you choose the good, you have greater freedom to live out your humanity more fully.

> **discernment** The process of discovering what God wants of you in a given situation.
>
> **free will** The capacity to choose among alternatives. Free will is "the power, rooted in reason and will . . . to perform deliberate actions on one's own responsibility" (*CCC*, 1731). True freedom is at the service of what is good and true.

Steps in the Discernment Process

It's hard to believe at times, but God loves you even more than you could possibly love yourself. He wants your happiness and fulfillment even more than you desire it. If you are convinced of this reality, you know that following his will is always better for you, though it may not be easy. Acknowledging the truth of God's love for you is the first step of discernment. Connected with this first step is the necessity for prayer: you can only know what God wants by listening to him and reflecting on his Word through, for example, reading Sacred Scripture.

A second step in discernment is gathering information about your various options. For example, if you are discerning your college major, you will need to know how many years it would take to finish the major and what courses are required.

A third step in discernment involves taking active steps toward a decision. For example, you may think the Lord is calling you to be a religious sister or brother. In this case, part of this discernment step would be actually visiting a convent or monastery to see what the life there is like. During this time of action, you would seek the **fruits of the Holy Spirit**, such as peace and joy, as a way to confirm the decision you should make.

Eventually, your final step will be to make a decision. If you did your best to work with God's grace in discerning his will, you can have hope that though the path may be difficult, in the end it will lead to your greater happiness. More information on how to discern your vocation is in the Appendix subsection "Next Steps for Discerning Your Vocation."

> **fruits of the Holy Spirit** "The perfections that the Holy Spirit forms in us as the 'first fruits' of eternal glory. The tradition of the Church identifies twelve fruits of the Holy Spirit: charity, joy, peace, patience, kindness, goodness, generosity, gentleness, faithfulness, modesty, self-control, and chastity" (*CCC*, Glossary).

12 FRUITS of the Holy Spirit

charity
joy
peace
patience
kindness
goodness
generosity
gentleness
faithfulness
modesty
self-control
chastity

Growing Your Faith in COLLEGE

As you prayerfully discern your "*What's next?*" after high school, you may well choose to go to a college or university. Something to keep in mind as you are discerning your options is how you will keep your faith strong in these years. Unfortunately, recent statistics paint a dire picture, with one study maintaining that nearly 80 percent of baptized Catholics have stopped practicing the Catholic faith by the age of twenty-three.[2] Studies have also shown that often college-aged Catholics who leave the Church did not make one premeditated, intentional decision to do so; rather, they just stopped going to Mass, stopped praying, and stopped taking time to see how Catholicism was relevant in their lives. These small, daily decisions eventually led to a complete withdrawal from the practice of faith.

While the university or college you choose will not be responsible for making sure you continue to practice your Catholic faith, most have programs that help you foster your faith while living a vibrant life on campus. Here are a few examples:

- **Catholic colleges and universities.** There are hundreds of Catholic colleges and universities in the United States. They provide theology courses that will help you learn about the faith. Many of these universities have parishes and campus ministry programs associated with them so that students may grow in their relationship with God and with fellow Catholics. For a full list of Catholic colleges in the United States, visit the "Catholic Colleges and Universities in the United States" page at www.usccb.org.

- **Newman Centers.** These are places of ministry at non-Catholic universities. They are named in honor of St. John Henry Newman, a famous British cardinal and academic who was a convert to the Catholic faith. Newman Centers usually provide Mass and the sacraments, along with community-building activities and fellowship. You can research either through your intended college or through the Newman Connection site to see if there is a Newman Center nearby.

- **Fellowship of Catholic University Students (FOCUS).** This is a successful campus outreach program in which young missionaries lead Bible studies and other initiatives to encourage college students into a deeper relationship with Christ. FOCUS also has specific programs geared toward those involved in collegiate athletics and fraternity and sorority life. FOCUS missionaries have a presence at more than one hundred campuses in the United States.

- **St. Paul's Outreach (SPO).** Another program that sends young missionaries to help build up Catholic communities on college campuses, SPO is known for its enthusiastic evangelistic outreach. They often have retreats, prayer events, and other formation programs on campus to help foster the faith of college students.

SECTION ASSESSMENT

NOTE TAKING

Use the list you created to help you answer the following questions.

1. What is the first step of discernment?
2. What does it mean to gather information about various options?
3. What is an example of an active step a person can take toward making a decision?

COMPREHENSION

4. What are the roots of the word *discernment*?
5. When do you need to use the process of discernment?

VOCABULARY

6. What is the role of your *free will* in the discernment process?

REFLECTION

7. How is prayer part of the discernment process?

Section Summaries

Focus Question

Are you willing to make a lifelong commitment?

Complete one of the following:

 Define the term *vow* in a religious sense (see *CCC*, Glossary) and from the dictionary. How are they the same? How do they differ?

 Describe a decision you have already made that will have lifelong ramifications.

 Rate yourself on a scale of 1 to 5 (with 5 being excellent) on how good you are at keeping commitments. Explain your rating. Share an example of a time you kept (or broke) a commitment.

INTRODUCTION
You Are at a Crossroads

This is a time in your life in which you will have to make many decisions. Self-reflection is important when looking at your future. Some of these choices involve a commitment of your life, such as to a vocation.

 Share about a recent time when someone has asked you, "*What's next?*" How did you reply? Respond in one or two paragraphs.

SECTION 1
The Difference between Vocations and Careers

A vocation is answering a call from God in your life. Vocations tend to have a *vertical dimension*, concerning how you relate to God. A career is what you dedicate yourself to in a professional sense. A career should always be at the service of, not in opposition to, one's vocation. Careers typically have more of a *horizontal dimension*, helping you to connect to the world.

 Read the complete definition of *vocation* from the Glossary of the *Catechism of the Catholic Church*. Summarize three additional components of the definition not introduced in Section 1.

SECTION 2

What Is Discernment?

Discernment is the process of discovering what God wants for you, even when you are deciding between two good choices. Key steps to discernment include gathering information and, especially, prayer.

Name something in your life that needs discernment (for example: choosing a major, choosing a college, deciding upon a summer job). List some practical steps you can take to discern this decision.

Chapter Assignments

Choose and complete at least one of the following three assignments assessing your understanding of the material in this chapter.

1. Choosing a Major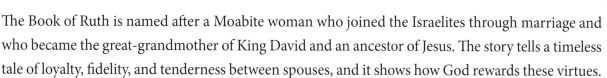

Determine three possible college majors you might consider based on your skills and interests. Answer each question in writing.

1. Assess your existing skills. In what subjects do you perform well at school? What are some other tasks you do well at home or work? What are some talents others have told you that you possess?

2. Identify your personal interests. What is something that inspires you? What do you enjoy doing? What do you want to achieve?

3. Think about some life goals. What are your main motivations for a career? Do you want to work for a large organization or on your own? Why?

4. Think about your relationship with God. How will study in this field and a subsequent related career help to improve your relationship with God?

Write up an assessment of your skills and interests. Then work through one or more college websites (search "choosing a major" on the websites) to attempt to match your profile with a college major. Write a report of your findings.

2. Discernment and the Fruits of the Holy Spirit

Research more about the twelve fruits of the Holy Spirit as found in paragraph 1832 of the *Catechism of the Catholic Church,* and write a short definition for each. Then describe a decision you have been trying to discern, such as where to go to school or whether to apply for a certain job, and how the fruits of the Holy Spirit might be expressed in that decision.

3. Lessons from Ruth

The Book of Ruth is named after a Moabite woman who joined the Israelites through marriage and who became the great-grandmother of King David and an ancestor of Jesus. The story tells a timeless tale of loyalty, fidelity, and tenderness between spouses, and it shows how God rewards these virtues.

The story begins in Moab, a land hostile to Israel, where the Israelites Naomi, her husband, and their two sons have settled to avoid famine. After Naomi's husband and two sons die, she decides to go back to Israel because the famine has ended. Her two daughters-in-law, Orpah and Ruth, accompany her. But Naomi encourages them to stay in Moab with their families.

However, Ruth tells her mother-in-law, "Do not press me to go back and abandon you! Wherever you go I will go, wherever you lodge I will lodge. Your people shall be my people and your God, my God" (Ru 1:16). Ruth goes with Naomi to Israel, where Boaz, a rich landowner and distant relative of her husband, notices her and eventually marries her. Boaz and Ruth's son, Obed, was the father of Jesse, who in turn fathered David, the great king from whose line Jesus was born.

Read the entire Book of Ruth. Then do the following:

- List three qualities that describe Ruth's character. Cite verses that support your descriptions.

- Write three paragraphs about a time when you were loyal to a friend or a friend was loyal to you.

- Why is loyalty important in one's life, especially in one's vocation? Explain in three well-constructed paragraphs.

Faithful Disciple

St. Joan of Arc

Jeanne d'Arc—more commonly known as St. Joan of Arc—was born in 1412 and grew up on a forty-acre farm in the little French village of Domrémy, which had remained loyal to the king of France in the midst of the Hundred Years' War with the English.

Around the age of thirteen, Joan began to hear voices and see visions of angels and saints. She recognized the saints individually as St. Michael the Archangel, St. Margaret of Antioch, and St. Catherine of Alexandria, along with some others. While she rarely discussed the details of these visions, later at her trial she told her accusers, "I saw them with these very eyes, as well as I see you." What the voices of the saints told her was that it would be her role to free France from its enemies.

Of course Joan of Arc met with doubt from those older than her and in authority. But she persevered by sharing her dreams and message with anyone who would listen. She went to a commander in the French army and told him that she was commissioned to win back France's lost kingdom and set the crown upon the head of the

St. Joan of Arc

uncrowned King Charles VII. The commander responded, "What, you? You are only a child." He sent her back to her village and told his advisers that she should have her ears boxed.

Joan did not give up. She said God had spoken to her and inspired the course of her life. She came back time and time again; the commander finally yielded, gave her a troop of soldiers, took off his sword, and gave it to her as well: "Go—and let come what may," he said. Eventually Joan was able to meet with

King Charles himself and convince him and his advisers that it was God and not Satan who had commissioned her.

At age seventeen, with the prince of the king's house and veteran generals as subordinates, she became head of an army set to engage in the pivotal battle of Orléans. While there is historical debate over Joan's exact role in the battle—for example, some insist she had influence over decisions made in battle, while others say she may have only carried a banner—after ten days and three separate assaults on the English at the fortress at Orléans, France did triumph.

Eventually, jealousy within the French army and the lack of support from King Charles led to Joan's capture by the English and trial for witchcraft. One of the most serious charges leveled against her was that she put on men's clothes (which she wore while in battle). Her accusers also said the voices she heard were the devil's.

Joan of Arc was convicted and ordered burned at the stake on May 30, 1431. She confessed her sins and asked for Holy Communion. She held a cross as she suffered a torturous death, crying out the name of Jesus. Joan of Arc's ashes were scattered in the river so that her followers could not venerate them at a shrine. Yet just a few short years later her cause for sainthood was introduced. Pope Benedict XV canonized St. Joan of Arc in 1920. She is the patron saint of France.

Reading Comprehension

1. What did the voices of the saints tell Joan of Arc?

2. What is the name of the pivotal battle Joan of Arc led in the Hundred Years' War?

3. What led to Joan of Arc's arrest and trial by the English?

4. What were the charges leveled against Joan of Arc?

Writing Task

Answer the following questions in complete sentences: How do you hear the voice of God? How is God calling you? How are you enacting God's will?

Explaining the Faith

Isn't the real measure of success in life the degree of one's financial security and material comfort?

It might seem as though money, financial security, and living a comfortable lifestyle make for a successful life, but this is not how Jesus lived or taught. In the Beatitudes (see Matthew 5:1–12), Jesus teaches his disciples what is essential for true happiness. Though the Beatitudes seem to oppose the natural desire for comfort, they encourage you to prioritize holy ways of acting and deepening your relationship with Jesus, rather than depending on things that will pass away such as money, careers, houses, etc. Your ultimate goal in life should be holiness, which is found in a personal relationship with Jesus Christ and in your relationships with and attitudes toward others.

 Writing Task

List the eight Beatitudes from Matthew 5:3–12. Describe how each Beatitude can form virtue in a person that will lead to lasting happiness.

Prayer

Prayer for Discernment

Lord, I know that you love me and that you have great plans for me,

but sometimes I am overwhelmed thinking about my future.

Show me how to walk forward one day at a time.

As I explore the various options that lie before me, help me to listen openly to others and to pay attention
to what is in the depth of my own heart.

May I hear your call to a way of life that will allow me to love as only I can and to serve others with the
special gifts you have given me.

Amen.

YOUR **CALL** TO
HOLINESS

1

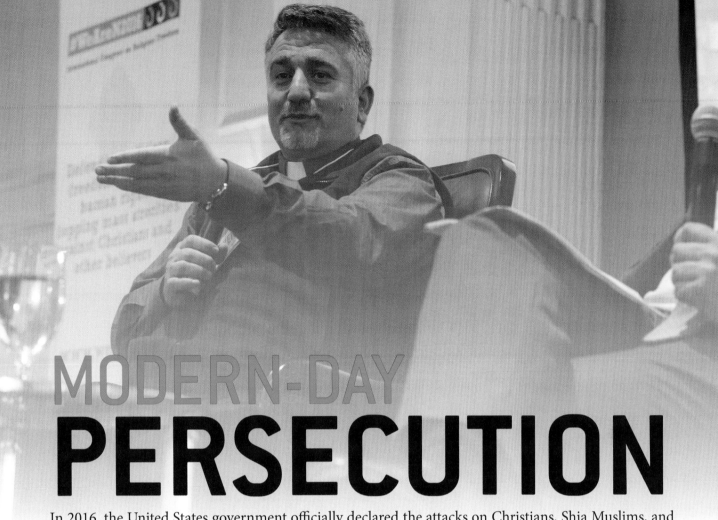

MODERN-DAY
PERSECUTION

In 2016, the United States government officially declared the attacks on Christians, Shia Muslims, and Yazidi (a religious minority) in the Middle East, primarily made by a radical Islamist group known as ISIS (Islamic State in Iraq and Syria), as genocide. Although this declaration was important for humanitarian reasons, it was not a surprise for advocates of the persecuted Christians. They had been decrying for years the attacks on Christians, which regularly included rape, enslavement, kidnapping, and murder.

One story among many reported in the genocide was that of "Khalia," a middle-aged woman captured and held hostage with forty-seven others. "During her fifteen days in captivity, she rebuffed demands to convert, despite a gun being put to her head and a sword to her neck," the report said. "She literally fought off ISIS militants as they tried to rape the girls, and again later when they tried to take a nine-year-old as a bride."[1] Eventually, their captors left the hostages in the desert to walk a long distance to Erbil, Iraq.

Fr. Douglas Al-Bazi (above), a parish priest of the Chaldean Catholic Church in Baghdad, Iraq, who was himself once kidnapped and held captive by a criminal gang, speaks for many Christians living in the Middle East: "Please don't look at me as a hero. Who am I to complain what happened to me? As a priest in Iraq and the Middle East, we live like a one-way mission. We never know when we go out of a church if we will go back alive."[2]

Yet Fr. Al-Bazi maintains a Christlike gaze upon his persecutors, a clear sign of his personal holiness. "We cannot play that game, eye for an eye," he says. "We do love you, we do forgive you, and we actually do feel sorry about you. And the message to you, it is please, put the weapon down and let's open a new page, a page with forgiveness."[3]

FOCUS QUESTION

What is **ESSENTIAL** in **ORDER TO BE HAPPY** in this life and to **ACHIEVE ETERNAL HAPPINESS**?

Chapter Overview

Introduction **Who Are You?**

Section 1 **The Universal Call to Holiness**

Section 2 **Your Personal Call**

Section 3 **The Specific Primary Vocations**

Section 4 **Your Vocation to Self-Giving**

INTRODUCTION
Who Are You?

Self-reflection is important at this crossroads moment of your life. If you have engaged in meaningful introspection, at some point you have probably asked yourself questions such as

- "What is the purpose of my life?"
- "Why am I here?"
- "For what do I exist?"

In order to understand where you should be going with your life, you must begin with another question: "From where did I come?" On the surface, this question may seem unrelated to the others, but in reality they are inseparable. Indeed, knowing where you come from and where you are going illuminates the meaning of your existence in the present.

If you walked into your bedroom and saw a beautiful present, wrapped impeccably with ribbons and bows, most likely your first reaction would be "Who gave this to me?" The beauty and thoughtfulness of the gift would convey to you that the one who gave it knows and loves you.

The same goes for the world around you. Consider that creation is a gift, lovingly fashioned by a Creator. God created the world out of wisdom and love; it is not the result of blind chance. "How

NOTE TAKING

Categorizing Concepts. Draw a concept web like the one below. As you read the subsection "The Human Person," fill in the blank circles with the attributes unique to the human person.

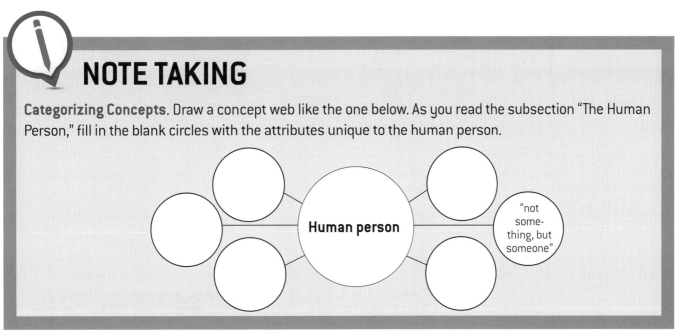

Michelangelo's The Creation of Adam—*which depicts God giving Adam the spark of life—is one of nine frescos that adorn the ceiling of of the Sistine chapel in Vatican City. Each of the nine frescos depicts important scenes from the Book of Genesis: the first three are devoted to the creation of the world, the second three to the creation and Fall of Adam and Eve, and the last three to the story of Noah.*

varied are your works, LORD! In wisdom you have made them all; the earth is full of your creatures" (Ps 104:24). God creates out of goodness, and his creation shares in this goodness.

Not only is the world God's gift to you, but you are also part of his creation, the pinnacle of his work. He created *you* out of wisdom and goodness. Your origin is with God. Creation is the God's first **covenant** with his people; that is, he created you in order to be in relationship with you. Adam and Eve rejected this covenant (their rejection is known as **the Fall**), but God continued to invite his people to loving relationship with him over and over again, as recorded in the Old

> **covenant** "A solemn agreement between human beings or between God and a human being involving mutual commitments or guarantees" (*CCC*, Glossary).
>
> **the Fall** The disobedience of Adam and Eve, which introduced sin, death, and their effects into the world.

Testament. This offering of a covenantal relationship culminated in God the Father's sending his only Son, Jesus Christ, to redeem the world and offer all people the opportunity for salvation. Christ is the new and definitive covenant for all people. Creation is the foundation for God's saving action, which was fulfilled in Christ.

When you look at creation and examine the beauty of God's work, you cannot escape looking into the saving actions of the life, Death, and Resurrection of Christ. "The mystery of Christ casts conclusive light on the mystery of creation and reveals the end for which 'in the beginning God created the heavens and the earth': from the beginning, God envisaged the glory of the new creation in Christ" (*CCC*, 280, quoting Genesis 1:1).

God created the world to glorify him. God created you to bring him glory through the way you live your life: "In love he destined us for adoption to himself through Jesus Christ, in accord with the favor of his will, for the praise of the glory of his grace that he granted us in the beloved" (Eph 1:4b–6). St. Irenaeus said that God is glorified when people are "'fully alive'" (*CCC*, 294). But what does this mean? What does it mean to be human?

The Human Person

Yes, the human person is part of creation, but you are different from all of creation. Humans are the pinnacle of creation. A human person is not something but rather *someone*. Humans are unique in that they are a unity of body and soul. Angelic beings are purely spiritual and the matter of this earth is purely physical, but within the human person is a joining of these spiritual and material worlds. Humans have an immortal soul, which is their spiritual principle, their inner life. The soul is not "trapped" within the body, but rather united to it: the body expresses the soul. Humans have a free will, which, you will recall, means they can choose and make decisions on more than just instinct. Humans also have a rational intellect; they can think and reason in an abstract manner—quite different from animals.

Don't ever forget that you, along with all of humanity, were made in the image and likeness of God. Take a moment to let that truly sink in. You were actually created to be like God, to share in his very life. In fact, humans are only called "persons" because God is a **communion of Persons**, and humans are made in his image. God is a Trinitarian communion of self-gift and love. You image the Trinity most clearly when you give of yourself to another. Section 4 will examine the concept of self-giving more thoroughly.

Even though you were made in God's image, your personal likeness to God has been distorted by sin, first by **Original Sin** and then by your own personal sin. Every person can understand the brokenness that sin causes. For example, if you've ever felt hurt by gossip or felt guilty after yelling at your parents, you have experienced the effects of the sins of others and your own sin. But Jesus Christ brings Good News: "It is in Christ, Redeemer and Savior, that the divine image, disfigured in man by the first sin, has been restored to its original beauty and ennobled by the grace of God" (*CCC*, 1701).

The covenant God offers his people in Christ is not some vague, general concept. Rather, it is a specific and deeply personal invitation to *you* to share in his very life. You received the redemptive grace of Christ at your Baptism. It was through the waters of this **sacrament** that you were made a new creation, "washed clean . . . from all the squalor of the life of old" (Rite of Baptism) and called to life in the Holy Spirit. This life is strengthened in the Sacrament of Confirmation, nourished by the Eucharist, and restored by the graces of the Sacrament of Penance.

The answer to the question "From where did I come?" is "From God." He created you out of love to share in his life. Section 1 will address the question "Where am I going?"—the other key to understanding your current state in life.

---

communion of Persons A complete giving-of-self, shown perfectly in the life of the Divine Persons of the Blessed Trinity.

Original Sin The personal sin of the first two people, called Adam and Eve, which in an analogous way describes the fallen state of human nature into which all generations are born. Adam and Eve transmitted Original Sin to their human descendants. Christ Jesus came to save the world from Original Sin and all personal sin.

sacrament "An efficacious sign of grace, instituted by Christ and entrusted to the Church, by which divine life is" given to those who receive it, "through the work of the Holy Spirit" (*CCC*, 1131).

SECTION ASSESSMENT

NOTE TAKING

Use the concept web you created to help you answer the following questions.

1. Name six ways the human person is unique within creation.
2. What does it mean to say a human has an immortal soul?

COMPREHENSION

3. Why can humans be called "persons"?

VOCABULARY

4. Define *covenant*.

CRITICAL THINKING

5. What does it mean to say that the mystery of Christ "casts conclusive light" upon creation?

SECTION 1
The Universal Call to Holiness

MAIN IDEA
You will feel most fulfilled when you have union with Christ. This is called *holiness* or *saintliness*.

Everyone wants to be happy. This is the common human experience that transcends time and culture. Every person searches for happiness in various ways, such as in friendships, entertainment, or success. However, even the greatest moment here on earth will never completely satisfy you. The party always comes to a close, the friendship goes through difficult periods, the money runs out. Every moment of happiness always ends. This is because you were made for a deeper, more profound fulfillment than anything this world can offer.

God created you out of love. When he created you, he created you *for himself*. "The desire for God is written in the human heart, because man is created by God and for God; and God never ceases to draw man to himself. Only in God will he find the truth and happiness he never stops searching for" (*CCC*, 27). Nothing on this earth will ever fully satisfy. This is because you were made for more than this earth: you were made for communion with the infinite God. When you recognize and rejoice in the love God has for you, you are living out the full truth of your existence.

NOTE TAKING

Main Ideas. Create a chart like this one to help you organize your answers to the following questions.

What were you created for?	
What is holiness?	
Who is called to be a saint?	
What is your destination?	

It Is Jesus That You Seek

At World Youth Day in Rome in 2000, Pope John Paul II gave a famous address to the youth. Carefully read his words below, and answer the questions that follow.

It is Jesus in fact that you seek when you dream of happiness; he is waiting for you when nothing else you find satisfies you; he is the beauty to which you are so attracted; it is he who provoked you with that thirst for fullness that will not let you settle for compromise; it is he who urges you to shed the masks of a false life; it is he who reads in your hearts your most genuine choices, the choices that others try to stifle. It is Jesus who stirs in you the desire to do something great with your lives, the will to follow an ideal, the refusal to allow yourselves to be ground down by mediocrity, the courage to commit yourselves humbly and patiently to improving yourselves and society, making the world more human and more fraternal. (Address at Vigil of Prayer)

ASSIGNMENT

Answer the following questions.

1. What did Pope John Paul II mean when he said, "It is Jesus in fact that you seek when you dream of happiness"?

2. What do you think he meant by "it is he who urges you to shed the masks of a false life"? What are the "false masks" in your own life?

3. What great thing is Jesus stirring you to do with your life?

Holiness Is a Gift

God made you for the deeply profound, forever kind of happiness that only he can provide. Your happiness will not be complete until you have union with God. This is called **holiness**. To be holy means to be sanctified—that is, set apart for God, the Holy One. To be holy is the calling of every person: "This is the will of God, your holiness" (1 Thes 4:3). The **universal call to holiness** is rooted in Baptism, by which a person is conformed to Christ and brought into the very life of the Blessed Trinity. Baptism calls a person to the fullness of Christian life and perfect charity. Christ said that you must "be perfect, as your heavenly Father is perfect" (Mt 5:48).

Perfection may seem impossible. That is because it *is* impossible for you to be perfect by your own powers. Like all people, you are wounded and broken by sinfulness. Only by God's grace can you be united with him and thus obtain sanctity. Because holiness is an objective gift from Christ offered at Baptism, this gift makes you a son or daughter of God, thus sharing in his divine nature.

To put it succinctly, to be holy is to know and love Jesus and to conform your life to his. Pope Francis has emphasized repeatedly that although holiness is indeed for everyone, it is always a divine gift to be received: "First of all, we must bear clearly in mind that sanctity is not something we can procure for ourselves, that we can obtain by our own qualities and abilities. Sanctity is a gift, it is a gift granted to us by the Lord Jesus, when He takes us to Himself and clothes us in Himself, He makes us like Him" (General Audience, November

19, 2014). Because holiness is about having a relationship with the Lord, it is requisite that you cooperate with God's grace by striving for holiness. You are able to access this life of grace in the Church primarily through the sacraments. Holiness is the defining reality of the Church, the Bride of Christ. Jesus "loved the church and handed himself over for her to sanctify her . . . that she might be holy and without blemish" (Eph 5:25–27). The promises of this world will always leave you empty. It is only by pursuing holiness that your deepest desires will be satisfied. Carefully read these further words of Pope Francis:

> God says to you: do not be afraid of holiness, do not be afraid to aim high, to let yourself be loved and purified by God, do not be afraid to let yourself be guided by the Holy Spirit. Let

> **holiness** The state of being set apart for God.
>
> **universal call to holiness** The call to all Christians, no matter their state of life, to be sanctified. It is based on Jesus' words in the Sermon on the Mount: "So be perfect, just as your heavenly Father is perfect" (Mt 5:48).

us be infected by the holiness of God. Every Christian is called to sanctity (cf. *Lumen Gentium*, nn. 19–42); and sanctity does not consist especially in doing extraordinary things, but in allowing God to act. . . . Let us not lose the hope of holiness, let us follow this path. Do we want to be saints? The Lord awaits us, with open arms; he waits to accompany us on the path to sanctity. (General Audience, October 2, 2013)

Pope Francis emphasized that holiness is not an opportunity just for a few but rather a calling for everyone. That said, your holiness is not ultimately about your own actions: holiness consists primarily in allowing God to act in you.

Holiness Is about Becoming a Saint

Pope Francis asks, "Do we want to be saints?" You can experience holiness here on earth through a relationship with Jesus Christ. But this relationship and your quest for saintliness will ultimately be fulfilled in heaven. You were created to live forever in the love of the Blessed Trinity. On a basic level, a **saint** is any person in heaven. And since you are called to the **beatific vision** of heaven, you are called to be a saint.

The Church goes through a process of **canonization** for certain saints, to state that they are indeed with God in heaven. The canonization process is not intended to hold up saints as some unattainable ideal but rather to show that they practiced "heroic virtue"

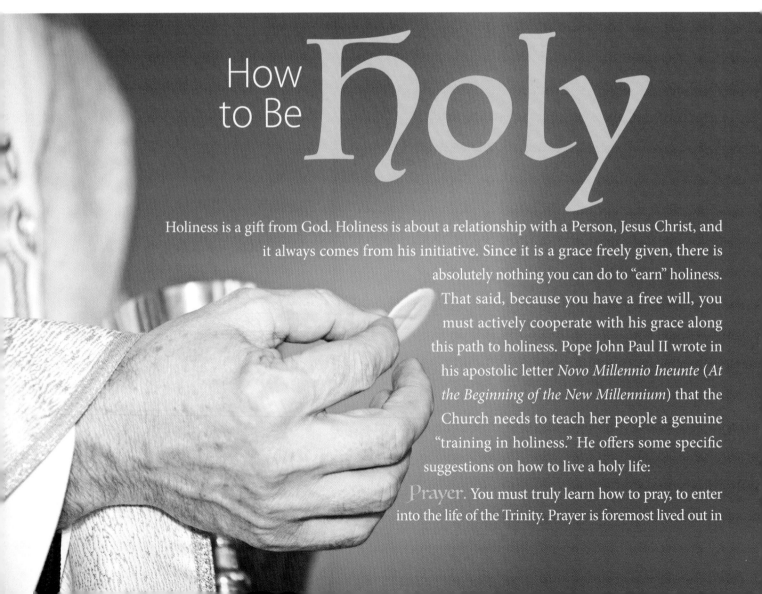

How to Be Holy

Holiness is a gift from God. Holiness is about a relationship with a Person, Jesus Christ, and it always comes from his initiative. Since it is a grace freely given, there is absolutely nothing you can do to "earn" holiness. That said, because you have a free will, you must actively cooperate with his grace along this path to holiness. Pope John Paul II wrote in his apostolic letter *Novo Millennio Ineunte* (*At the Beginning of the New Millennium*) that the Church needs to teach her people a genuine "training in holiness." He offers some specific suggestions on how to live a holy life:

Prayer. You must truly learn how to pray, to enter into the life of the Trinity. Prayer is foremost lived out in and that they are our "models and intercessors" (*CCC*, 828). In other words, the declaration of saints affirms the holiness of God working in his people, and thus it gives you hope to become a saint too.

> **saint** "The 'holy one' who leads a life in union with God through the grace of Christ and receives the reward of eternal life. The Church is called the communion of saints, of the holy ones" (*CCC*, Glossary).
>
> **beatific vision** "The contemplation of God in heavenly glory, a gift of God which is a constitutive element of the happiness (or *beatitude*) of heaven" (*CCC*, Glossary).
>
> **canonization** "The solemn declaration by the Pope that a deceased member of the faithful may be proposed as a model and intercessor to the Christian faithful and venerated as a saint on the basis of the fact that the person lived a life of heroic virtue or remained faithful to God through martyrdom" (*CCC*, Glossary).

St. Thérèse of Lisieux felt the call to religious life and entered the same Carmelite order that her two older sisters had when she was only fifteen. She was canonized in 1925, only twenty-eight years after her death.

the liturgy of the Church, but it must also take on a personal dimension. Living a full life of prayer is the "secret of a truly vital Christianity, which has no reason to fear the future, because it returns continually to the sources and finds in them new life" (*Novo Millennio Ineunte*, 32).

The Eucharist. The Mass is "the summit towards which the Church's action tends and at the same time the source from which comes all her strength" (*Sacrosanctum Concilium*, 10). This means that the Eucharist is both the highest point and the foundation for the entire Christian life. If your goal is union with Christ, it would make sense to make an effort to receive worthily his very Body, Blood, soul, and divinity in the Sacrament of the Eucharist. Pope John Paul II emphasized the importance of the Sunday Eucharist; it should be the heart of the Lord's Day that you have set aside for worship of God.

The Sacrament of Penance. Pope John Paul II highlighted the need to be awake to the reality of sin, to be aware of your own weakness and brokenness. However, your sinfulness is nothing compared to salvation offered in Christ. He has bound his graces of forgiveness to the Sacrament of Penance. Partaking of the Sacrament of Penance is essential in the journey to holiness.

The primacy of grace. Sometimes on the path to holiness, you can fall into the trap of thinking that results depend entirely upon your own effort and ability. "God of course asks us really to cooperate with his grace, and therefore invites us to invest all our resources of intelligence and energy in serving the cause of the Kingdom. But it is fatal to forget that 'without Christ we can do nothing' (cf. Jn 15:5)" (*Novo Millennio Ineunte*, 38). Returning again and again to prayer reminds you that the source of all sanctity is God himself.

Listening to and proclaiming the Word. The role of Scripture in your journey of holiness is indispensable. Pope John Paul II encouraged *lectio divina*, which is the prayerful reading of Scripture seeking how it specifically applies to your life. Once you encounter the Word, you become a "servant of the word" and are compelled to share the encounter with others.

This painting by Fra Angelico, The Forerunners of Christ with Saints and Martyrs, *depicts men and women of all ages who dedicated their lives, and often their deaths, to Christ.*

It is important to clear up the misconception that a saint is the "opposite" of a sinner. This is not so. Instead, a saint is a sinner who has embraced the redemptive graces of Christ. Remember that holiness does not mean sinlessness; it means being set apart, ultimately for the happiness of heaven. Becoming a saint is not about stifling yourself; instead, it is about becoming your true self—your most fulfilled, happiest self. A fish was made for water, so it is most free when it is in the water. You were made for sainthood and will be the most fulfilled when you accept this path. Contemporary Catholic writer Peter Kreeft writes:

> You can become a saint. Absolutely no one and nothing can stop you. It is your free choice. Here is one of the truest and most terrifying sentences I have ever read (from William Law's *Serious Call*): "If you will look into your own heart in complete honesty, you must admit that

there is one and only one reason why you are not a saint: you do not wholly want to be."

> That insight is terrifying because it is an indictment. But it is also thrillingly hopeful because it is an offer, an open door. Each of us can become a saint. We really can. (*How to Win the Culture War*)

Your calling is to become a saint. You can choose at every moment whether to say yes to this calling or not. Christians are not supposed to be completely comfortable in this world, because life on earth is not their ultimate destination. St. Thérèse of Lisieux famously said, "The world is your ship, not your home." You were made for heaven. That means both your origin and your destination are with God. This is the answer to the question "Where am I going?"

SECTION ASSESSMENT

NOTE TAKING

Use the chart you made to help you answer the following questions.

1. Why will nothing on this earth fully satisfy you?
2. What does it mean to be holy?

COMPREHENSION

3. Why is it inaccurate to say that a saint is the opposite of a sinner?

CRITICAL THINKING

4. Explain the seeming contradiction that Jesus calls you to perfection and yet perfection is impossible on your own.

APPLICATION

5. Share your reaction to this famous quotation from the French convert Léon Bloy: "The only real sadness, the only real failure, the only great tragedy in life, is not to become a saint."

SECTION 2
Your Personal Call

MAIN IDEA
Your universal vocation is to holiness, but God has a unique path for you to reach this goal. Being a disciple is part of walking this path.

Recall that the term *vocation* comes from a word that means "to call" or "to cry out." A vocation is God calling out to you; it is an invitation from him. A vocation is God crying out to you to achieve the destiny he intends for your life both on earth and in heaven. You are personally called to communion with God the Father through Christ. You cannot find your vocation apart from Christ, who brings light to your specific vocation. This is true for every human person. You are called to holiness. You are called to be a saint in Christ's name.

A Vocation Is a Call

God provides a unique path for every person to reach this ultimate vocation to holiness. God does not just call *people*; he calls *you*. He knew you before you were born (see Jeremiah 1:5). He has counted the hairs on your head (see Luke 12:7). He knows you better than you know yourself.

God revealed himself progressively over time throughout the Old Covenant in order to make his people "capable of responding to him, and of knowing him, and of loving him far beyond [our] own natural capacity" (*CCC*, 52). The fullness of his self-revelation came in the Divine Person of Jesus Christ. "In times past, God spoke in partial and various ways

NOTE TAKING

Identifying Supporting Details. Make a chart like this one. As you read this section, fill in the corresponding details.

Aspects of a vocation	Details
Personal call	
Lived in the Church	
Discipleship	

Mary, who was with the disciples at Pentecost, is known as the "first disciple." Her answer of "yes" to the angel's request of her to be the Mother of God was a human being's first acceptance of Christ.

to our ancestors through the prophets; in these last days, he spoke to us through a son, whom he made heir of all things and through whom he created the universe" (Heb 1:1–2). There is no further Revelation after Christ.

Some people know from a young age what God wants for them. Others may try different directions and their own methods, until they finally find what path is congruent with God's desires. Many aspects of the paths traveled to holiness are the same: there are prayers of petition to do God's will, reception of the sacraments, the offering up of your sufferings, and learning about the faith. While each person's path to holiness is otherwise varied, all paths to holiness do lead to Christ.

Your Vocation Is Lived in the Church

Jesus promised not to leave his people orphans (see John 14:18). He sent the Holy Spirit to guide his people, the Church. Transmission of God's Revelation is entrusted to the Church through two distinct modes: Sacred Scripture and Sacred Tradition. Sacred Scripture refers to the inspired Word of God found in the Bible. Sacred Tradition is the living transmission of the **Deposit of Faith** handed on through the successors of the Apostles. Both Sacred Scripture and Sacred Tradition are safeguarded by the **Magisterium**, the official teaching authority of the Church.

> **Deposit of Faith** The body of saving truths and the core beliefs of Catholicism that are contained in Sacred Scripture and Sacred Tradition and faithfully preserved and handed on by the Magisterium. The Deposit of Faith contains the fullness of God's Revelation.
>
> **Magisterium** The official teaching authority of the Church. Jesus bestowed the right and power to teach in his name on Peter and the Apostles and their successors—that is, the pope and the college of bishops. The authority of the Magisterium extends to specific precepts of the natural law because following these precepts is necessary for salvation.

This means that the Church, the Body of Christ, is crucial to your personal vocation to holiness and to your salvation. The Second Vatican Council emphasized that "it is through Christ's Catholic Church alone, which is the universal help toward salvation, that the fullness of the means of salvation can be obtained" (*CCC*, 816 quoting *Unitatis Redintegratio*, 3). Regarding holiness, the Church herself is holy. "The Church is sanctified by [Christ]; through him and with him she becomes sanctifying. 'All the activities of the Church are directed, as toward their end, to the sanctification of men in Christ and the glorification of God'" (*CCC*, 824, quoting *Sacrosanctum Concilium*, 10). The Church is holy because she is the Bride of Christ; she is joined to Christ's holiness. She also has one of Christ's means to holiness—that is, the sacraments.

Your Vocation Is Lived as a Disciple

Related to the call to holiness within the Church is your responsibility to be a **disciple**. Simply put, a disciple is a follower of Jesus. But discipleship goes deeper than this. Jesus invited his disciples into his own life. He called them to abide in him: "Remain in me, as I remain in you. . . . I am the vine, you are the branches" (Jn 15:4–5). And he declared a bodily communion with his followers: "Whoever eats my flesh and drinks my blood remains in me and I in him" (Jn 6:56).

Thus, to be a disciple means to share in Christ's very life, his "mission, joy, and sufferings" (*CCC*, 787). This leads to an important point about the pursuit of holiness through discipleship: it is not always easy. Jesus said to his disciples, "In the world you will have trouble"; however, he immediately assured them, "but take courage, I have conquered the world" (Jn 16:33). Christian discipleship demands that you take up your cross and follow him. Christ has promised to be united to you in your trials, such as your schoolwork,

Bl. Charles de Foucauld

difficulties with friends and family, and the disappointments of daily life. He won your redemption through the Cross, and you are baptized into this Cross, so that you might share in the Resurrection. Christ remains present to you always in the Catholic Church.

The vocation of each person lived through discipleship in Christ is paradoxically both universal and personal. This means that your personal choice of a vocation will have implications not only for yourself but for others as well.

> **disciple** A person "who accepted Jesus' message to follow him. . . . Jesus associated his disciples with his own life, revealed the mystery of the Kingdom of God to [them], and gave them a share in his mission, his joy, and his sufferings" (*CCC*, Glossary).

♥Abandonment to God's Will

Bl. Charles de Foucauld, who lived as a hermit in Northern Africa after a religious conversion in the early twentieth century, wrote this prayer as a statement of his abandonment to the will of God.

> Father,
>
> I abandon myself into your hands: do with me what you will.
>
> Whatever you may do, I thank you:
>
> I am ready for all, I accept all.
>
> Let only your will be done in me, and in all your creatures—
>
> I wish no more than this, O Lord.
>
> Into your hands I commend my soul;
>
> I offer it to you with all the love of my heart,
>
> for I love you, Lord, and so need to give myself,
>
> to surrender myself into your hands without reserve,
>
> and with boundless confidence,
>
> for you are my Father.
>
> —Bl. Charles de Foucauld

ASSIGNMENT

Research and print three other prayers that speak of surrendering to God's will. Then write your own heart-felt prayer surrendering your own will to the will of God.

SECTION ASSESSMENT

NOTE TAKING

Use the chart you made to help you answer the following questions.

1. How is vocation both personal and universal?
2. Why must a Christian vocation be lived in the Church?
3. What does it mean to be a disciple?

COMPREHENSION

4. What is the importance of the Church in the life of the Christian?

REFLECTION

5. What is the meaning of this statement: "You cannot find your vocation apart from Christ"?

SECTION 3
The Specific Primary Vocations

All people are called to a relationship with Christ, a life of holiness. Then each person has a specific path and calling for his or her own life. The Church has held up certain states of life, known as *primary vocations*, as a means to union with God.

The primary vocations are traditionally categorized as the vocations to marriage, priesthood, and consecrated life. Much of the material in this course is devoted to explaining the discernment of, preparation for, celebration of, and grace-filled effects of these vocations. This section briefly introduces each of these vocational states of life, which later chapters cover in greater detail.

Marriage

Marriage has existed since the beginning of humankind. Note that "Sacred Scripture begins with the creation of man and woman in the image and likeness of God [see Genesis 1:27] and concludes with a vision of 'the wedding feast of the Lamb' [see Revelation 19:7, 9]" (*CCC*, 1602). Marriage is a lifelong union of a man and woman, for their own good and for the purpose of procreation: "The matrimonial covenant, by which a man and a woman establish between themselves a partnership of the whole of life, is by its nature ordered toward the good of the spouses and the procreation

NOTE TAKING

Tree Web. Create a tree web like the one below that helps you remember the different vocational states of life. In the box next to each name, write its meaning.

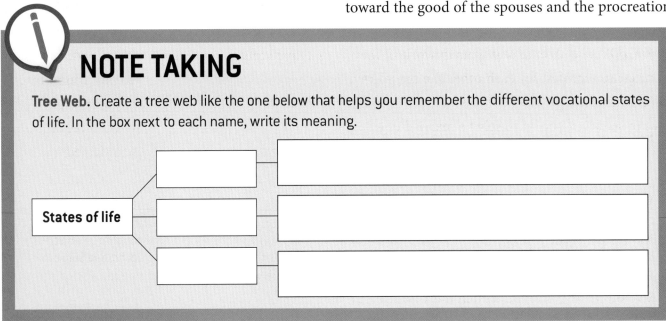

Mass is celebrated at the Church of the Holy Sepulchre in Jerusalem, the place that marks the site of the tomb of Christ.

and education of offspring; this covenant between baptized persons has been raised by Christ the Lord to the dignity of a sacrament" (*CCC*, 1601, quoting *Gaudium et Spes*, 48).

The New Covenant of Christ images the union of Christ and his Church, along with the inner life of the Trinity. The vocation to marriage is one that springs from God's love. A man and woman work in their marriage to manifest for each other the committed and eternal love that God has shown to them. On the basis of statistics, you will likely be married one day. If so, you will be called to a covenantal bond of self-gift to your spouse and children that lasts until death. Chapters 2, 3, 4, and 5 cover the vocation to marriage.

Priesthood

As with marriage, a man enters the vocation to the priesthood through a sacrament; in this case, it is the Sacrament of Holy Orders. The Sacrament of Holy Orders confers a sacred power on the priest for the service of the faithful. Following the example of Jesus, who chose only men to be his Apostles, and the example of the Apostles, who called only men to be bishops, the sacrament is conferred only on baptized men. In the Latin Church, priests live celibate lives and promise to remain celibate as a witness to the Kingdom of God. In the **Eastern Churches**, married men can be priests and deacons, while bishops are chosen among celibate men. The sacrament is received in three degrees—bishop, priest, and deacon. These ordained ministers

> **Eastern Churches** "Churches of the East in union with Rome (the Latin Church), but not of Roman rite, with their own liturgical, theological, and administrative traditions," such as those of the Byzantine, Coptic, and Syriac rites (*CCC*, Glossary).

serve the Church by teaching, by leading worship, and by their governance.

Priests can be members of religious communities—for example, the Jesuits or the Franciscans. A religious-order priest takes the same vows of poverty, chastity, and obedience as the other members of the religious community (i.e., the brothers). The difference is that the religious priest is ordained and a brother is not. Diocesan priests are not members of religious communities. They are ordained to serve in a particular diocese, giving obedience to the local bishop. The diocesan priest makes a promise of celibacy along with the promise of obedience. Most often, his bishop assigns a diocesan priest to work in a parish or another apostolate within the diocese.

Chapters 6 and 7 offer more information on each degree of ordained ministry, on the preparation men typically undergo on the road to priesthood, and on the rite and effects of the Sacrament of Holy Orders.

Consecrated Life

Consecrated life is a life dedicated to living by the **evangelical counsels** of poverty, chastity, and obedience. All Christians are called to live these counsels according to their state of life. However, public profession of these counsels within a permanent state of life recognized by the Church is what characterizes a life consecrated to God. Those who follow the call to consecrated life have made a commitment to follow Christ more completely, to give themselves to God above all things, and to seek out the perfection that comes with loving God and loving other people. Consecrated life

is a bold witness that there is more to life than what we experience on earth. Consecrated life proclaims the glory of the world to come. Consecrated life is "one way of experiencing a 'more intimate' consecration, rooted in Baptism and dedicated totally to God" (*CCC*, 916). Further, the *Catechism of the Catholic Church* explains: "In the consecrated life, Christ's faithful, moved by the Holy Spirit, propose to follow Christ more nearly, to give themselves to God who is loved above all and, pursuing the perfection of charity in the service of the Kingdom, to signify and proclaim in the Church the glory of the world to come" (*CCC*, 916).

Consecrated life has been with the Church since her earliest days. The most common practice of consecrated life is as a sister or brother in a religious community; this is called the "religious life." Other styles of consecrated life include an eremitic lifestyle as a hermit, taking a vow as a consecrated virgin or widow, or participating in a secular institute of consecrated life or a society of apostolic life. All of these models include an embrace of the evangelical counsels. You will look more closely at the vocation to consecrated life in Chapter 8.

> **evangelical counsels** "In general, the teachings of the New Law proposed by Jesus to his disciples which lead to the perfection of Christian life. . . . The public profession of the evangelical counsels of poverty, chastity, and obedience is a constitutive element of state of consecrated life in the Church" (*CCC*, Glossary).

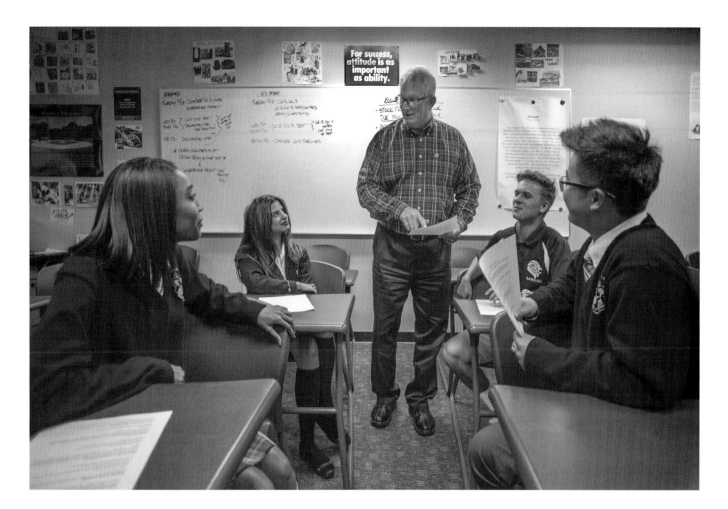

The Laity

Both those called to marriage and those in the committed single life (see the feature "The Committed Single Life" later in this chapter) are considered part of the Church **laity**, or laypeople. Essentially, the laity are those Catholics who are not part of the priesthood or consecrated life. They have a specific mission to live in the world by consecrating their daily activities to God. The Second Vatican Council document *Lumen Gentium* (*Dogmatic Constitution on the Church*) teaches, "By reason of their special vocation it belongs to the laity to seek the kingdom of God by engaging in temporal affairs and directing them according to God's will. . . . It pertains to them in a special way so to illuminate and order all temporal things with which they are closely associated that these may always be effected and grow according to Christ and maybe to the glory of the Creator and Redeemer" (*CCC*, 898 quoting *Lumen Gentium*, 31). "Temporal affairs" refers to the matters of this world, such as family, work, involvement in the local community, and participation in the parish. By the nature of their vocations, priests and consecrated persons are not in as direct contact with the world as is the laity. Thus, laypeople have a specific mission to **evangelize** the world in their normal, everyday activities. The workplace, the classroom, the athletic field, and the coffee shop all can be places in which laypeople bring others to Christ.

> **laity** All the baptized faithful except those who have received the Sacrament of Holy Orders or who have taken solemn vows in consecrated life.
>
> **evangelize** To proclaim "Christ and his Gospel (Greek *evangelion*) by word and the testimony of life, in fulfillment of Christ's command" (*CCC*, Glossary).

The reality is that the majority of people in the world will never meet a priest or consecrated person; therefore, the laity have a crucial role in bringing Christ to those whom they encounter. Evangelizing the world is not separate from normal, daily life. Quite the opposite. The laity are to offer up their everyday tasks in their families, parishes, and workplaces to the Lord.

The Complementarity of Vocations

At their core, all vocations have the same purpose: to love God. Since vocations have the same goal or purpose, they can complement one another. The three primary vocations may seem very different on the surface. For example, the day-to-day life of a wife and mother may appear very different from that of a religious sister. And yet the Church speaks of a **complementarity** of vocations; this is partly because all Catholics in every state of life have the same foundation of Baptism, strengthened by Confirmation, and nourished by the Eucharist.

A key to understanding this complementarity is to see how vocations are all rooted in the mystery of Christ. "In the unity of the Christian life, the various vocations are like so many rays of the one light of Christ, whose radiance 'brightens the countenance of the Church'" (*Vita Consecrata*, 16). Christ is married to his Bride, the Church (see Ephesians 5:21–33). He is also the Good Shepherd (see John 10:1–18) and the great High Priest (see Hebrews 4:14–16). Christ lived a perfect life of poverty, chastity, and obedience consecrated to the Father. All the vocations reflect the mystery of Christ, but in different ways:

> **complementarity** A way to describe two realities that belong together, producing a whole that neither is nor can be alone.

"Sacred ministers . . . are living images of Christ the Head and Shepherd, who guides his people during this time of 'already and not yet,' as they await his coming in glory."

The laity . . . reflect the mystery of the Incarnate Word particularly insofar as he is the Alpha and the Omega of the world. . . . *Sacred ministers*, for their part, are living images of Christ the Head and Shepherd who guides his people during this time of "already and not yet," as they await his coming in glory. It is the duty of the *consecrated life* to show that the Incarnate Son of God is *the eschatological goal towards which all things tend*, the splendor before which every other light pales, and the infinite beauty which alone can fully satisfy the human heart. (*Vita Consecrata*, 16)

The vocations can also complement one another in practical ways. For example, the total self-gift a consecrated person makes to Christ can inspire a married couple and thus move them to a deeper self-gift to each other and to God. A priest can see a family endure great sacrifice and struggles but still have strong faith and be motivated by their witness to offer up his day-to-day difficulties for a deeper adherence to Christ.

THE COMMITTED
SINGLE LIFE

An important and sizable group of people within the Church comprises those who are single but have not taken vows like consecrated persons. Clearly, all Catholics are committed singles at some point in their lives. *You* are single right now. Widows and widowers are singles. Even a person in a dating relationship or in the seminary is considered single in the eyes of the Church. For most people, the single life is a temporary state, in that it leads to one of the permanent primary vocations. However, some people never get married or become a priest or enter consecrated life. In this case, their singlehood is more long-lasting.

The primary vocational states of life mentioned in this section are all marked by vows and a permanent self-gift to another. The married couple give themselves to each other. The priest gives himself to Christ's Church. And the consecrated woman gives herself directly to God. These are not transitory commitments; they are lifelong.

The absence of inherent and permanent self-gift to another is what makes the committed single life different from the primary vocations. The reasons why a person might remain an unconsecrated single are countless. Sometimes due to accident, sickness, poverty, poor timing, or other effects of living in a fallen, broken world, people who greatly desire to be married or enter into another vocation simply cannot. In other cases, people do not answer God's call to marriage, priesthood, or consecrated life; just because God calls someone, does not mean the person has to answer.

Regardless of the reason, the Church is compassionate toward and has regard for those in the committed single life. In fact, single people have a certain availability and access that those in the married life, priesthood, or consecrated life do not possess. For example, a single person may be able to care for an elderly parent in a manner someone within another vocation cannot. "Some live their situation in the spirit of the Beatitudes, serving God and neighbor in exemplary fashion" (*CCC*, 1658).

In other words, single people can use their state of life, whether chosen or not, to pursue their universal call to holiness. A person who remains permanently single can become a saint, just like those living a permanent primary vocation.

Lay Ecclesial Movements

Emerging within the Church primarily after the Second Vatican Council have been many lay ecclesial movements. These are Catholic associations whose members are primarily laypeople. They usually have a particular aim or way of life. The formation of groups of laypeople for a specific purpose is not at all new in the history of the Church. "However, in modern times such lay groups have received a special stimulus, resulting in the birth and spread of a multiplicity of group forms. . . . We can speak of a *new era of group endeavors* of the lay faithful" (*Christifideles Laici*, 29).

These associations provide ways for married and committed single people to live out their faith in a specific manner. Each movement has a certain charism, which influences its activities and prayer life. Pope Benedict XVI remarked that "the ecclesial movements and new communities are a luminous sign of the beauty of Christ and of the Church, his Bride."[4]

A lay ecclesial movement begins in a specific diocese with the approval of the local bishop, but many of them have spread throughout various dioceses and even different countries. Members may be part of an

> **lay ecclesial movements** Associations of laypersons who come together with a common purpose and way of life.
> **charism** "A specific gift or grace of the Holy Spirit which directly or indirectly benefits the Church, given in order to help a person live out the Christian life, or to serve the common good in building up the Church" (*CCC*, Glossary).

ASSIGNMENT

Choose any two lay ecclesial movements, and complete the following items for each movement.

1. Who founded the movement? When? Where?
2. How many members of the movement are there worldwide?
3. What are some of the charisms of the movement?
4. Pick a quotation from the founder that encapsulates the mission of the movement.

association on a local level but connected with other members throughout the world. Generally, the leaders of the movements decide on their structure and commitments, but all of the movements exist under the guidance and authority of the universal Church. Once a lay ecclesial movement grows internationally, the Dicastery for Laity, Family and Life oversees it to make sure its aim is always authentic communion within the Church.

The number of lay ecclesial communities is vast; some you may have heard of are Emmanuel Community, Fraternity of Communion and Liberation, L'Arche International, International Catholic Charismatic Renewal Services, Focolare Movement (Work of Mary), and the World Organization of the Cursillo Movement. A full list and explanation of these international associations can be found on the website for the Dicastery for Laity, Family and Life, under "Directory of Associations."

SECTION ASSESSMENT

NOTE TAKING

Use the tree web you created to help you answer the following questions.

1. What are the three primary vocations?

2. What do the three primary vocations have in common?

3. What is one unique element of each of the primary vocations?

COMPREHENSION

4. What is the goal or purpose of every vocation?

VOCABULARY

5. Why do the laity have a specific task to *evangelize*?

APPLICATION

6. Give an example not mentioned in the section of how two different vocations can complement each other.

Your Vocation to Self-Giving

Every vocation is highly personal, since it concerns a person's relationship with God. Inseparable from your vocation is your relationship with others. This fact is rooted in the truth that God himself is a communion of Divine Persons.

The Trinity as a Communion of Persons

The foundation for understanding the nature of God and how you can relate to him is the reality that "God is love" (1 Jn 4:8, 16). Love is not something that God *does* but rather it is *who he is*. Love is his very essence. Love by its nature is given and received. Thus, the inner life of God is an eternal exchange of love.

Contemporary Catholic evangelist Bishop Robert Barron explains the Blessed Trinity as the interplay of lover (the Father), the beloved (the Son), and the love between them (the Holy Spirit).[5] From all eternity, the Father has loved the Son, who in turn has loved the Father for all eternity. The love between them is so great that it *is* a person, the Holy Spirit. The *Catechism of the Catholic Church* proclaims, "God has revealed his innermost secret: God himself is an eternal exchange of love, Father, Son, and Holy Spirit, and he has destined us to share that in exchange" (*CCC*, 221).

NOTE TAKING

Summarizing Cited Works. Create a flowchart like the one here, adding circle pairs for each cited work. As you read this section, summarize in the left circle what each of the following cited works says about the call to self-gift: *CCC*, 221; John 15:12; *Gaudium et Spes*, 24; and *CCC*, 1534.

Catechism of the Catholic Church, 221 ⟶

St. Teresa of Calcutta, founder of the Missionaries of Charity, said that "by giving wholehearted free service to the poorest of the poor we are doing it for Jesus. If it were not for Jesus, it would not be worth doing."

The Incarnation fully revealed God as Three Divine Persons. Jesus again and again revealed God as a loving Father—for example, in these words, "Righteous Father, the world also does not know you, but I know you, and they know that you sent me. I made known to them your name and I will make it known, that the love with which you loved me may be in them and I in them" (Jn 17:25–26). Christ also promised to send the Advocate, the Holy Spirit (who fully manifested himself to the world at Pentecost): "I will ask the Father, and he will give you another Advocate to be with you always, the Spirit of truth, which the world cannot accept, because it neither sees nor knows it. But you know it, because it remains with you, and will be in you" (Jn 14:16–17).

Law of Self-Giving

When you reflect on the fact that you were made in the image of God, you must do so with the understanding that you were made in the image of a Triune God, a God who is a communion of Divine Persons. You are called to reflect the Trinitarian life by the way you live your own life. This is crucial for your understanding and practice of vocation.

Inherent in any vocation is the **law of self-giving**, which essentially means that you are called to a complete self-donation or self-gift; you are called to love as God loves. Most people know that Jesus said to "love one another," but that is not the full statement. Jesus said, "Love one another, *as I have loved you*" (Jn 15:12; emphasis added). How did Christ love? He loved until his Death. He had a complete, total, self-giving love for others.

> **law of self-giving** The principle that encapsulates one's call to communion and self-donation with another. It means that you can discover your true self only through a sincere gift of self (cf. *Gaudium et Spes*, 24).

This is the paradox of the Christian life: in giving of yourself, you become who you are truly meant to be. According to the Second Vatican Council, "It follows, then, that if man is the only creature on earth that God has wanted for its own sake, man can fully discover his true self only in a sincere giving of himself" (*Gaudium et Spes*, 24). Read that again: you can *fully discover your true self* only by giving of yourself to others. This is written into your very being as a human person. Just as the world is a gift to you, so must you be a gift to others. Your own self-giving is at the heart of whatever primary vocation you follow. But this kind of love is not possible on your own. Indeed, a vocation is a *participation* in the perfect self-gift of God's divine love.

At the Service of Communion

Whereas the Sacraments of Initiation (Baptism, Confirmation, and Eucharist) are directed toward one's own personal holiness and the mission of evangelizing the world, the Sacraments of Matrimony and

Holy Orders "are directed towards the salvation of others; if they contribute as well to personal salvation, it is through services to others that they do so" (*CCC*, 1534). They are categorized as Sacraments at the Service of Communion. In other words, through these sacraments, you become holy by giving yourself to others. In the case of marriage, a husband and wife give themselves to each other and to their children; in Holy Orders, an ordained man offers himself in service of the people of the Church.

No vocation is lived in isolation. Matrimony is a sacrament given to foster the good of the human family, society, and the Church. Holy Orders is a sacrament given to foster the good of the spiritual family, the Church. Even though consecrated life is not a sacrament like Matrimony and Holy Orders, it is still an inherent call to communion with God and other members of one's community. Even a person who follows the vocation of a consecrated hermit is still called to practice self-gift in prayer and sacrifice for others in the Body of Christ.

This call to communion that is intrinsic to vocation goes against many modern mentalities. Society tells you that life is merely about your own satisfaction and what you can get out of a given situation. Media and advertising say you must be satisfied bodily at every moment with instant food, entertainment, and sex whenever you feel like it. This goes completely against the law of self-giving, which often involves self-denial.

God never forces you to give of yourself to others, even though he knows this is how you will be the most satisfied. Rather, he invites you to enter into his love more profoundly by so doing. Because of the free will inherent to your humanity, you can choose whether to accept his invitation.

Planning a Vocations Week

Help to plan the initial stages of a "Vocations Week" for your school in order to call attention to various Christian vocations. Do the following:

- Design a poster that emphasizes words such as *call*, *prayer*, *vocation*, and *discernment* as well as particular Christian vocations.

- Suggest three names for a panel of speakers who could address the student body on specific preparation and practices for the vocations of marriage, priesthood, and consecrated life. Write a one-paragraph biography of each speaker you suggest.

- Write your own "Prayer for Vocations" that could be prayed by students throughout a Vocations Week.

To actually enact a Vocations Week at your school, work with your teacher, campus minister, and classmates to form a committee that can schedule and implement some of your ideas and the ideas of your classmates from this assignment.

Discernment *of* Vocational *States of Life*

A key question to keep in mind throughout this course and beyond is "To what state of life is God calling *me*?" You were briefly introduced to the concept of discernment in Section 2 of the Introduction. There are many methods and approaches to discernment of your vocation. Fr. Michael Schmitz proposes a simple method to begin to discern one's vocation.[6]

First, Fr. Schmitz says, you must understand two fundamental truths:

- *God knows you better than you know yourself.* This means he knows what will make you happiest, most fulfilled. God alone knows what vocation will be best for you as a unique individual.
- *God loves you better than you love yourself.* This means that God genuinely wants you to know your vocation. You can trust him.

Fr. Schmitz says that after you realize those two truths, there are three questions you should ask yourself on a regular basis, even every day.

1 *Am I in a state of grace?* In other words, is there any mortal, serious sin on your soul? If so, then go to receive the Sacrament of Penance. If not, then move on to question two.

2 *Am I doing my daily duty?* Are you faithful to the small duties in your daily life? For example, do you show up to class on time? Are you doing your homework? Are you fulfilling your obligations to your parents and other authority figures? If not, then start doing these things. If so, then move onto question three.

3 *Did I pray today?* If you want to know what God wants you to do with your life, it makes sense to spend time listening to him. God speaks in a special way through Scripture and the liturgy.

If you have said yes to all three questions, then you can be at peace in waiting for God to reveal his will. These three practices train you to say yes to God in the little moments of your life, so when the "big" moment comes regarding your vocational state of life, you are prepared to say the most important yes.

SECTION ASSESSMENT

NOTE TAKING

Use the flowchart summaries you made to help you answer the following questions.

1. What can be called God's "innermost secret"?

2. How can you fully find yourself?

3. How can the Sacraments of Matrimony and Holy Orders contribute to the personal salvation of those who receive them?

COMPREHENSION

4. What does it mean to say "God is love"?

5. How did Jesus love?

6. How are the Sacraments at the Service of Communion different from the Sacraments of Initiation?

CRITICAL THINKING

7. Read the following quotation from the *Catechism of the Catholic Church*, and explain how it relates to the Main Idea of Section 4: "God is love and in himself he lives a mystery of personal loving communion. . . . God inscribed in the humanity of man and woman the vocation, and thus the capacity and responsibility, of love and communion" (*CCC*, 2331, quoting *Familiaris Consortio*, 11).

Section Summaries

Focus Question

What is essential in order to be happy in this life and to achieve eternal happiness?
Complete one of the following:

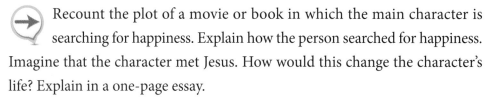 Recount the plot of a movie or book in which the main character is searching for happiness. Explain how the person searched for happiness. Imagine that the character met Jesus. How would this change the character's life? Explain in a one-page essay.

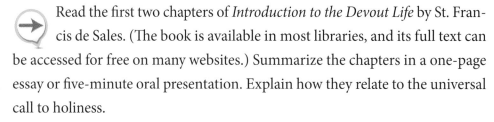 Read the first two chapters of *Introduction to the Devout Life* by St. Francis de Sales. (The book is available in most libraries, and its full text can be accessed for free on many websites.) Summarize the chapters in a one-page essay or five-minute oral presentation. Explain how they relate to the universal call to holiness.

→ Write a one-page profile of someone you know in a specific vocation (married person, priest, consecrated person). Explain with specific examples how he or she lives the law of self-giving in his or her vocation.

INTRODUCTION
Who Are You?

Creation is a gift from God. The pinnacle of all creation is human beings, who are made in God's image and likeness. Humans are broken because of sin, but they have a covenant of redemption offered through Christ.

 Read Psalm 139. Explain this psalm's connection with the dignity of the human person in two paragraphs.

SECTION 1
The Universal Call to Holiness

Every human person desires happiness. Because you were created by God and for God, only in him will you ever be completely satisfied. Having union with God is the state of being sanctified or being made holy. Related to your desire for lasting happiness is your call to be a saint. This is referred to as the *universal call to holiness*. Only by God's grace can you reach this perfection. Indeed, holiness is ultimately a gift to be received.

→ Write one paragraph explaining this quotation from St. Thérèse of Lisieux: "Holiness consists simply in doing God's will, and being just what God wants us to be."

SECTION 2
Your Personal Call

A vocation is a call from God. Even though everyone has the universal vocation to holiness, there is a specific path for each person. The Church is given to you as a means to help you discover and accept your primary vocation, specifically through your call to discipleship.

 Think back on the past twenty-four hours. List three ways you acted as a disciple during that time.

SECTION 3
The Specific Primary Vocations

The Church holds up certain states of life as paths to holiness. Marriage is entered into through the Sacrament of Matrimony. It is a lifelong, permanent union of a man and woman, who promise fidelity and openness to life. The priesthood is entered into through the Sacrament of Holy Orders. Priests are men who share in the priesthood of Christ in a special way. They serve the Body of Christ, especially through the administration of sacraments, primarily the Eucharist. Consecrated persons are those who make a vow to live the evangelical counsels of poverty, chastity, and obedience in a permanent state of life. The laity are those who are unordained and unconsecrated, both married and single; they are to bring Christ to the temporal world.

 Write three to four paragraphs explaining how you can incorporate the evangelical counsels—poverty, chastity, and obedience—into your current lifestyle.

SECTION 4
Your Vocation to Self-Giving

You are made to love as God loves. God himself is a perfectly eternal, self-donative communion of Divine Persons. You are to image this law of self-giving by loving as Christ loved, which was until death. You are able to fully discover yourself only within this self-gift to others. Self-gift is at the heart of a primary vocation. In fact, Matrimony and Holy Orders are called Sacraments at the Service of Communion, which means that those who receive them experience holiness through serving others.

Summarize in your own words the concept of "love" as described in this section. Give three concrete examples of this love being lived out. (Example: a mother losing her own sleep to get up and feed her baby.)

Chapter Assignments

Choose and complete at least one of the following three assignments assessing your understanding of the material in this chapter.

1. Artwork and Presentation: "Eucharist—Heart of Vocations"

Pope John Paul II said, "Each believer finds in the Eucharist not only the interpretative key of his or her own existence, but the courage to actualize it, indeed to build up, in the diversity of charisms and vocations, the one Body of Christ in history."[7] The Eucharist has been described as the "heart of vocations."

- Find the "Eucharist—Heart of Vocations" section on the United States Conference of Catholic Bishops' website (www.usccb.org). Spend some time reading and watching what is available on this site.

- Create an artistic presentation, such as a sculpture, collage, or painting, that has the theme of the Eucharist as the heart of vocations.

- Present the artwork to your class with a five-minute oral presentation, or record a video presentation to share with your teacher.

2. Digital Presentation on the State of Catholic Vocations

Prepare a digital presentation that summarizes with words and images each of the primary vocations: marriage, priesthood, and consecrated life. Use charts and graphs to detail current statistics on these vocations. In the notes section of your presentation, include further details that explain reasons and trends for the statistics labeled in the slides. Share this presentation with your class, or record it on video so that you can share it with your teacher.

3. The Beauty of Creation

Create a video presentation or slide show accompanied by Haydn's *The Creation* or Beethoven's Ninth Symphony. Use images that reflect the beauty of creation and connect with the music.

- The presentation should have a natural flow to convey the creation theme. For example, you could represent the beginning of God's creation of the world out of nothingness. Or you might focus on the beginning, development, and growth of one part of creation, perhaps one species or even one individual person.

- You must also visually depict how Christ's Paschal Mystery "casts conclusive light on the mystery of creation" (*CCC*, 280) (see Chapter 1 Introduction).

- For your final frame or slide, include a two- to three-paragraph essay or a short poem that is your personal reflection on the human person's unique place within creation.

- Finally, footnote background information on the piece of music you chose for this presentation.

Faithful Disciple

St. Aloysius Gonzaga

Born into a wealthy family in Lombardy (a region in northern Italy) in 1568—the height of the Renaissance—Luigi Gonzaga, the eldest son of Ferrante Gonzaga, was his father's pride, joy, and hope for the future. When Luigi was only four years old, Ferrante dressed his son as a soldier, gave him a set of miniature guns, and took him on his own military-training expeditions so that Luigi might get a taste of the life that would be his future.

However, by age seven, Luigi was already repelled by what he perceived to be the decadent lifestyle of the aristocracy. At this early age he began to practice on his own very strict religious penances that his family and others close to him found odd. He fasted three days a week on bread and water. He refused to have his

St. Aloysius Gonzaga

bedroom warmed with fire even on the coldest nights of winter. And he typically rose at midnight to kneel and pray on the stone floor near his bed.

When Luigi was twelve, his father sent him and his younger brother Rodolfo to board with relatives in Florence. This family had a private chapel in their home, and Luigi spent much of his time there, praying and reading the lives of the saints. This was the place where Luigi first thought he might want to be a priest. When he returned home, he made his First Communion (prepared, incidentally, by another future saint, Charles Borromeo).

In spite of all of these clues, Ferrante was caught off guard when Luigi approached him at age sixteen to tell him that he wanted to enter the Society of Jesus and become a Jesuit priest. His father was angry and brought Luigi home to the family castle before sending him and Rodolfo off on an eighteen-month tour of the courts of Italy in the hope that Luigi would give up his plan. At the end of the tour, Luigi's resolve was just as firm; he soon renounced his inheritance and left home to join the Jesuits in Rome.

Soon after, Ferrante Gonzaga relented and gave his permission to his son to enter religious life. He sent a letter with Luigi—now known more commonly by the Latin form of his name, Aloysius—to the Jesuit superior; it read, "I merely say that I am giving into your Reverence's hands the most precious thing I possess in all the world."

As a seminarian, Aloysius conformed with the other novices and ended some of his most extreme penances. By 1591, a plague had broken out in Rome, and Aloysius ministered to the sick and dying, often carrying them from the streets to a Jesuit-run hospital. He washed the patients, helped them into bed, and cleaned their bed coverings. Eventually he contracted the disease himself.

Aloysius Gonzaga had a premonition that he would die on the Feast of Corpus Christi (the Body of Christ). In fact, though he seemed to recover as the feast approached, he died on the Octave of the Feast of Corpus Christi, June 21, 1591. He was twenty-three years old. Aloysius's cause for sainthood began within fifteen years of his death. Pope Benedict XIII canonized him on December 31, 1726, naming him the patron saint of youth. His feast day is on June 21.

 ## Reading Comprehension

1. What kind of life did Aloysius's father wish for his son?

2. What was one of the extreme penances Aloysius undertook as a child?

3. What type of ministry did Aloysius undertake as a Jesuit?

4. What is Aloysius patron saint of?

 ## Writing Task

Aloysius had a different plan for his own life than his father had for him. How do your own plans for your life differ from expectations your parents have for you? How do your plans align with God's plan for holiness?

Explaining the Faith

Isn't having the right vocation, job, or career essential for a person's happiness?

No, the foundational call from God is not to a particular vocation, job, career, or way of life but to holiness and communion with him. Holiness and communion with God are the basis of all happiness. Your particular vocation or career can certainly serve your greater call to union with God, but they are not the end or purpose of your life. Often the key to happiness is using one's gifts fully for God by using them to serve others in Christian love. It is important to add that a refusal to answer God's particular call to holiness may result in a more difficult road to eternal life, or it may even jeopardize a person's salvation.

 ## Writing Task

- Read paragraphs 2012–2015 of the *Catechism of the Catholic Church*. Explain this quotation in your own words: "There is no holiness without renunciation and spiritual battle" (*CCC*, 2015).

Prayer
Some Definite Service

God has created me to do him some definite service.

He has committed some work to me which he has not committed to another.

I have my mission. I may never know it in this life, but I shall be told it in the next. . . .

I am a link in a chain, a bond of connection between persons.

He has not created me for naught.

I shall do good; I shall do his work.

I shall be an angel of peace, a preacher of truth in my own place, while not intending it if I do but keep his commandments and serve him in my calling.

Therefore, I will trust him. Whatever, wherever I am, I can never be thrown away.

If I am in sickness, my sickness may serve him; in perplexity, my perplexity may serve him.

If I am in sorrow, my sorrow may serve him.

He does nothing in vain. He knows what he is about.

He may take away my friends. He may throw me among strangers.

He may make me feel desolate, make my spirits sink, hide my future from me.

Still, he knows what he is about.

—St. John Henry Newman

THE
VOCATION
TO MARRIAGE

2

Enrico and Chiara Corbella Petrillo:
A Witness to Joy

"I promise to be true to you in good times and in bad, in sickness and in health. I will honor you all the days of my life."

For Chiara Corbella Petrillo and her husband, Enrico Petrillo, challenges came early on in their relationship. Chiara became pregnant shortly after their wedding. A sonogram at fourteen weeks determined that the baby was anencephalic, a condition that leaves the child with an underdeveloped brain and partial skull. The prognosis is fatal. Doctors encouraged the couple to opt for an abortion. They declined. Maria Grazia Letizia was born on June 10, 2009. She died thirty minutes later, after receiving the Sacrament of Baptism.

Again Chiara became pregnant. However, doctors told her that the child, a little boy the couple named Davide Giovanni, would not be able to live outside the womb. He was born on June 24, 2010, and lived only thirty-eight minutes, just long enough for Enrico and Chiara to be able to hold him.

Although everyone who loved them was fearful, again Chiara became pregnant. The young couple, however, were serene, and the baby was healthy. Yet as the pregnancy progressed a tumor was discovered on Chiara's tongue that spread to her neck and eyes. She refused any treatment that would endanger the baby's life, and so a healthy baby boy, Francesco, was born. For a time Enrico and Chiara were able to revel in the joys of family life. However, the tumor, which was malignant, had spread during the pregnancy. Enrico told Chiara in the hospital chapel the news that little could be done. They prayed together before the Blessed Sacrament and repeated their marriage vows: "In good times and bad, in sickness and health. I will love you and honor you all the days of my life." Only a few months later she died.

Chiara's short but impactful life is a bittersweet story but ultimately a joyful one. Rather than facing their trials with resentment and fear, Chiara and Enrico let their love for each other be caught up in their deep love for God, a love which both held firmly as Chiara went to be reunited with her two children in heaven.[1]

FOCUS QUESTION

What is the **NATURE OF MARRIAGE**, and how does one **PREPARE** for this **VOCATION**?

Chapter Overview

Introduction	God Is the Author of Marriage
Section 1	The Nature of Marriage
Section 2	Promises and Benefits of Marriage
Section 3	Complementarity and Chastity within Marriage
Section 4	Discerning and Preparing for the Vocation to Marriage

INTRODUCTION
God Is the Author of Marriage

MAIN IDEA
God is the author of marriage from the very beginning of time. Sacred Scripture teaches that God's plan for marriage is a covenant of love.

Within your universal call to holiness—that is, your work to be a saint—God calls you to a specific primary vocation. God wants you to connect with him most profoundly through your primary vocation. In fact, your vocation is the best means for you to become happy and holy in this life and in heaven.

Although many young people are called to the priesthood or religious life, most are called to and do accept the vocation to marriage. You are likely very familiar with marriage already from witnessing several examples of married couples. Think about the best marriages you know of, in which the married couples truly love, honor, and respect each other. How long have those couples been married? Have they had difficult, even seemingly impossible experiences during their marriage that they overcame? What is it about their marriages that make them stand out as exceptional?

Perhaps the couples who came to mind were your parents, grandparents, or other relatives. Perhaps you thought of a younger couple at your parish or a couple living in your neighborhood whom you have grown to admire. Although there are no two marriages alike, good marriages, such as the ones you have witnessed, have a few things in common. For example:

NOTE TAKING

Summarizing Key Concepts. Make a table like the one here and use it to highlight key scriptural elements from this section. In one column, list Scripture citations. In the second column, write short summaries of what the verses say about marriage. As you add citations to this table, you may also cite longer Scripture passages adjacent to those referenced in the text.

Verses	Summary
Genesis 1:26–31	God creates humankind in his image, male and female; he gives humankind charge over creation and tells them to be fruitful.
Genesis 2:24	
Tobit 8:6–7	

- The couples are *committed* from the very beginning to making their marriage one that will last, no matter what happens. Commitment bonds a couple together when they are tired, angry, or stressed in life or with each other.

- The couples have learned and developed good *communication skills*. Some couples have learned these skills intuitively, and others have had to work hard to develop them. However, couples who know how to discuss their problems fairly have strong marriages.

- The couples have *common values* in such areas as practicing faith, raising children, handling money, and supporting family life. Tensions arise when couples don't agree on basic issues; even good communication can't solve this problem.[2]

Good marriages remind the world of a basic principle about the human person: everyone desires to love and to be loved. This desire for love and communion is built into God's design of the human person. People exist both as individuals and in relationship with

Ten Reasons Marriage Makes a Difference

Marriage is a personal, but not private, relationship that carries great public significance. Marriage is both good for the couple and makes vital contributions to the common good of society as a whole. Listed below are ten benefits of marriage for couples and society:

 01 On average, married couples are healthier, happier, and enjoy longer lives than those who are not married.

 02 Those who are married are more productive, have higher incomes, and enjoy more family time than those who are unmarried.

 03 Married women are significantly less likely to be the victims of violent crime than single or divorced women. Married men are less likely to perpetrate violent crimes than unmarried men.

 04 Boys raised in single-parent homes are more likely to engage in criminal behavior than those raised by married parents.

others. As discussed in Chapter 1, God has made you so that you find fulfillment in the giving of yourself. One of the most profound yet basic expressions of the law of self-giving (see Chapter 1, Section 4) can be found in the vocation to marriage, when a man and woman join their lives together and pledge mutual self-giving in their love and their family life.

God himself wrote the vocation to marriage into the very nature of men and women from the beginning. The Second Vatican Council document *Gaudium et Spes* (*The Church in the Modern World*) reminds the Church that "the intimate community of life and love which constitutes the married state has been established by the Creator and endowed by him with its own proper laws. . . . God himself is the author of marriage" (*Gaudium et Spes*, 48). Though marriage can be thought of as a "natural" vocation that is ratified by human laws and customs, it is not a purely human institution.

 05 Children raised by their own married mother and father are more likely to stay in school, have fewer behavioral and attendance problems, and earn four-year degrees.

 06 Children raised by their married mother and father are less likely to struggle with serious emotional illness, depression, or suicide.

 07 Married women have lower rates of depression than single or cohabiting women.

 08 Married men show the most physical health benefits from marriage and suffer the greatest health consequences if they divorce.

 09 Marriage changes people's lifestyles and habits in ways that are personally and socially beneficial. Marriage is a seedbed of positive social behavior.

 10 Marriage generates social capital. The familial and social bonds created through marriage yield benefits for the family and society at large.[3]

ASSIGNMENT

Choose one of the following items. Write three paragraphs summarizing your findings.

- Citing another recent study, name two other benefits of marriage not on this list.

- Explain to someone who isn't Catholic why marriage is good for individuals and society.

This depiction of Adam and Eve in the Garden of Eden was done by a Kuna Indian artist. Kuna Indians are native to the Kuna Yala region of Panama.

Marriage "In the Beginning"

The Church looks first to Sacred Scripture to learn about marriage. The Book of Genesis begins with two accounts of creation, each telling something important about man and woman. In the first account (see Genesis 1:1–31) God creates humans "in his image; in the image of God he created them; male and female he created them" (Gn 1:27). People are unique in that God has created nothing else in his image and likeness.

God's plan for humanity includes companionship shared between male and female. Companionship is a special relationship between man and woman that is unique among God's creatures. Genesis says that God blesses humans, finds them "very good" (Gn 1:31), and tasks them to "be fertile and multiply; fill the earth and subdue it" (Gn 1:28). God gave the first couple both a blessing and a responsibility: the blessing of unity and community and the responsibility of caring for creation and being fruitful in family life.

The second account of creation (see Genesis 2:4–3:24) has similar themes; man is settled in the garden to "cultivate and care for it" (Gn 2:15). Additionally, Scripture affirms that "it is not good for man to be alone" and that the woman is created as "bone of his bone, flesh of his flesh," to be the man's helper (Gn 2:18). Even more than the first account, the second creation account emphasizes the companionship and unbreakable union between man and woman in marriage, saying "a man leaves his father and mother and clings to his wife, and the two of them become one body" (Gn 2:24). Their relationship is built on mutual support and the complementarity of masculinity and femininity.

Marriage in Salvation History

The two creation accounts illustrate what the *Catechism of the Catholic Church* teaches: "God created man and woman together and willed each for the other" (*CCC,*

Jesus' first recorded miracle is turning water into wine during the marriage at Cana. His presence at the wedding blesses the marriage and signals the importance of marriage in God's plan.

371). Scripture continues to speak about God's plan for marriage, even with the difficulties resulting from sin. Marriage is a remedy for sin after the Fall, in that it helps men and women to overcome their selfishness. Marriage requires spouses to provide mutual support to each other.

Under the **Mosaic Law**, the Jewish people held the practice of marriage up to a high standard. The Jews considered marriage indissoluble, though divorce was permitted under certain circumstances. The Books of Ruth and Tobit describe faithful and loving relationships between spouses. Consider the prayer of Tobiah and Sarah on their wedding night from the Book of Tobit:

> You made Adam, and you made his wife Eve
>> to be his helper and support;
>> and from these two the human race has
>> come.
> You said, "It is not good for man to be alone;
>> let us make a helper like himself."
> Now, not with lust,
>> but with fidelity I take this kinswoman as my
>> wife.
> Send down your mercy on me and on her,
>> and grant that we may grow old together.
> Bless us with children. (Tb 8:6–7)

The Song of Songs gives beautiful imagery of the love between spouses that is deep and strong. It shows marriage as exclusive and faithful:

> Set me as a seal upon your heart,
>> as a seal upon your arm;
> For Love is strong as Death,
>> longing is fierce as Sheol.
> Its arrows are arrows of fire,
>> flames of the divine.
> Deep waters cannot quench love,
>> nor rivers sweep it away. (Sg 8:6–7a)

The faithfulness and passionate love between spouses found in the Song of Songs is a foretaste of the great love that God has for each human heart and that Jesus has for the Church, his Bride.

In the New Testament, Jesus' first public miracle, initiated by his mother, happened at a wedding feast in Cana (see John 2:1–12). In this first miracle, Jesus signals the great importance of marriage in God's plan by making himself a part of it. Jesus blesses marriage and shows that he intends for marriage to become an **efficacious** sign of his presence.

When he taught the crowds during his public ministry, Jesus affirmed the original intent of the Creator for marriage as an indissoluble union where the two "become one flesh" (Mt 19:5). He said, "Therefore,

> **Mosaic Law** The laws, beginning with the Ten Commandments, that God gave to Moses for the Israelites. It includes rules for ritual religious observance as well as rules for everyday life.
>
> **efficacious** Effecting or accomplishing that which a thing represents.

what God has joined together, no human being must separate" (Mt 19:6). Due to sin, this was a hard teaching for some to accept. Jesus knew the teaching would be difficult, which is why he promises his grace to aid spouses by raising marriage to a sacrament in the New Covenant. The graces of the Sacrament of Matrimony come from Christ's **Paschal Mystery**. According to the *Catechism of the Catholic Church*, "By coming to restore the original order of creation disturbed by sin, he himself gives the strength and grace to live marriage in the new dimension of the Reign of God. . . . This grace of Christian marriage is a fruit of Christ's cross, the source of all Christian life" (*CCC*, 1615).

When Jesus blessed marriage and raised it to the level of a sacrament, it became a sign of the covenant of love between Christ and the Church. St. Paul wrote about the love of spouses reflecting the love of Christ for the Church, calling husbands to "love your wives, even as Christ loved the church and handed himself over for her" (Eph 5:25). Marriage should point ultimately to the consummation of that love in heaven, which the Book of Revelation describes as the "wedding feast of the Lamb" (Rv 19:9)—that is, the union of Christ with his Church.

> **Paschal Mystery** Christ's work of redemption accomplished through his Passion, Death, Resurrection, and Ascension. It is celebrated and made present in the liturgy of the Church (see *CCC*, Glossary).

SECTION ASSESSMENT

NOTE TAKING

Use the table you made to help you complete the following items.

1. Compare and contrast the two creation accounts in the Book of Genesis.

2. Describe the practice of marriage in the Old Testament.

COMPREHENSION

3. In what ways does marriage become a remedy for sin in the Old Testament verses?

4. What original elements of marriage did Jesus come to restore?

5. What does Jesus do to aid spouses?

REFLECTION

6. What does the "wedding feast of the Lamb" in the Book of Revelation symbolize?

7. Reread the excerpted portion of paragraph 1615 of the *Catechism of the Catholic Church* and consider marriages with which you are familiar. How might couples live out the original intent of marriage to be self-giving and indissoluble? How do you think couples today rely on the fruits of Christ's Cross in their marriages?

SECTION 1
The Nature of Marriage

MAIN IDEA
Although marriage was distorted by sin, it still retains its original purpose of being an image of the love of the Divine Persons of the Blessed Trinity. Christian spouses are called to be witnesses to the self-giving love of Christ and the Church.

The two creation accounts you studied in the last section are important because they explain two fundamental truths: (1) humans are individuals created to live in communion with one another, and (2) family life nurtured in marriage is the core of human society. In his wisdom and mercy, God wants humans to enjoy the companionship and fruitfulness of marriage. As studies have shown (see "Ten Reasons Marriage Makes a Difference" in this chapter's Introduction), married people are generally happier and healthier and live longer. In short, marriage is a good for couples and society. However, Christian marriage is much more than a human contract between a man and a woman. It is a covenant inviting God himself to enter into the union between a man and woman and transform it into a living reflection of God's own love.

Marriage Images the Blessed Trinity

God reveals his very nature as a social being, meant to interact in love. The love of the Three Persons of the Blessed Trinity—Father, Son, and Holy Spirit—flows from their sharing in one divine nature. Humans and human society are a reflection of that Trinitarian

NOTE TAKING

Identifying Main Ideas. Create a chart like the one here to help you understand the nature of marriage. Fill in at least two details explaining each main idea.

Main ideas	Explanation
Marriage images the Trinity.	Married love flows from and reflects the love of the Trinity.
Christ restores the original goodness of marriage.	
Marriage images Christ and his Church.	

love, called the **Divine Economy**, to which the creation accounts allude. In Genesis 1:26, God says, "Let us make human beings in our image, after our likeness." In a Christian marriage, a baptized man and a baptized woman participate in the love shared by the Divine Persons of the Blessed Trinity. "Authentic married love is caught up into divine love" (*Gaudium et Spes*, 48 § 2). The human love between a husband and wife is made holy by sharing in the love of the Blessed Trinity. This is lived most profoundly in the marital act, the consummation of marriage.

Christ Restores the Original Goodness of Marriage

Infidelity, divorce, and spousal abuse are all results of the distortion of sin on what God intended for marriage. Although these distortions are extremely painful and do great harm to society, they do not occur because of God, because of the nature of the human person, or because of the nature of marriage; rather, they occur only because of sin. Directly following the disobedience of Adam and Eve, one of the first consequences of sin was a rupture in the harmonious relationship between man and woman. Although their relationship was not broken completely, it was seriously disfigured.

However, God did not abandon humans after the Fall when sin entered the world. Humanity needed God, and so God provided a remedy to some of the effects of sin on marriage. For example, the toil and hard work of providing for a family mitigates the effects of self-absorption and the desire to pursue one's own pleasures above the good of other persons. The

> **Divine Economy** The name for the divine plan of salvation. "The ultimate end of the whole divine economy is the entry of God's creatures into the perfect unity of the Blessed Trinity" (*CCC*, 260).

The prophet Nathan reproached King David for his sin of adultery. "Why have you despised the Lord and done what is evil in his sight" (2 Sm 12:9).

difficulty of having and raising children opens parents to allowing others to help them and often calls for heroic self-giving on the part of spouses.

The Old Testament reveals a developing understanding about the unity and indissolubility of marriage through the history of the Chosen People, the Jews. In some of the historical books of the Bible, patriarchs and kings practiced polygamy, which was not explicitly condemned. Yet through the development of covenants between God and the Chosen People, there was a growing understanding of the design of marriage by God. The Mosaic Law, while allowing for divorce due to the "hardness of man's heart," aimed to protect the wife from being dominated by her husband (see Matthew 19:8). Over time, the Chosen People were being formed in a deeper understanding of the original permanence and tenderness for which marriage was created.

When Jesus came to redeem humanity, he also came to restore marriage to its original goodness. Jesus is the source of grace in marriage. In his preaching, Jesus taught clearly the original meaning of marriage as it was intended from the beginning: marriage was to be indissoluble to death. "It is by following Christ, renouncing themselves, and taking up their crosses that spouses will be able to 'receive' the original meaning of marriage and live it with the help of Christ" (*CCC*, 1615).

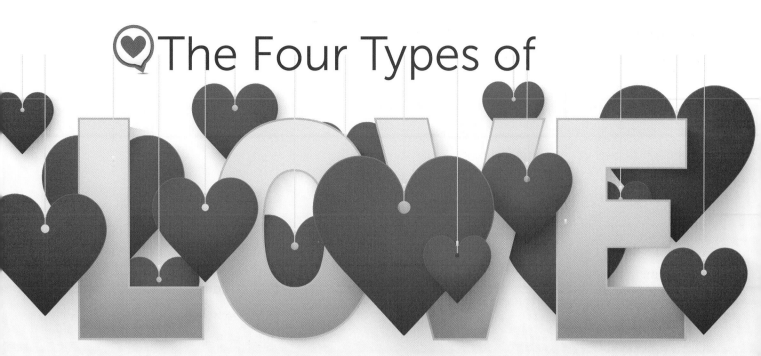

The Four Types of LOVE

Love encompasses the entire Christian vocation. Love—of God, between spouses, and for children—is essential to Christian marriage. Yet love is among the most misunderstood and misused words in society today. People say they love a candy bar or a song in the same breath as they express love for a friend or their mother. One way to better grasp what love means is to look at four different words the ancient Greeks used for love. In his book *The Four Loves*, C. S. Lewis distinguished between four types of love:

- *Storge* is the unconditional, emotional love between family members.

- *Philia* is the natural love between friends, often translated as "brotherly love" (e.g., Philadelphia is "the city of brotherly love"). This love is often expressed through shared values, interests, and activities.

- *Eros* is the love associated with the natural feeling of sexual desire. This is the passionate and intense love that often comes with emotion-based romance and that can often vanish when there is trouble in a relationship.

- *Agape* is godly love that is unconditional and unselfish, seeking the good of others first.

Lewis described *agape* love as a committed and chosen type of love that fulfills the other types of human love. *Agape* love chooses to love *this person*, seeking first what is best for him or her, and in spite of his or her faults. It rises above the feelings of *storge*, *philia*, or *eros* love to imitate the love of Christ himself, who desires that each person come into relationship with him.

ASSIGNMENT

Do each of the following:

- Read what St. Paul has to say about *agape* love in 1 Corinthians 13:4–8a. Create a song lyric, short poem, or simple collage using at least one verse from St. Paul's description of love and/or a passage on love from the Song of Songs.

- Write a "Prayer for an Increase in *Agape* Love" that incorporates ideas from these passages.

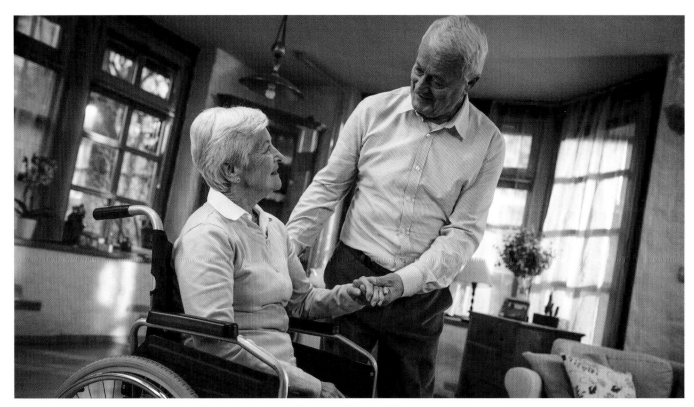

Marriage Images Christ and His Church

Another aspect of marriage is that it images the relationship between Christ and his Church. St. Paul referred to this aspect when he instructed about the mutual love and respect spouses should give to each other: "Be subordinate to one another out of reverence for Christ" (Eph 5:21). St. Paul went on to name the Church as Christ's beloved Bride for whom he gave himself up so that she would become holy. Husbands and wives are called to love each other in the same way Christ loves his Church: with a faithfulness that does not end until death. Each spouse is called to love in different ways: "Wives should be subordinate to their husbands as to the Lord. For the husband is head of his wife just as Christ is head of the church. . . . Husbands, love your wives, even as Christ loved the church and handed himself over for her to sanctify her. . . . 'For this reason a man shall leave [his] father and [his] mother and be joined to his wife, and the two shall become one flesh'" (Eph 5:22–23, 25–26a, 31).

Husbands, therefore, should love their wives with the same depth and self-sacrifice with which Christ loves his Church. Wives should reciprocate, honoring their husbands in the same way the Church honors and serves Christ. These different ways of showing love allow the couple's love to flourish.

It can be easy to mistake the meaning of this Scripture passage when it is taken out of the context of marriage as an image of Christ and his Church. As a member of Christ's Body, the Church, you have been called to a spousal relationship with Christ. Your Baptism initiated you into the Church, which allowed Christ to lay down his life for you and perfect you. In turn, as a member of the Church, you took on a special relationship with Christ. You promised to follow Christ, the Head. The *Catechism of the Catholic Church* teaches that "the entire Christian life bears the mark of the spousal love of Christ and the Church" (*CCC*, 1617). When a baptized man and a baptized woman are married, their love becomes a sign of the love between Christ, who gave himself up, and his Church.

SECTION ASSESSMENT

NOTE TAKING

Use the chart you created to help you complete this item.

1. Explain the following aspects of marriage:

   - images the Trinity
   - was restored to goodness by Christ
   - images Christ and his Church

COMPREHENSION

2. What understanding of the unity and indissolubility of marriage does the Old Testament reveal?

3. Explain how the marital love between a baptized man and a baptized woman is like the love between Christ and his Church.

VOCABULARY

4. Define the *Divine Economy*.

CRITICAL THINKING

5. How could St. Paul's words in Ephesians 5:22–31 be misunderstood when taken out of the context of married love imitating Christ and his Church? How would you respond to such a misunderstanding?

6. "Authentic married love is caught up into divine love." Explain this statement by referring to the love of the Three Persons of the Blessed Trinity.

SECTION 2
Promises and Benefits of Marriage

MAIN IDEA

Christian marriage is a sacred covenant between a husband and wife requiring promises of indissolubility, faithfulness, and fruitfulness. Keeping these promises aids the married couple in living out their vocation as God intended.

When a baptized man and a baptized woman are married, they enter into covenant relationship through the promises they make to each other. These promises, to which the spouses give their full consent, are a sign of the total self-gift between the couple. The promises each have associated benefits (goods) that will aid the married couple in living out the Sacrament of Matrimony.

Indissolubility

Indissolubility is what God intended for marriage from the beginning: "That is why a man leaves his father and mother and clings to his wife, and the two of them become one body" (Gn 2:24). You read earlier that Jesus said of the husband and wife: "They are no longer two, but one flesh. Therefore, what God has joined together, no human being must separate" (Mt 19:6). In this verse, Jesus ratified God's original intent for marriage, confirming that marriage was designed to be indissoluble. When a couple make

> **indissolubility** Permanence. In relation to marriage, indissolubility means that a marriage cannot be dissolved either by the withdrawal of consent of the married partners or by civil authorities.

NOTE TAKING

Concept Webs. Make three concept webs like the one here. In the large circles, write the three promises made in marriage. In the smaller circles, name the benefits or goods associated with the promises.

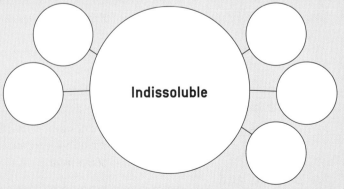

Indissoluble

their vows, they promise to live within their marriage covenant until they are separated by death. In order for the marriage to be valid, the man and woman must each understand and each have the intention of indissolubility when they enter into the Sacrament of Matrimony.

Can you imagine the prospects for a marriage in which both parties are only "trying out" marriage to see if it is a "good fit"? The modern mentality is often to see a lifelong promise as a burden or as impossible to keep. The promise of indissolubility holds the couple to a higher standard and reminds a husband and wife that, although marriage can be difficult, it is ultimately for their greater good to work through problems and support each other through hard times. A commitment to the indissolubility of marriage helps them grow in mutual self-giving. The grace offered by Christ in the Sacrament of Matrimony aids the couple in working toward what is right and good for the other, promoting unity within their marriage. When spouses work for what is good for each other, they grow in affection and mutual respect for each other's dignity, which brings them closer together.

Faithfulness

Because married love involves a total self-gift of the spouses to each other, it must be a totally faithful love. Married love rests on the promise of a husband and wife to remain true to each other emotionally, mentally, and sexually from the first moments of their marriage onward. The benefit of faithfulness protects and builds up their unity. Often, couples who have been married for many years will say that they love each other more after ten, twenty, or forty years of marriage. Because they have pledged a permanent commitment of **fidelity** to each other, they receive grace to build up that bond through a lifetime of learning to selflessly give and receive love.

There are many circumstances that might make keeping the vow of faithfulness difficult. The Church certainly provides resources such as counseling to couples in difficult circumstances where sin has deeply affected their relationship. At the same time, the Church reminds married couples that they share in the totally faithful and indissoluble love of God in the Sacrament of Matrimony. Their fidelity reflects the love of Christ for the Church and the love of the Divine Persons of the Blessed Trinity for one another. These are models for the relationship of husband and wife.

Fruitfulness

Indissolubility and faithfulness refer primarily to the relationship between husband and wife, though their keeping those promises also benefits their children. A third promise of marriage relates directly to the benefit of children. This good is named fruitfulness or **fecundity**. Going back to the intention of God in the beginning, "married love is ordered to the procreation and education" of children (*CCC*, 1652). The Second

---

fidelity Faithfulness. In relation to marriage, fidelity refers to one of the promises of marriage. Both spouses "give of themselves definitely and totally to one another. They are no longer two; from now on they form one flesh. The covenant they freely contracted imposes on the spouses the obligation to preserve it as unique and indissoluble" (*CCC*, 2364).

fecundity Fruitfulness. In relation to marriage, fecundity refers to procreation and education of children as one of the promises of marriage.

Vatican Council document *Gaudium et Spes* teaches, "Children are the supreme gift of marriage and contribute greatly to the good of the parents themselves. . . . True married love and the whole structure of family life which results from it, without diminishment of the other ends of marriage, are directed to disposing the spouses to cooperate valiantly with the love of the Creator and Savior, who through them will increase and enrich his family from day to day" (*Gaudium et Spes*, 50, quoted in *CCC*, 1652).

Fruitfulness in marriage means, first, that spouses are willing to welcome children into their family. Second, fruitfulness refers to the primary responsibility parents have for the educational, moral, spiritual, and physical needs of their children. This requires a great amount of self-giving, which, as you will recall, is a way husbands and wives serve each other and God. They often would not experience these opportunities for self-giving without the gift of children.

The promise of fecundity is frequently misunderstood as a burden the Church puts on married couples. The view of children as troublesome and difficult is absorbed from current culture, not from the nature of children or persons in general. The Church encourages couples to look at a child through God's eyes—that is, as a supreme gift. The Church teaches married couples to practice responsible procreation through means that do not place a barrier between the spouses or affect their fertility. The Church thus advocates the practice of **Natural Family Planning (NFP)**. You will find more information on Natural Family Planning in Chapter 4.

> **Natural Family Planning (NFP)** A method approved by the Church for naturally planning and spacing the birth of children in marriage that honors the unitive and procreative purposes of the sexual act.

SECTION ASSESSMENT

NOTE TAKING

Use the concept webs you created to help you complete the following items.

1. Name and describe in your own words each of the three promises of marriage.
2. Name at least one benefit associated with each of the promises.
3. How do each of the three promises of marriage relate to marriage as God intended it from the beginning?

COMPREHENSION

4. How does a modern view of promises and commitments contradict the promise of indissolubility in marriage?
5. In what ways are couples to remain faithful to each other in marriage?
6. What are two responsibilities that come with fruitfulness in marriage?

REFLECTION

7. What are appropriate ways you can learn to practice these three promises of marriage in your current relationships?

SECTION 3
Complementarity and Chastity within Marriage

MAIN IDEA
All persons are called to live chastely in their state of life. Chastity within marriage is based on respect for the complementarity of men and women and on respect for the two ends of the sexual act: union and procreation.

You have learned that marriage is rooted in God's plan from the very beginning. God created persons for communion and love by creating them "male and female" (Gn 1:27). Each is made equal in dignity. Each is made in God's image. They are also different, though their differences highlight their complementarity. Understanding sexuality is key to understanding the human person. Sexuality "affects all aspects of the human person in the unity of [the person's] body and soul" (*CCC*, 2332).

Men and Women Are Designed to Be Complementary

Your sexual identity comes from the physical reality of the body given to you at birth. Sexual identity is not changeable or subjective according to a person's wishes. While there are different ways to express maleness and femaleness, there are only two sexual identities possible for the human person. The sexual differences—male and female—complement each other; they "are necessary toward the goods of marriage and the flourishing of family life" (*CCC*, 2333). Complementarity of the sexes leads to fruitfulness: "Each of the two sexes is an

NOTE TAKING

Summarizing Key References. Create a chart like the one here. Summarize what the Church teaches on the following issues. Paraphrase a quotation from the *Catechism of the Catholic Church* or another Church document cited in this section. List the citation.

Issue	Church teaching	Document citation
Complementarity of men and women	Men and women, equal in dignity, have physical, moral, and spiritual differences that complement each other.	*CCC*, 2332–2333
Unitive end of marriage		
Procreative end of marriage		
Chastity in marriage		

POPE JOHN PAUL II and
Theology of the *Body*

From September 1979 to November 1984, Pope John Paul II gave a series of 129 Wednesday addresses (called audiences) to groups of pilgrims visiting the Vatican. In this series, the pope addressed the meaning of human sexuality, the complementarity of the sexes, and the calling to marriage and family life. The talks are known collectively as Theology of the Body.

An astute observer of society and the human person, Pope John Paul II saw that the Church needed to find new ways to speak about the noble callings of love, marriage, and family life that would engage modern people.

Using the language of **personalism**, Pope John Paul II described the vocation to love as carved into every person's very humanity. He explained that the creation stories draw people into the great mystery that God wants each person to know him through a full human experience of sexuality, mind, relationships, joys, and struggles.

Throughout his Wednesday addresses, Pope John Paul II reflected on the words of Scripture and the application of doctrine to **celibacy**, marriage, contraception, and the complementarity of the sexes. The most important principle of his Theology of the Body talks is that human persons, made up of body and soul, have unparalleled dignity and value. The body, not just the soul, participates in this dignity because it is a unique expression of the person. Each individual person is an unrepeatable and distinctive being. Pope John Paul II's message in Theology of the Body "proposes a fresh view of God's love that leads to deep awareness of human dignity, identity, and purpose."[4]

personalism A philosophical movement that emphasizes the meaning and value of human persons and their relationality to each other and God.

celibacy "The state or condition of those who have chosen to remain unmarried for the sake of the kingdom of heaven in order to give themselves entirely to God and to the service of his people" (*CCC*, Glossary).

image of the power and tenderness of God, with equal dignity though in a different way. The union of man and woman in marriage is a way of imitating in the flesh the Creator's generosity and fecundity" (*CCC*, 2335).

Complementarity also recognizes that men and women are different in their responses and tendencies because of their different masculine and feminine identities. St. Edith Stein emphasized that maleness and femaleness are more than mere biological makeups; they are grounded in the very soul of each person.[5] The beauty of the complementarity of the sexes is that both the differences between masculinity and femininity *and* the equality of all human persons are important.

Humans need each other in their maleness and femaleness. This is evident in the second creation account when God says, "It is not good for the man to be alone," and the man responds, "This one, at last, is bone of my bones and flesh of my flesh" (Gn 2:18, 23). Jesus restored creation to the original purity intended by God in the beginning. This original plan intended spouses to be gifts of love totally and exclusively for each other.

The Two Ends of the Sexual Act in Marriage: Unity and Procreation

Sexuality is a gift for all persons from the Creator, yet its full expression is ordered to the love between one man and one woman in marriage. God designed the sexual act to be reserved for marriage as a sign of the couple's union in body and soul. There is a tendency in today's culture to view the sexual act as a purely emotional or biological action, as if sex can be disconnected from the whole human person. Yet if the sexual act is to be lived in the most full and human way as "an integral part of the love by which a man and woman commit themselves totally to one another" (*Familiaris Consortio*, 11), it must be reserved only for marriage.

Sexual love expresses love for the whole human person; it is not simply a biological need or an emotional connection. Therefore the Church identifies two ends (purposes) of the sexual act. The first end is the union of the spouses. This means that the sexual act connects spouses more deeply with each other. The sexual act can be a source of joy and pleasure, and, when practiced intimately and chastely, is noble and honorable. Unity in the sexual act is an expression of deep, mutual self-giving. Sexual love expresses bodily the union that has happened on a spiritual level in the Sacrament of Matrimony.

The second end of the sexual act is the procreation of children. Fruitfulness is intimately connected to the first end of sexual love, union. Children spring from the very heart of the mutual love between spouses as a fulfillment of this love.

In an age that can see children within marriage merely as cute accessories, the Church calls Christian married couples to a deeper and fuller understanding of fruitfulness. Procreation includes an attitude of openness to children in both body and soul and to the gift of fatherhood and motherhood. This proper attitude sees the procreation and education of children as part of the mission of married love, in which spouses are "cooperating with the love of God the Creator" (*Gaudium et Spes*, 50). All married couples are called to this mission. Couples who, through no fault of their own, are unable to conceive children are also called to fruitfulness, which can be expressed in many different ways, such as fostering children, offering their time in service to other families and the Church, supporting missions for family and children, or even adoption.

The call to fruitfulness also emphasizes the importance of responsible parenthood. The Church recognizes that in many situations there are just reasons for spacing the birth of children. Parents have a duty to meet the current needs (e.g., emotional, financial) of their family, while at the same time making certain that their desire to refrain from procreation at a given time is not motivated by selfishness. Responsible parenthood should always be practiced within "criteria that respect the total meaning of mutual self-giving and human procreation in the context of true love" (*Gaudium et Spes*, 51). This means that contraception and other forms of birth control cannot be accepted because they do not respect both the unitive and procreative ends of the sexual act.

When you think about the sexual act in marriage, it is important that you see the two ends of unity and procreation as both necessary and good. As the *Catechism of the Catholic Church* states, "The spouses' union achieves the twofold end of marriage: the good of the spouses themselves and the transmission of life.

These two meanings or values of marriage cannot be separated without altering the couple's spiritual life and compromising the goods of marriage and the future of the family" (*CCC*, 2363).

All People Are Called to Chastity

It is easy to think that once people are married they are no longer called to live chaste lives. However, **chastity** is different from **continence**—that is, refraining from any sexual acts. Chastity means successfully integrating your sexuality into your identity as a human person made up of body and soul, both for yourself as well as in relation to others. Chastity means that a person's sexuality is understood as a personal gift meant to be given fully in the mutual self-giving of married love.

Though chastity can look different in the various states of life and vocations, *everyone* is called to chastity as an "*apprenticeship in self-mastery* which is a training in human freedom" (*CCC*, 2339). Self-mastery does not mean denying one's sexuality or the goodness of the sexual act. Rather, it means using self-knowledge, temperance, prayer, and obedience to God's commandments to place the human passions under the use of reason. The chaste person does not stifle or reject human passions but rather governs the passions in such a way that freedom is not subject to impulse. True chastity respects that real freedom means freedom for excellence, which can depend at times on restraining oneself from passing desires.

Everyone is called to chastity in whatever state of life they are in. For the single person, consecrated religious, and priest, the call to chastity includes continence. Consecrated persons and priests are called to celibacy, "which enables them to give themselves to God alone with an undivided heart in a remarkable manner" (*CCC*, 2349). For married couples, chastity is lived by respecting the promises of indissolubility, faithfulness, and fruitfulness. Chastity is the work of both the individual person and society in general. Here's how:

> **For the individual, growing in chastity includes the following:**
> - understanding one's own sexual identity as part of one's identity as a son or daughter of God
> - knowing God's commandments and morality
> - depending on the grace of the sacraments and prayer
> - practicing restraint

In summary, individual chastity involves the mutual respect of persons toward one another.

> **Chastity is also the work of society, including the following:**
> - educating people both morally and socially to respect the whole human person
> - acknowledging the goods and responsibilities of human sexuality
> - acting for a virtuous society as it relates to the interdependence of all people

Governments and those who influence public policy should also uphold and support family life, virtuous living, and examples of authentic love in the media.

chastity The moral virtue which provides for the successful integration of sexuality within one's whole identity, leading to the inner unity of the physical and spiritual being (see *CCC*, 2337).

continence Refraining from use of the sexual faculties and any sexual act through self-control, which is a fruit of the Holy Spirit and is granted a person through the aid of prayer.

Offenses against Chastity

Understanding chastity begins with a proper respect for the dignity of persons and an understanding of the proper place of the sexual act within marriage. However, you will encounter many situations, actions, and beliefs in modern culture that directly offend against chastity. It is important for you to recognize their immorality and how they can harm both you as an individual and society. Offenses against chastity include the following:

- *Lust*. The disordered desire for sexual pleasure that prizes the feelings of sexual pleasure above the unitive and procreative purposes of the sexual act.

- *Fornication*. **Fornication** disregards the nature of the sexual act, which is a total gift of self within marriage. Fornication asks the body to promise itself, without the spiritual and emotional totality of marriage.

- *Masturbation*. "The deliberate stimulation of genital organs in order to derive sexual pleasure" (*CCC*, 2352). Masturbation is a disordered use of a person's sexuality for the purpose of personal pleasure. It is contrary to the understanding of the sexual act as a gift of self to be given in the bond of marriage. It trains the person to use the gift of his or her sexuality selfishly, as a means of temporary pleasure.

> **fornication** "Sexual intercourse between an unmarried man and unmarried woman. Fornication is a serious violation of the Sixth Commandment of God" (see *CCC*, Glossary).

- *Rape*. The sexual violation of another person by imposed force or deception. Rape is an intrinsically evil act that "deeply wounds the respect, freedom, and physical and moral integrity to which every person has a right" (*CCC*, 2356).

- *Prostitution*. Paying or providing a commodity in exchange for sex. Prostitution is a gravely sinful act that treats the human person as an object. It often leads to other sins: human trafficking, abuse of all kinds, exposure to disease, separation from family, and children born out of marriage.

- *Pornography*. The display of real or simulated sexual acts or nudity to provoke a sexual response. Pornography perverts the sexual act, reduces people to objects, and promotes a selfish view of sexuality.

One way to practice chastity is to avoid offenses such as these that are against the moral norms of chastity taught by the Church.

SECTION ASSESSMENT

NOTE TAKING

Use the chart you created to help you complete the following items.

1. Name the two ends of the sexual act in marriage.

2. Explain the similarities and differences between chastity as a single person and chastity as a married person.

VOCABULARY

3. How is *chastity* different from *continence*?

COMPREHENSION

4. Explain the following sentence in your own words: "The beauty of the complementarity of the sexes is that both the differences of masculinity and femininity *and* the equality of all human persons are important."

5. What does it mean that chastity is a work of both the individual and society?

CRITICAL THINKING

6. Write an explanation of what you think is meant by "freedom for excellence" in regard to chastity.

Discerning and Preparing for the Vocation to Marriage

MAIN IDEA
Making wise decisions and choosing good experiences now will help you to discern well if you are later called to the married life.

The decisions you make now and the experiences you choose in developing moral and virtuous skills will affect whatever vocation you are called to, especially if your vocation is to marriage. Making intentional and wise decisions now will help form you into a person who is able to embrace both the joys and difficulties of married life as well as help you discern well the qualities of a good spouse.

Family Life

Preparation for marriage begins at a young age. Ideally, family life is where children begin to form an understanding of unselfish love through the example of their parents. The Church puts great importance on the role of parents in the whole formation of their children, including moral and sexual education, and the good use of freedom. Family life is an "initiation into life in society" (*CCC*, 2207).

Though no family is without struggles, many young people come from homes that are more troubled due to divorce, abuse, single parenthood, or other issues that strain relationships between family members. Even if your own family situation has not been ideal, you still have control over your own formation, especially as you mature. You can choose to develop good friendships, practice your faith, and seek out healthy examples of marriage.

NOTE TAKING

Identifying Details. Use a chart like this one to keep track of details about the three ways you can discern and prepare for the vocation to marriage.

Family life	Friendship	Dating for discernment
• Example of parents • •	• Imitates Christ's friendship with us • •	• Seeks clarity • •

Dating and Courtship

You know from reading this chapter that sacramental marriage reflects Christ's relationship to the Church. Marriage is a beautiful and joyful calling that has external consequences. This means that if you are called to marriage, then finding a spouse is serious business. However, what contemporary society offers for meeting and getting to know a potential spouse isn't always successful and is often harmful. Studies have shown that modern trends of dating in high school and college—such as "hooking up" and forming early, codependent attachments—have significant negative physical and emotional consequences that can lead to depression, insecurity, and rape as well as emotional problems in later relationships.[6] In many ways, even the use of the term *dating* as it once applied to meeting a person of the opposite sex and getting to know him or her better is now foreign. If you feel called to marriage, an important task for you now is to develop skills that will serve you in a future marriage without suffering the pitfalls of the dating culture.

The Church points teens to a few key ideas about what exactly dating is meant for in order to help them decide whether they are ready to begin. First, it is important to realize the difference between dating for entertainment and dating for discernment.

Dating for Entertainment

Much of what passes for dating in high schools and colleges today would be considered dating for entertainment. The underlying attitude in this type of dating is that the person you are dating is source of entertainment or enjoyment for you. The emphasis is not to determine whether the other person might one day make a good spouse but rather to be entertained by each other's company. While there is nothing wrong with enjoying another person's company, you should always keep in mind that persons are not merely objects of enjoyment. The ultimate reason and purpose for dating is discernment.

In dating for entertainment, then, there are several dangers—for example:

- *Dangers against chastity.* Dating for entertainment encourages one-on-one dating, often to the exclusion of others. There is pressure to move further along physically. This progression can come either in "hooking up," in which there is an expectation of sexual affection without any commitment, or in a couple making emotional, mental, or physical commitments too soon.

- *Dangers against disturbing the peace of the community.* Unfortunately, dating for entertainment can be entertaining, but for all the wrong reasons. When the couple have differing expectations, physical and emotional commitments have been made prematurely, or other things have gone wrong, there is often drama that affects others outside the relationship—that includes friends, family members, school peers, and coworkers. Many times parents and siblings are called in to pick up the pieces of a broken relationship. This type of drama can affect the person's academics, extracurricular activities, and other social relationships.

- *Dangers of resentment, detraction, and calumny.* These progress naturally from drama. When a couple break up, or one person gets hurt, there is a desire to hurt the other person back. Often information that should remain private is passed around, and gossip and rumors spread. This is called **detraction**. False stories are often made up in the process, leading to **calumny**, and friendships that might have lasted are often ruined.

Dating for Discernment

In contrast to dating for entertainment, dating for discernment emphasizes respect for the dignity of the other person. Discernment through dating models prayer, reflection, and discussion to determine whether God is calling you to the vocational path of marriage. This type of dating is intended to create lasting emotional, mental, and physical connections.

Since dating for discernment is meant to move in the direction of choosing a spouse, it is important for the couple to be open to the possibility that their relationship could lead to marriage. *Courtship* is another term for dating for discernment. Though courtship can sound old-fashioned, it emphasizes more clearly what is lost in the term *dating*. Courtship emphasizes respect for the other person's family and getting to know the character of the other person in a spirit of discernment. For example, many men will begin a courtship by asking permission of the father of the woman. The couple will typically spend more time getting to know each other in a family and group setting than on individual dates.

Dating for discernment is beneficial in that it respects both the dignity of the individual and the call to married life. It calls the man and woman to seek out clarity in their relationship through interacting with each other in a variety of circumstances and by discussing important topics. It also upholds chastity through appropriate expressions of affection, so that early attachments, which might cloud good judgment and hinder discernment, do not form. Even if they do not marry the person they are dating, people who date for discernment will develop much-needed communication skills and will learn about what a good marriage requires.

Dating for discernment may seem foreign to your own experience as a teenager, but you should not brush it off as something you would never consider trying. If you truly reflect on this form of dating in the quiet of your heart, there is a good chance you will recognize its benefits and value for encouraging good choices and developing good friendships—with the chance, also, of finding out if you are suited for marriage and finding a lifelong marriage partner.

> **detraction** Disclosure of another's faults and sins, without an objectively valid reason, to persons who did not know about them, thus causing unjust injury to that person's reputation (see *CCC*, 2477).
>
> **calumny** A false statement that "harms the reputation of others and gives occasion for false judgments concerning them" (*CCC*, 2477).

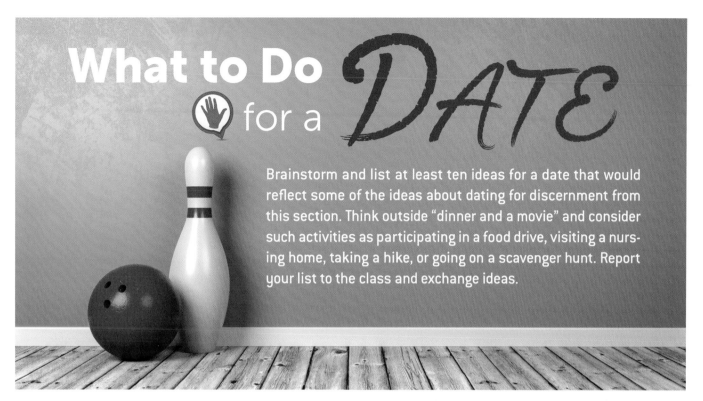

What to Do for a DATE

Brainstorm and list at least ten ideas for a date that would reflect some of the ideas about dating for discernment from this section. Think outside "dinner and a movie" and consider such activities as participating in a food drive, visiting a nursing home, taking a hike, or going on a scavenger hunt. Report your list to the class and exchange ideas.

Determining Your Readiness for Dating

Once you have a clearer understanding of dating, it is easier to decide whether you are ready to begin. The Church points specifically to the importance of friendship in developing meaningful relationship skills and following the example of Christ, who called you his friend. Skills that will be helpful in marriage (communicating through disagreements, mutual self-giving, desiring the good of another, and chastity) can all be developed in a friendship. You cannot be a good spouse without first knowing how to be a good friend.

This means that a good first step in dating is to go out with groups of people. Group dating helps to bypass some of the dangers of dating for entertainment, and it does not add undue pressure to a relationship. A second step would be going on a casual individual date with someone you have gotten to know from the group. Going on a casual date usually means that you have an appropriate level of interest in the other person and are ready to know that person better and to be known better

yourself. "Appropriate level of interest" means recognizing the dignity of the other person. This cannot happen unless you first recognize your own dignity.

If the relationship continues, it is important to bring in the other elements of dating for discernment:

- getting to know the other person's friends and family
- having discussions about important topics
- praying individually and together for good discernment
- keeping chastity as a goal by managing your time alone
- seeing each other in various environments so you come to understand the other person's character

Dating for discernment does not necessarily mean you will marry the first person you date. It does place discernment at the head of the relationship. This helps each person both to look inward at his or her own desires for a spouse and to care for the good of the other person.

SECTION ASSESSMENT

NOTE TAKING

Use the chart you made to help you complete the following items.

1. What are some ways in which family life can prepare you for the vocation to marriage?

2. In what ways does friendship help you to discern the vocation to marriage?

3. Describe the difference between dating for entertainment and dating for discernment.

COMPREHENSION

4. What are some of the dangers that can arise in a relationship that treats dating as entertainment?

5. In what ways does dating for discernment (courtship) respect and honor the other person?

REFLECTION

6. Think about friendships in your own life. What in those friendships might help you in a relationship with a future spouse?

Section Summaries

Focus Question

What is the nature of marriage, and how does one prepare for this vocation?
Complete one of the following:

 Look up and write down dictionary definitions for the following terms: *covenant, indissoluble, fidelity, fecundity, complementarity*. How do these definitions compare to what you have learned in this chapter?

 Read paragraphs 1601–1617 of the *Catechism of the Catholic Church*. Answer this question: How is God the "author of marriage"? Write four to five paragraphs. Cite references from the *Catechism*.

 Write a letter to your possible future husband or wife that tells what you are doing right now to keep yourself chaste and pure and how you are developing yourself as a person while awaiting your time of marriage.

INTRODUCTION
God Is the Author of Marriage

The vocation to marriage is an expression of the law of self-giving. Sacred Scripture tells that God is the author of marriage and that he made man and woman in his image, forming an unbreakable union between them in marriage. Jesus affirms the original intent of marriage and raises it to the level of a sacrament. The graces of marriage emanate from the Paschal Mystery.

 Read the two creation accounts found in Genesis 1 and 2. Copy two relevant verses about marriage and explain the significance of each.

SECTION 1
The Nature of Marriage

Marriage images and is a participation in the love of the Three Divine Persons of the Blessed Trinity. Humans are created to reflect Trinitarian love, called the Divine Economy. Even though marriage was distorted through sin, Christ restored marriage to its original goodness by his Passion, Death, and Resurrection. Jesus calls all baptized married persons to become signs of the love between Christ and his Church.

 Read Ephesians 5:21–33. Write a paragraph about its meaning in the context of marriage.

SECTION 2

Promises and Benefits of Marriage

Marriage is a covenant that involves a lifelong commitment and a total gift of self between spouses. The marriage covenant has certain requirements that spouses must give their full consent to; these promises in turn have associated benefits (goods) that will aid the married couple in living out their sacrament. These promises and goods are indissolubility, faithfulness, and fruitfulness.

→ Make a chart of the three promises and associated benefits of marriage: indissolubility, faithfulness, and fruitfulness. Under each heading, list suggestions for keeping the promise. For example, under indissolubility you might write: don't joke about or threaten divorce, strive to work through problems, don't go to bed angry, etc. Write two or three examples for each promise and benefit.

SECTION 3

Complementarity and Chastity within Marriage

God created humans as male and female and expressed that the two sexes are complementary and equal in dignity. The two ends of the sexual act in marriage are unity and procreation. Church teaching on procreation encompasses the importance of responsible parenthood. All persons, including married couples, are called to chastity.

 Research ways teenagers have made a commitment to chastity. Cite several benefits of chastity shared by teens you read about in your research.

SECTION 4

Discerning and Preparing for the Vocation to Marriage

Decisions made in your teenage years will prepare you for marriage. These include formation in one's family, virtuous friendships, and choosing to date for the purpose of discerning one's vocation. Perfecting the elements of friendship can help you to determine your readiness for dating for discernment.

 Name at least five reasons you find dating for discernment compelling and worthwhile.

Chapter Assignments

Choose and complete at least one of the following three assignments assessing your understanding of the material in this chapter.

1. Media Evaluation

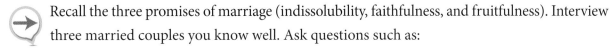

Choose a television episode or movie that you think portrays a good marriage. Evaluate the marriage represented based on the information in the opening section of this chapter's Introduction. Pretend you are a media critic for an online video magazine. Create and video record a five- to seven-minute review of the episode or movie in which you compare the marriage depicted to what you have learned about God's plan for marriage. Use specific examples from the movie or episode to illustrate your points in the review.

2. Interview about Marriage

Recall the three promises of marriage (indissolubility, faithfulness, and fruitfulness). Interview three married couples you know well. Ask questions such as:

- What is the main purpose of marriage?
- What do you see as your responsibilities in marriage?
- What kinds of promises to each other did you make during your wedding?

Video record their responses and note how the interviewees express their thoughts about the responsibilities and purpose of marriage. Record your summary of the interview and your comparison of their answers to what you have learned in this chapter. Save the video on a platform that your teacher and, optionally, your classmates can view.

3. Beginning Discernment

One of the vocational discernment tools proposed and offered on the United States Conference of Catholic Bishops' website is to create a personal timeline by recalling your life story from birth to the present, reflecting on and answering several questions grouped from different categories. For example:

Significant Persons in My Life
- Who have been important people in your life?
- Reflect on the experience of family.

Educational Experience
- What are your favorite memories of school?
- What did you learn about life that you want to remember?

Social Development

- What do you enjoy doing with others?

- What impact have various relationships had on you?

Work History

- What jobs and positions of responsibility have you held?

- What skills have you acquired in the process?

Faith Development

- What is your earliest recollection of God?

- Who taught you about God?

- Who has had the greatest influence on your faith development?

- How were Church, faith, and God in your family?

- What practices do you do to care for your faith life?

- Where did you learn about these practices?

- Who is God in your life?

- Name your experiences of God in your life.

- How did these experiences feel; what impact did they have?

- How do you see God in the everyday circumstances of your life?

- How do you nurture this relationship?

Life Choice

- When did you first think about religious life?

- What is the pattern of this thought?

Review your life by creating a timeline from the year of your birth until the present. Include some of these questions with your answers at different years on the timeline. It is okay to repeat questions and answers at different years in your life. Add a one-page essay reflecting on what this exercise taught you about discerning a vocation.

Optional: There are several free timeline generators online. Use one of these or one of your own to record the information from this assignment.

Resource: "Discernment Tools" at the USCCB website.

Faithful Disciples

Bl. Luigi Beltrame Quattrocchi and Bl. Maria Corsini

On October 21, 2001, Bl. Luigi Beltrame Quattrocchi and Bl. Maria Corsini became the first people beatified in the twenty-first century, and the first married couple ever beatified together.

In his homily for the occasion, Pope John Paul II pointed out that even though the couple lived in Rome in the first half of the twentieth century, a time marked by war, fascism, and the Nazi invasion, "the husband and wife, Luigi and Maria, kept the lamp of faith burning—*lumen Christi*—and passed it on to their four children." Three of their children were at St. Peter's Basilica to witness their parents' beatification. In fact, three of Luigi and Maria's children had religious vocations. Stefania became a Benedictine nun, Filippo (Fr. Tarcisio) a diocesan priest, and Cesare (Fr. Paolino) a Trappist monk.

Fr. Paolino remembers his parents sharing their spirituality with all their children: "There was always a supernatural, serene, and happy atmosphere in our home, but not excessively pious. No matter what the issues facing us, they always resolved it by saying that it had to be 'appealed to the heavens.'"

Bl. Maria Corsini and Bl. Luigi Beltrame Quattrocchi

Luigi was born in Catania in 1880. He received a law degree and worked as a lawyer for the Inland Revenue in Rome. His children said that he was not a strong spiritual or religious man prior to meeting their mother.

Maria, four years younger than Luigi, met him at her family's home in Florence. They married on November 25, 1905, at the Basilica of St. Mary Major in Rome. As the years of married life went on, the couple took on the challenge of growing spiritually. Fr. Paolino remembers: "There was a kind of race between Father and Mother to grow in spirituality. She began in the 'pole position' as she already lived an intense faith experience, while he was certainly a good man, just and honest, but not very practicing."

The couple began to go to daily morning Mass together. Every evening they prayed the Rosary with the family, and their family was consecrated to the Sacred Heart of Jesus. The family kept the holy hour on the eve of the first Friday of the month and participated in the night vigil prayer and weekend retreats organized by a local monastery. Maria was a volunteer nurse during World War II, and together with their children, Luigi and Maria started a scouting group for poor children in Rome. They also took in Jewish refugees displaced by the Nazis.

Their greatest challenge of faith occurred in 1913 after Maria found out that she was pregnant with the couple's fourth child. It was a difficult pregnancy, and doctors ultimately told the couple that there was barely a 5 percent chance of Maria surviving childbirth. Doctors recommended an abortion. Their oldest daughter, Stefania, recalls seeing her father crying in a conversation with a priest during that time. However, the couple gave thanks to God when their youngest daughter, Enrichetta, was born in 1914 with no lasting problems. Luigi died in November 1951 after suffering a heart attack at home. Maria lived for another fourteen years. On August 26, 1965, she died in the arms of Enrichetta.

Pope John Paul II described the witness of Luigi and Maria this way: "Drawing on the word of God and the witness of the saints, this blessed couple lived an ordinary life in an extraordinary way. Among the joys and anxieties of a normal family, they knew how to live an extraordinarily rich spiritual life."

 ## Reading Comprehension

1. What was Luigi's occupation?

2. What was the couple's son Fr. Paolino referring to when he said that his mother began in the "pole position"?

3. Name two of Luigi and Maria's religious practices.

4. What was the couple's greatest challenge of faith in their marriage?

 ## Writing Task

Pope John Paul II quoted his apostolic exhortation *Familiaris Consortio* (*On the Christian Family*) in his homily at the beatification of Bl. Luigi and Bl. Maria. He said that the sacramental grace of marriage "is not exhausted in the actual celebration of the sacrament of marriage, but rather accompanies the married couple through their lives" (*FC*, 56). How might these words encourage couples preparing for marriage to put more focus on the life after the wedding than on the wedding itself? Write three paragraphs to explain your response.

Explaining the Faith

Does dating really need to be so serious? Can't I just have fun?

Dating can be rewarding, challenging, fun, and a lot of work all at the same time. One problem with dating is the gameplaying: mock-disinterestedness, gossip, and dishonesty can often lead to confusion and heartache. Also, when a relationship is treated *just* as something fun—sexually, emotionally, or in any other way—things become not fun very quickly. Dating should be a healthy relationship built on mutual respect, and there should be boundaries. The fact is, everyone wants to be treated with dignity, truthfulness, and kindness, especially in an activity as emotionally charged as dating.

However, it shouldn't take a résumé to go out on a date with someone! Marriage is certainly good to keep in mind; after all, why would you date someone you could never see yourself potentially marrying? But it is also good to take dating and relationships one step at a time. Friendship is always a good place to start, but if you want to get to know someone better, going on a casual date is a great way to do that and to learn about relationships in general. Casual dates are usually a great deal of fun too!

Further Research

Make a list of important conversations to have with someone you might date. Discuss your list with a trusted married couple, and ask whether there are any conversations missing from your list.

Prayer
Prayer for Your Future Spouse

Loving Father, if I am called to the sacramental life of Matrimony, hear my prayer now for the person who will be my spouse. Be with that person today and every day. Help them through the challenges of becoming an adult and send my support in prayer through any difficulties. In this way, may I genuinely love this person even before we meet.

I ask for help ahead of time to be respectful and honorable when we meet and begin a relationship. I ask for help ahead of time to be faithful, supportive, strong, and as loving as I can be when we are married. If I am privileged to help create new human beings, I pray today for my children. You exist outside of time, and you know who they will be, so I can pray for them now. Help me to do everything I can now to become the best parent I can be for them, from the day they are born to the day you call me home to heaven.

Amen.

THE CELEBRATION OF THE SACRAMENT OF MATRIMONY

SUPPORTING
COUPLES AFTER
"I DO"

When Sue Haggerty and her husband, Pat, got engaged, Sue confesses that she was "an idealistic engaged woman in love. I naively thought our marriage would never face challenges or be tested."

Then they had their first real fight over what color they should paint their living room. Sue saw that if something as frivolous as paint color had led to an argument, the challenges of newlywed life would be plenty.

The Haggertys found help from their parish's marriage mentoring program. Each newly married couple that enrolled was matched up with a mentor couple with whom they would meet several times over the year, perhaps over coffee or dinner. When they met, the two couples would discuss a range of topics, such as reflective listening, ways to defuse anger and fight fairly, how to deal with unexpected changes, good communication skills, and financial planning. As the years went on, Sue and Pat were matched with new mentor couples, who could provide different perspectives on married life.

Sue attests to how much their marriage has grown through mentoring. She and her husband have deepened their relationship in ways they might not have been able to in working through issues on their own. They have also formed lasting friendships with other couples "who are all striving to deepen and better their marriages."

Sue Haggerty says she is a witness to how effective marriage mentoring can be in spreading the truth about the Church's teaching on marriage and building strong marriages. "These strong marriages, in turn, create stronger families, which results in stronger communities," she explains.

FOCUS QUESTION

How does a CATHOLIC COUPLE prepare for and CELEBRATE the SACRAMENT OF MATRIMONY, and what are its EFFECTS?

Chapter Overview

INTRODUCTION
Marriage Is a Sacred Covenant

MAIN IDEA
Sacramental marriage is a participation in the New Covenant of Christ and, when celebrated validly, is a sign to the world of God's love.

Have you ever heard the saying that "great marriages are not 50/50 but 100/100"? This quote expresses the sentiment that approaching marriage as if each person only has to give a certain percentage of their effort, love, and time will lead to a failed marriage. For a marriage to work, both spouses must be committed to giving of themselves totally.

A contract does take a 50/50 approach: "I'll give half of myself; you give half of yourself." A contract is an exchange of goods and services that can be voided by either party. A contract can become invalid or be destroyed if one or both parties don't keep their end of the deal.

For Catholics, marriage is not simply a contract between a man and a woman. Rather, it is a covenant relationship based on promises made. If one party of the covenant breaks it, the covenant still remains. Marriage is a sacred covenant between the man and woman, who pledge to one another a lifelong, faithful, and fruitful love, and between the couple and God. In marriage, the spouses are the ministers of Christ's grace through a promise that involves a total gift of self—in other words, a gift of persons, not of goods and services. Pope John Paul II explained, "Conjugal love involves a totality, in which all the elements of the

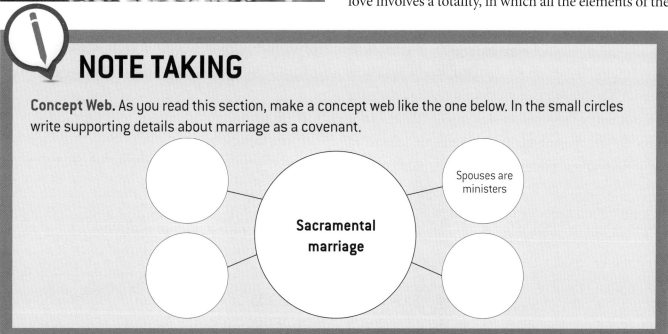

NOTE TAKING

Concept Web. As you read this section, make a concept web like the one below. In the small circles write supporting details about marriage as a covenant.

Sacramental marriage

Spouses are ministers

A Catholic marriage is not primarily a social event, but a sacrament of the Church. For this reason marriages between Catholics or between Catholics and other Christians should be celebrated in the parish church of one of the spouses. Only the local bishop can permit a marriage to be celebrated in another place. (See Explaining the Faith: "Why shouldn't Catholics get married on a beach?" in this Chapter's review section.)

person enter—appeal of the body and instinct, power of feeling and affectivity, aspiration of the spirit and of will. It aims at a deeply personal unity, a unity that, beyond union in one flesh, leads to forming one's heart and soul" (*Familiaris Consortio*, 13).

The marriage covenant is modeled on the faithfulness God exhibited in his covenants made with the Israelites in the Old Testament and on the New Covenant established by Christ on the Cross.

Marriage Is a Public Act within a Liturgical Celebration

In the celebration of the Sacrament of Matrimony, the spouses give Christ's grace to each other through their **consent** to their vows. For marriage in the **Latin Church**, the ministers of the sacrament are the man and woman being joined in Matrimony. The priest or deacon present at a marriage is there as a witness of the Church to receive the consent of the spouses and to make sure that all the elements of a valid marriage are present. (In the Eastern Churches, the bishop or priest *confers* the Sacrament of Matrimony.) The presence of the priest or deacon, the official witnesses (often the best man and maid of honor), and the other guests to listen and watch the couple visibly and publicly express their vows expresses that the marriage is a reality.

Another important sign of the covenant being made between the couple and God is that the marriage takes place in a church, signifying that God is a party to the marriage. The Sacrament of Matrimony usually takes place within the Mass. This is to remind the couple and all Christians that marriage (like all sacraments) is connected with the Paschal Mystery. The Eucharist is a memorial of the New Covenant, in which Christ has united himself to the Church, his bride, by his Passion and Death. "It is therefore fitting that the spouses should seal their consent to give themselves to each other through the offering of their own lives by uniting it to the offering of Christ for his Church made present in the Eucharistic sacrifice, and by receiving the Eucharist so that, communicating in the same Body and the same Blood of Christ, they may form but 'one body' in Christ" (*CCC*, 1621).

In the celebration of marriage, certain elements of the wedding Mass are emphasized:

- the Liturgy of the Word, which shows the importance of Christian marriage in the history of salvation

consent In the context of marriage, a free and unconstrained act of the will in which spouses promise to give themselves to each other in marriage.

Latin Church The vast majority of the Roman Catholic Church which uses the Latin Rite liturgies and has its own distinctive canon law.

- the consent of the spouses to marry, which the couple give to each other
- the special **nuptial blessing**
- the reception of Holy Communion by the groom and bride, and by all present

Section 2 has more information on these topics.

Natural Marriage vs. Sacramental Marriage

Marriage has existed since the beginning of time; God created it as a natural institution. Most cultures and religions throughout history have regarded marriage as a permanent bond from which a family grows, very similar to the scriptural understanding of marriage. The Catholic Church understands how central marriage is to all cultures and thus regards any marriage, whether between Christians or non-Christians, as a true, permanent bond, rooted in the divine origin intended from the beginning by God. Because marriage is a natural institution, marriages that are not between Catholics or are between a Catholic and a nonbaptized person are considered *natural marriages*. Thus, a marriage in a Jewish or Hindu ceremony or even a civil marriage between a nonbaptized man and a nonbaptized woman can share in the fundamental nature of marriage.

A *sacramental marriage* differs from a natural marriage in that a sacramental marriage recognizes and participates in the New Covenant of Christ, and is thus a sign to the world of God's love. Sacramental marriages are those entered into by a baptized man and a baptized woman in a liturgical setting.

When a man and a woman are seeking to be married in the Church, part of the initial preparation for marriage involves their learning both Church and state requirements for a valid marriage. Civil laws determine the legality of marriage according to the government of a country. In the United States, there are age requirements that vary from state to state. Church laws set the conditions for a valid, lawful Catholic marriage. Before beginning preparation for a sacramental marriage, the couple are asked if they meet the basic requirements to receive the Sacrament of Matrimony:

- They have received the Sacraments of Initiation (or, for non-Catholics, Christian Baptism).
- They are not already married or bound by a previous vow.
- They are coming freely to be married.
- They are of the legal age to marry.

These questions help to determine if there are any **impediments**, or obstacles, for the couple to a valid and licit celebration of the Sacrament of Matrimony. Impediments are discussed in more detail in the feature "Understanding Impediments." If there are no impediments, then a valid marriage can be celebrated in the Church.

The Church wants couples to have all the graces available to aid them as they enter married life. Having the proper **disposition** is a necessary precursor to being able to fruitfully receive the graces of their sacrament. Thus, each baptized Catholic in the couple must make sure they have no mortal sins on their souls. Receiving the Sacrament of Penance right before the wedding is strongly encouraged.

Section 2 details other important tasks the Church asks of a couple prior to their reception of the Sacrament of Matrimony.

nuptial blessing "Prayers for the blessing of a couple being married, especially of the bride," after the couple have given their consent to be married (*CCC*, Glossary).

impediments External circumstances or facts that make a person ineligible for entering into a sacramental or legal marriage.

disposition An interior and exterior attitude that reflects openness to receiving the graces of a sacrament.

Understanding
IMPEDIMENTS

An impediment is an obstacle that would prevent a marriage from being valid (actually occurring). There are twelve impediments to the Sacrament of Matrimony, sometimes called *diriment impediments*. *Diriment* comes from the Latin word *dirimens*, meaning "separating." Thus, a diriment impediment is one that prevents a couple from being joined. Some diriment impediments can be removed, or dispensed, while others cannot. The first three are based on Divine Law and cannot be dispensed. The next three are "reserved," meaning they can only be dispensed by the pope. The last six are dispensable by a local bishop.

01 **IMPOTENCE**. A person who is unable to consummate the marriage through the sexual act is not free to marry. This is not the same as sterility.

02 **PRIOR MARRIAGE**. If a person is married, and the marriage has not been declared null (see the subsection "Annulment" in Chapter 5, Section 1, "Marriage Is until Death"), then a person is not free to marry.

03 **CONSANGUINITY**. Direct line (father-daughter) and "up to the fourth degree consanguinity" (first cousins) blood relations cannot marry.

04 **CONJUCIDE**. A person who has killed a spouse so as to be free to marry another may not marry without permission from the pope.

05 **HOLY ORDERS**. Bishops, priests, and deacons cannot move from their present state of life without going through the process of *laicization* (becoming a layperson) and must have specific permission to marry from the pope.

06 **PERPETUAL VOW OF CHASTITY.** A person who has taken a perpetual vow of chastity is not free to marry without papal permission and release from the vow.

07 **AGE.** The Church has set the minimum age for marriage as sixteen for a man and fourteen for a woman; however, most dioceses use the legal state requirements as the minimum age.

08 **AFFINITY.** Those who are related by marriage cannot marry each other. Thus, an uncle-by-marriage cannot marry his niece.

09 **DISPARITY OF CULT.** A Catholic cannot marry a non-Christian without an express dispensation. This is discussed further in Section 4, "Mixed Marriage and Marriage with Disparity of Cult."

10 **ABDUCTION.** If an intended spouse is abducted by the other intended spouse, this impedes the marriage from validly occurring.

11 **ADOPTION.** If persons are related through adoption, they cannot validly be married.

12 **PUBLIC PROPRIETY.** A person cannot marry a first-degree relation of a previous spouse, such as the mother of a previous spouse.

In addition to these twelve diriment impediments, there are *general impediments*, such as *coercion* (forcing someone to marry); *refusing procreation* (if a spouse declares he or she does not want to have children); and *exclusion of fidelity* (if a spouse refuses to be faithful or says he or she cannot), which directly oppose the promises and benefits of marriage (see Chapter 2 Introduction). *Lack of form* (not following the rites of the Church in a marriage, such as getting married on a beach by a non-Catholic minister) and *mental incapacity* are other impediments.[1]

SECTION ASSESSMENT

NOTE TAKING

Use the concept web you made to help you complete the following items.

1. Name some of the characteristics of a sacramental marriage.

COMPREHENSION

2. Why does a marriage take place publicly?

3. What are some similarities between a natural and a sacramental marriage?

4. What are the basic requirements to enter into the Sacrament of Matrimony?

VOCABULARY

5. As found in the feature "Understanding Impediments," name one *impediment* to marriage that may be dispensed only by the pope.

CRITICAL THINKING

6. What are some reasons that marriage has always been central to all cultures?

Preparation for the Sacrament of Matrimony

MAIN IDEA

Remote preparation for the Sacrament of Matrimony begins in each individual family. Proximate and immediate preparations occur when a man and a woman become engaged and desire to be married in the Church.

The Church desires that all people should understand the beautiful plan God has for married love; but she desires this in a special way for engaged couples, so that they can approach with freedom and responsibility the commitment they will make to each other. Because marriage is a lifelong commitment that asks for complete fidelity, marriage preparation is of "prime importance" so that the "marriage covenant may have solid and lasting human and Christian foundations" (*CCC*, 1632).

In fact, marriage preparation is ideally *lifelong*, beginning when children witness the loving relationship of their parents, who live out the graces of the Sacrament of Matrimony. Thus, marriage preparation can be divided into periods of remote, proximate, and immediate preparation for the Sacrament of Matrimony.

Remote Preparation

Remote preparation for marriage begins in the family during infancy and extends through childhood and adolescence. Through the example of your parents and relatives, family life is potentially your first "school" to learn about love. It is in the family that you learn how to give generously and selflessly. The

NOTE TAKING

Tracking Examples. Draw a timeline like the one here with segments for remote, proximate, and immediate preparation for marriage. Above each segment, print details about each type of preparation named in this section.

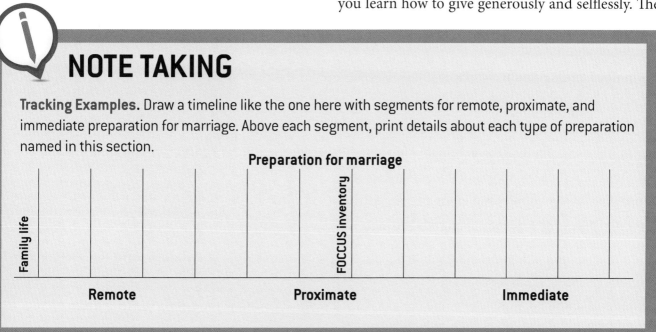

Second Vatican Council teaches: "It is imperative to give suitable and timely instruction to young people, above all in the heart of their own families, about the dignity of married love, its role and its exercise, so that, having learned the value of chastity, they will be able at a suitable age to engage in honorable courtship and enter upon a marriage of their own" (*Gaudium et Spes*, 48, quoted in *CCC*, 1632).

The Church places great importance on the role of parents in the whole formation of their children, including their sexual education, in preparation for their vocation. The *Catechism of the Catholic Church* teaches that "the family is the community in which, from childhood, one can learn moral values, begin to honor God, and make good use of freedom. Family life is an initiation into life in society" (*CCC*, 2207). Your own parents have probably tried to pass along to you their values in these areas. At its best the family is a **domestic church**, a place where you can learn that:

- every person should have a healthy understanding of himself or herself;

- sexuality is a part of a your intimate self, a part of your personality;

- from creation God made man and woman for each other, complementary as masculine and feminine;

- marriage involves total self-giving, emotionally and physically; and

- healthy sexual relations in marriage are an expression of mutual love, not selfish pleasures.

Every family will have its own struggles and weaknesses. Therefore, some of these formative ideas might not have been imparted to you or encouraged in your upbringing. Many young people benefit greatly from the extension of the domestic church through the

> **domestic church** *Ecclesia domestica*, a name for the family that signifies a miniature Church.

examples of other trusted adults who can help them grow in wisdom and virtue. There are probably many trusted adults you know, such as grandparents, godparents, catechists, or teachers, who witness healthy and holy marriage.

The remote period of marriage preparation also includes forming friendships and dating for discernment, as described in Chapter 2 Section 4. The time of remote preparation extends into adulthood.

Proximate Preparation

The time of proximate preparation for marriage begins when a couple become engaged. It is the couple's responsibility to inform the pastor of their parish when they want to be married; it is the Church's responsibility to prepare couples well for marriage by taking care that they have assimilated the lessons of remote preparation and, if necessary, educating them in areas that were never taught.

In the United States, the preparation time before marriage in each diocese is at least six months. The pastor or his representative will interview the couple initially to determine whether there are any impediments preventing their marriage in the Church. Then a team usually made up of a priest or deacon, catechists, and marriage mentors will focus on the three promises couples make to each other at their wedding:

Indissolubility
Faithfulness
Fruitfulness

Often the couple will take a premarital inventory to gauge their similarities and differences, communication styles, and the like. The FOCCUS (Facilitating Open Couple Communication, Understanding, and Study) inventory is one of the most widely used Catholic inventories, with more than two hundred questions on topics such as finances, communication, sexuality, family of origin, and views on religion and morality.

Other components of marriage preparation are presentations to help the couple understand the inherent goodness of sexual intercourse and its connection to welcoming children. Often this is done through Natural Family Planning (NFP) classes. NFP helps the couple to become more aware of the woman's biological and physiological signs of fertility so that they can morally postpone or try to achieve pregnancy.

The couple's introduction to NFP should also include information about why the Church does not allow contraception.

An overall purpose of marriage preparation is to help engaged couples to grow in self-knowledge, knowledge of their intended spouse, and knowledge of the strengths and weaknesses of their relationship. All marriage preparation is done in the context of encouraging the couple to deepen their personal and communal prayer, spirituality, and practice of their Catholic faith. Marriage preparation also focuses on teaching the couple practical skills that will help them to remain committed to the three promises of marriage. Special adjustments are often made to marriage preparation classes when one spouse is not Catholic.

Marriage Preparation in Your Diocese

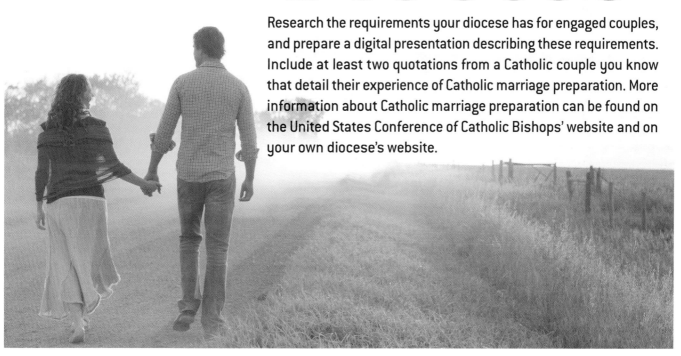

Research the requirements your diocese has for engaged couples, and prepare a digital presentation describing these requirements. Include at least two quotations from a Catholic couple you know that detail their experience of Catholic marriage preparation. More information about Catholic marriage preparation can be found on the United States Conference of Catholic Bishops' website and on your own diocese's website.

Immediate Preparation

In the weeks and days prior to the wedding, the couple should be invited to reflect more intensely on their previous preparation, especially the "doctrinal, moral and spiritual content" of married love (*Preparation for the Sacrament of Marriage*, 50). Often this takes the form of directed experiences of prayer, such as at an Engaged Encounter or a Pre-Cana retreat, during which the couple can reflect and pray together to encounter the Lord in the Sacrament of Matrimony.

The immediate preparation period also involves working with the priest who will officiate the wedding to plan a meaningful nuptial Mass. Special focus is placed on the choice of Scripture readings (see the feature "Choosing Readings for a Wedding Mass" in Section 2). The couple may also choose various prayers and blessings as well as select the music for the wedding with the help of a liturgical musician. Most dioceses and parishes have rules (or at least strong suggestions) for appropriate music for weddings. The couple can compose specific intercessory prayers to be included in the Liturgy of the Word. There is also opportunity for family members and friends to participate in some of the liturgical ministries, as lectors, extraordinary ministers of Holy Communion, altar servers, musicians, and more.

The couple usually celebrate the Sacrament of Penance close to the wedding date, often during the wedding rehearsal a day or two before.

SECTION ASSESSMENT

 NOTE TAKING

Use the timeline you drew to help you answer the following questions.

1. Why is it accurate to say that remote preparation for marriage begins in infancy?
2. Name one task of proximate preparation for marriage.
3. What is typically the subject of the meeting between the priest and the couple during the time of immediate preparation before their marriage?

 COMPREHENSION

4. Who might be part of the team assisting a couple during the time of proximate preparation for marriage?
5. What is the purpose of a premarital inventory?

 APPLICATION

6. What are some important things you can learn as a child within a family about marriage and married love?

 REFLECTION

7. Think about a friend you might choose to be the best man or maid of honor in your wedding. What do you imagine this person's advice for your successful future marriage might be?

The Order of Celebrating Matrimony

MAIN IDEA
The Sacrament of Matrimony is based on the free and mutual consent of the spouses given during the profession of vows to each other at a wedding Mass.

When two baptized persons come to be married in the Church, their marriage is based on their free and mutual consent. In other words, the Church depends on the man and woman making a free choice to be married; they must not be forced into the marriage or constrained in any way. The *Catechism of the Catholic Church* explains the importance of consent:

> Since marriage is a state of life in the Church, certainty about it is necessary. . . . The public character of the consent protects the "I do" once given and helps the spouses remain faithful to it. So that the "I do" of the spouses may be a free and responsible act and so that the marriage covenant may have solid and lasting human and Christian foundations, preparation for marriage is of prime importance. (*CCC*, 1631–1632)

Every Christian sacrament has matter and form. *Matter* is the physical element or gesture of a sacrament. For marriage, the matter is the mutual and free consent of the man and woman. *Form* refers to the words spoken during the sacrament to confer God's grace. The exchange of vows by the spouses using an approved formula to express their consent is the form of marriage. The consent of the couple determines the validity of the marriage.

NOTE TAKING

Identifying Details. Create a table like the one here. In the first column, make a list of the key elements of matrimonial consent. In the second column, list the key elements of a wedding Mass.

Key elements of matrimonial consent	Key elements of a wedding Mass
• No impediments	• Scripture readings
•	•
•	•
•	•
•	•

The Church realizes that couples must know what marriage is and what it asks of them as a couple in order to fully consent to be married. This is why marriage preparation and a sincere understanding of the marriage vows carry so much weight for those being married. The fundamental points of matrimonial consent are the following:

- There are no impediments hindering their union (see the feature "Understanding Impediments" in this Chapter's Introduction).

- The couple have come freely and without coercion.

- They intend to marry for life, to be faithful to one another, and to be open to children.

- They give their consent in the presence of two witnesses and a minister authorized by the Catholic Church.

The essential rite of the Sacrament of Matrimony—the consent of the couple to marriage—takes place directly after the Liturgy of the Word. The consent to marriage is received and accepted (typically by the priest or deacon in the name of the Church). Most couples then exchange rings, although this practice is optional. The priest then blesses the rings of the bride and groom and they exchange them. The circular ring is a sign of the eternal love of the couple and of their marriage that will last until death.

The following subsection details the form of matrimonial consent.

Matrimonial Vows and Consent

During the essential rite of the Sacrament of Matrimony, the priest or deacon asks the couple a series of questions so that they may express their consent and desires. The three promises made in the marriage vows correspond to the three promises and benefits of marriage named in Chapter 2's Introduction. The couple take turns answering the questions separately to establish that they are each coming freely into the bond of marriage. Here is one form of the marriage vows:

> N. and N., have you come here to enter into
>   Marriage
> without coercion,
> freely and wholeheartedly?
>
> Are you prepared, as you follow the path of
>   Marriage,
> to love and honor each other
> for as long as you both shall live?
>
> Are you prepared to accept children lovingly
>   from God
> and to bring them up
> according to the law of Christ and his Church?

After this, the priest will invite them to declare their consent by joining hands and repeating to each other:

> I, N., take you, N., to be my wife/husband.
> I promise to be faithful to you,
> in good times and in bad,
> in sickness and in health, to love you and to
>   honor you
> all the days of my life.

Another option in the United States is for the couple to repeat to each other:

> I, N., take you, N., for my lawful husband/wife,
>   to have and to hold, from this day forward,
>   for better, for worse,
>   for richer, for poorer,

in sickness and in health,
until death do us part.

It is important that the matrimonial consent is given publicly in a church and follows the form established by the Church; these actions lead the couple to certain rights and responsibilities within the Church, both regarding each other and regarding their children. Also, the public and official nature of the couple's consent "protects the 'I do' once given and helps the spouses remain faithful to it" (*CCC*, 1632).

As soon as the wedding concludes, the pastor of the parish records the name of the priest or deacon, the names of the witnesses, and the date and place of the wedding in the parish register.

Elements of the Wedding Mass

It is very appropriate that the Sacrament of Matrimony happens in the Mass, since the Eucharist is a sign of the union of Christ and his Church, which the married couple represent, now being "'one body' in Christ" (*CCC*, 1621). The wedding Mass proceeds as a normal Mass would but with special readings, Responsorial Psalm, and prayers that relate to marriage. The couple usually choose these Scripture readings, which allows them to personalize the wedding Mass. The couple exchange their vows and rings after the homily.

The Mass then continues with the Liturgy of the Eucharist. During the **epiclesis**, which calls down the Holy Spirit, "the spouses receive the Holy Spirit as the communion of love of Christ and the Church. The Holy Spirit is the seal of their covenant, the ever-available

> **epiclesis** The prayer, said in every sacrament, petitioning God to send down the sanctifying power of the Holy Spirit (see *CCC*, Glossary).

source of their love and the strength to renew their fidelity" (*CCC*, 1624).

After the Our Father, the priest faces the couple and extends his hands over them, giving them a nuptial blessing. This blessing is intended to bring the love of God and all his graces on the couple throughout their marriage. The priest may say:

Father, stretch out your hand,
and bless N. and N.
Lord, grant that as they begin to live this
    sacrament
they may share with each other
the gifts of your love
and become one in heart and mind
as witnesses to your presence in their marriage.
Help them to create a home together
and give them children to be
formed by the Gospel
and to have a place in your family.
Give your blessings to N., your daughter,
so that she may be a good wife and mother,
caring for the home,
faithful in love for her husband,
generous and kind.
Give your blessings to N., your son,
so that he may be a faithful husband
and good father.
Father, grant that as they come together to your
table on earth,
so they may one day have the joy of sharing
    your
feast in heaven.
We ask this through Christ, our Lord.
Amen.

The married couple, properly disposed for the reception of Holy Communion by having quite recently received the Sacrament of Penance, are the first to receive Communion under both species, the

Body and Blood of Christ. It is appropriate for the man and woman, who have just been joined as one, to drink from a common cup. The Holy Eucharist communicates and nourishes their love and is to be the center of their entire married life.

The wedding Mass is an opportunity for others to experience the Catholic faith, in particular the beauty of the Church's understanding of love and marriage. It is an opportunity for evangelization, especially if either member of the couple has many relatives or friends who are not Catholic.

Finally, note that when a baptized Catholic marries a non-Catholic Christian, the wedding is often celebrated outside of the Mass. Depending on the preferences of the local bishop, the wedding may include a celebration of the Liturgy of the Word along with the Order of Celebrating Matrimony. A marriage between a nonbaptized person and a Catholic is also celebrated outside of the Mass; it is considered a nonsacramental marriage, though still blessed and validated by the Church.

♥ Choosing Readings for a Wedding Mass

One way a couple can make their wedding more meaningful for themselves and their guests is by putting special thought into the readings and Responsorial Psalm used in the wedding Mass. Look at the following suggested Scripture readings to choose ones you might like for your own wedding. Choose one from each category. Then write a one-page reflection connecting the themes of the readings you chose to the Sacrament of Matrimony.

Old Testament Reading	Responsorial Psalm	New Testament Reading	Gospel Reading
Genesis 1:26–28, 31a	Psalm 33:12, 18, 20–22	Romans 8:31b–35, 37–39	Matthew 5:1–12
Genesis 2:18–24	Psalm 34:2–4, 6–9	Ephesians 5:1–2a, 21–28	Matthew 7:12, 24–29
Tobit 7:9–10, 11–15	Psalm 103:1–2, 8, 13, 17–18a	Colossians 3:12–17	Matthew 19:3–6
Tobit 8:5–10	Psalm 128:1–5	1 Peter 3:1–9	Matthew 22:35–40
Song of Songs 2:8–10, 14, 16a	Psalm 145:8–10, 15, 17–18	1 John 3:18–24	Mark 10:6–9
Jeremiah 31:31–32a, 33–34a	Psalm 148:1–4, 9–14	Revelation 19:1, 5–9	John 2:1–11

SECTION ASSESSMENT

NOTE TAKING

Use the table you created to help you complete the following items.

1. Explain the foundational importance of consent for the Sacrament of Martrimony.

2. What are the three essential elements for the wedding Mass?

COMPREHENSION

3. How should a couple properly dispose themselves before celebrating the Sacrament of Matrimony?

4. Why is it appropriate to celebrate a Catholic wedding in a Mass?

5. What happens at the epiclesis of a wedding Mass?

REFLECTION

6. Imagine yourself as a non-Catholic attending a wedding that is part of a Catholic Mass. What would you find most interesting? What would you find most inspiring?

SECTION 3

Effects of the Sacrament of Matrimony

MAIN IDEA
The effects of the Sacrament of Matrimony create an unbreakable bond through which the couple are given grace to perfect their love, strengthen their unity, and grow in holiness.

When a couple enters into the Sacrament of Matrimony, the spouses become a sign of life and love for each other and, in the way they love each other and their family, a sign of love to the world. Marriage becomes the avenue through which a husband and wife grow together in perfection and holiness, while also contributing to the glory of God in their family and in the world around them. With Christ, the couple are bound together in an unbreakable covenant so that "authentic married love is caught up into divine love" (*Gaudium et Spes*, 48).

Partnered with Christ, the couple works toward their own salvation. Assuredly their life will have many ups and downs, tragedies and joys. There is the joy of welcoming children and nurturing them in life and faith. Later, the same children can be the cause of pain to their parents either through their own decision (e.g., abuse of drugs, abandoning the faith) or through their suffering serious illness or death.

The key trait of the marriage covenant is that it is caught up into the New Covenant of God's love—Jesus Christ's giving of his life for all humanity. By giving his Son, the Father showed his faithful love and fidelity. Jesus draws all people into one body, loves us

NOTE TAKING

Tree Web. Create a tree web like the one here to help you remember the different effects and graces of the Sacrament of Matrimony. Two of the effects and graces are filled in for you.

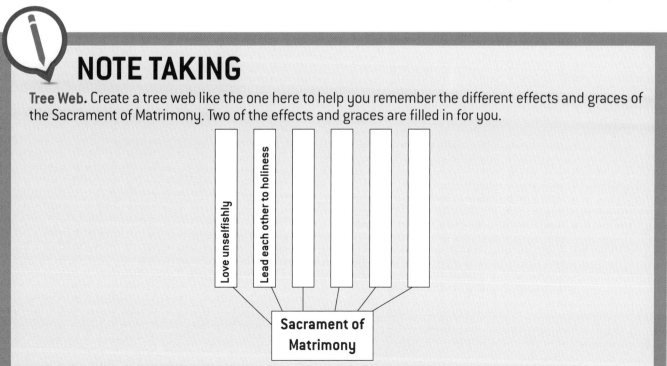

Love unselfishly — Lead each other to holiness — Sacrament of Matrimony

personally and unconditionally, and calls on us to grow in love by serving others. Hence, there are two main effects of the Sacrament of Matrimony:

1. The couple are united in a permanent bond. Human authority can never dissolve a consummated marriage between a baptized man and a baptized woman. The Church does not have the power to dissolve a bond that has been established by God.

2. The husband and wife are promised a lifetime of God's grace, by which their love is perfected and their unity is strengthened.

Humans are predestined to reproduce "the image of the invisible God" (*CCC*, 381). Through the witness of their married life, the couple bring the presence of Christ to the world. The following subsection examines some of the graces of the Sacrament of Matrimony.

Graces of Married Life

In the Introduction, marriage was described as a covenant of love between the two spouses and between the couple and God. Through their free consent in the Sacrament of Matrimony, couples are given the grace to be an image of Christ's New Covenant of unconditional love. The graces of the Sacrament of Matrimony help the couple to live out their promises of indissolubility, faithfulness, and fruitfulness in several ways:

- *Married couples are given the grace to love each other unselfishly, as Christ has loved us.* In marriage, a couple must be attentive to each other's needs, putting the other person first. For example, Jason is carrying a heavy load by working a full-time job, taking classes for an advanced degree, and attending to home life with his wife, Anna, and two children. Unselfish loves calls on Anna to be understanding when Jason is tired and skips some household tasks he is usually responsible for. Likewise, Jason is called to be aware that his wife is doing extra to manage the house and care for the children so that he can concentrate on his necessary tasks.

Unselfish love is also manifested through an attitude of self-giving and through always respecting the unitive and procreative dimensions of sexual intercourse. "The truly human performance of these acts fosters the self-giving they signify and enriches the spouses in joy and gratitude" (*Gaudium et Spes*, 49, quoted in *CCC*, 2362). Unselfish conjugal love (love relating to marriage) is concerned for the happiness and good of the other spouse.

- *The man and woman are given the grace to strengthen each other and lead each other to holiness.* Unselfish love spurs the husband and wife to be concerned about not just the physical and emotional well-being of the other but also their spiritual and eternal perfection. Each married couple works toward holiness in a unique way, always depending upon the grace of God first and foremost. The Second Vatican Council states that by the grace of Matrimony spouses "help one another to attain holiness in their married life" (*Lumen Gentium*, 11, quoted in *CCC*, 1641).

- *Married couples are given the grace to strengthen the indissoluble bond they have made, and to find joy in their union.* Through their union with the divine love of the Blessed Trinity, the love between a husband and wife is strengthened and purified. Couples who have been married twenty, thirty, or more years will often tell you that they are better at loving each other now than when they were first married. With God's help, spouses can learn to improve their love and anticipate each other's needs and desires and also how to express frustrations, disappointments, and anger in ways that will not damage their relationship. When a couple relies upon the graces of the Sacrament of Matrimony, their union deepens and becomes an even greater source of joy.

- *When a couple are blessed with children, they are given the grace to raise their children in faith and love.* God blessed marriage from the beginning of creation and desired that children should come from marriage. When married couples place their trust in God's plan, he will give them what they need to raise their children well.

The example given by faithful married couples is a witness that strengthens the Church and society. Imagine a couple sharing their testimony on the occasion of their sixtieth wedding anniversary. The praise and congratulations they received would not center on how much money they made, the jobs they had, or the cars they drove. Rather people would admire their marriage for

- the love and care they showed for each other even in difficult times,

- the fruitful lives of their children,

- their generosity to others,

- their faith and participation in the life of the Church, and

- the bold witness they give to living out married love.

The *Catechism of the Catholic Church* expresses this well: "In our own time, in a world often alien and even hostile to faith, believing families are of primary importance as centers of living, radiant faith. For this reason the Second Vatican Council, using an ancient expression, calls the family the *Ecclesia domestica* [domestic church]. . . . The home is the first school of Christian life and 'a school for human enrichment'" (*CCC*, 1656–1657, quoting *Gaudium et Spes*, 52). Through the love, care, and education they provide in their home, married couples enrich society, showing the Church and the world the goodness of God in family life.

NIGHT OUT

Offer your services (free of charge) as a babysitter to a married couple with young children. Instead of accepting money for your services, tell the couple you would like them to share three things with you about their relationship/marriage for a school project. Here are the three things:

1. How did you meet? Also, tell about the first time you had the feeling you would marry your spouse.

2. If you could change anything about your wedding day, what would it be?

3. What did you find to be the greatest adjustment to married life? How did you learn to make this adjustment?

Write a one- to two-page summary of what you found out from the husband and wife.

Don't forget to babysit the children. Have fun!

SECTION ASSESSMENT

NOTE TAKING

Use the tree web you created to help you answer the following questions.

1. How can the graces of the Sacrament of Matrimony benefit the spouses?

2. How does the example of faithful married couples strengthen the Church and society?

COMPREHENSION

3. What are the two main effects of the Sacrament of Matrimony?

CRITICAL THINKING

4. In the Sacrament of Matrimony, couples are given the grace to be an image of Christ's New Covenant of unconditional love through their free consent. Share two concrete examples of how this might be witnessed.

REFLECTION

5. Share two characteristics not mentioned in the section that you might admire in a couple who had been married for sixty years.

SECTION 4
Mixed Marriage and Marriage with Disparity of Cult

MAIN IDEA
Marriage between a Catholic and a non-Catholic requires special permissions and pastoral care from the Church. Couples should be aware of the challenges that face them in such cases.

It isn't hard to imagine that couples who share a religion and moral values have better odds for a happy and life-long marriage than those who don't. This is one reason the Church encourages Catholics to marry one another. Another reason is that when two Catholics marry, they are more likely to continue to practice their faith and to baptize and raise their children as Catholics.

Imagine the Church as a loving mother, who, out of care for what is best for her children, knows that marriage to someone who does not share the Catholic faith poses a challenge to the Catholic spouse. In those cases, the Church is aware that the Catholic spouse must preserve his or her faith without the benefit of completely sharing and growing in the faith with his or her spouse. Tensions may also arise because the Catholic spouse will be solely responsible for the raising of the couple's children in the faith.

Yet, though there are definitely challenges, with good preparation, open communication, and a committed faith on the part of the Catholic spouse, marriage between a Catholic and non-Catholic is not "an insurmountable obstacle" (*CCC*, 1634). Many of the saints of the Church—including St. Monica (see image at left), Sts. Woolos and Gladys Farfog (who converted together), and Servant of God Elizabeth Leseur—have lived either in a *mixed marriage* (a marriage between

NOTE TAKING

Writing Definitions and Examples. Create a table like the one here. As you read this section, write a one-sentence definition for each type of special marriage situation. Then tell what kind of permission is needed for each.

Type of marriage	Definition	Type of permission needed
Mixed marriage		
Marriage with disparity of cult		

a Catholic spouse and a non-Catholic but Christian spouse) or in a marriage described as having *disparity of cult* (a marriage between a baptized Catholic and a nonbaptized person). Each of these circumstances requires different permission, preparation, and care by the Church.

Mixed Marriage

In a mixed marriage, one spouse is a baptized Catholic, while the other is a baptized non-Catholic of another Christian community. In this case, the couple would work with their parish priest to seek express permission to be married from the local bishop. It is the responsibility of the local bishop to care for the spiritual well-being of the Catholics in his diocese, so he must be concerned about the welfare of the Catholic spouse. The Church recognizes that "the spouses risk experiencing the tragedy of Christian disunity even in the heart of their own home" (*CCC*, 1634). The Church wants neither to brush these difficulties aside as unimportant nor to allow them to cause disharmony within the home. The bishop will ask the priest preparing the couple to see to it that these necessary conditions for the marriage are met:

- The Catholic spouse declares that he or she is prepared to remove dangers from falling away from the faith.

- The Catholic spouse promises to do all in his or her power to have the children baptized and raised in the Catholic Church.

- The non-Catholic spouse is informed of these promises made by the Catholic spouse.

- The couple is instructed in the teachings of the Church, especially those on the Sacrament of Matrimony and family life.

It is the work of the Church, especially through their marriage preparation, to help couples entering into a mixed marriage to "live out their particular

"The practice of infant Baptism is an immemorial tradition of the Church. There is explicit testimony to this practice from the second century on, and it is quite possible that, from the beginning of the apostolic preaching, when whole 'households' received baptism, infants may also have been baptized" (CCC, 1252).

situation in the light of faith, overcome the tensions between the couple's obligations to each other and towards their ecclesial communities, and encourage the flowering of what is common to them in faith and respect for what separates them" (*CCC*, 1636). In their marriage preparation, the couple should have time to learn about and discuss each other's values and beliefs so that they can live and grow in unity.

Convalidation Brings One Couple Deeper into the Sacrament of Matrimony

Before having children, Frank and Allison Molnar of Wichita, Kansas, spent little time attending to religion or their faith lives. Allison had been raised as a Methodist, Frank as a "Chreaster" (Christmas and Easter) Catholic. Because Frank was not a practicing Catholic, they married in the Methodist Church.

When they began to have children, they realized that they wanted their kids to have some kind of faith. The Molnars tried out different worship services, but found it very difficult to get their young children ready on Sunday mornings. Frank suggested they attend the Catholic Church in their town since it had a Saturday evening Mass. The timing fit well for their family, and slowly they were drawn more into the life of the parish.

Gradually over four years, Allison was attracted to the truths of the Church and began to grow deeper in her relationship with Christ. She entered the Rite of Christian Initiation of Adults (RCIA) process to become a Catholic. She also noticed the difference that faith and practicing a common religion was having on her family and marriage. As Frank and Allison grew closer, they saw how important unity, especially in faith and morals, was to their family life. She notes, "No one, including Frank, pressured me to become Catholic. But I felt that I needed to do this."

After her conversion, Frank and Allison attended a Catholic Marriage Encounter weekend and began to take seriously "being Catholic in our marriage." The diocesan director of marriage and family life offered to do Pre-Cana classes with them so they could have their marriage blessed in the Catholic Church. "We wanted our marriage to reflect what we had been learning in those classes and in Marriage Encounter," says Frank. "That in dying to self and self-giving love we were reflecting Christ's love."

The Molnars decided to offer a new expression of their consent at a **convalidation** Mass. Now many photos from their convalidation and family life are displayed around their home. "We are sacrament to each other now," says Allison. "I used to put the kids first, and there was nothing left for Frank and the marriage. Now it's God, Frank, and the kids in that order. And the kids never ask, 'Are you getting a divorce?' anymore." Both Frank and Allison have noticed that the love between them has filtered down to their kids.

"We never used to pray," recalls Frank. "But now we get down on our knees and pray together." Frank says that often when they are out on a date one or the other will suggest that they stop by an Adoration chapel. This new life in Christ has made them a "family with focus and direction"; the Molnars devote their time and talents to helping with Marriage Encounters and marriage mentoring in their diocese. Their witness has also brought at least one other couple to have their marriage convalidated. "After our convalidation we have experienced how we are holier together than we could have ever been separate," says Allison.

Marriage with Disparity of Cult

A marriage with disparity of cult is a marriage between a baptized Catholic and a nonbaptized person; it requires even greater care by the Church and between the couple than a mixed marriage. The *Catechism of the Catholic Church* notes that "differences about faith and the very notion of marriage, but also different religious mentalities, can become sources of tension in marriage. . . . The temptation to religious indifference can then arise" (*CCC*, 1634). The Catholic person marrying an unbaptized person is challenged to preserve, practice, and pass on his or her faith without the benefit of being "one heart and mind."

A Catholic and a nonbaptized person seeking marriage must receive an **express dispensation**, or special exemption, from the local bishop because disparity of cult would usually be an impediment to a valid marriage. The bishop can give this dispensation if he believes it is justified in that particular case, and the marriage will be valid, though nonsacramental. The dispensation presupposes that the necessary conditions required for a mixed marriage are known and met. According to the *Catechism of the Catholic Church*,

> in marriages with disparity of cult the Catholic spouse has a particular task: "For the unbelieving husband is consecrated through his wife, and the unbelieving wife is consecrated through her husband." It is a great joy for the Christian spouse and for the Church if this "consecration" should lead to the free conversion of the other spouse to the Christian faith. Sincere married love, the humble and patient practice of the family virtues, and perseverance in prayer can prepare the non-believing spouse to accept the grace of conversion. (*CCC*, 1637, quoting 1 Corinthians 7:14)

The Catholic person marrying a nonbaptized person is challenged to preserve, practice, and pass on his or her faith to any children without the benefit of being of "one heart and mind" with the other parent.

---

convalidation Making an invalid marriage valid in the Church through new expression of the spouses' consent; sometimes referred to as the blessing of a marriage. The word *convalidation* derives from a Latin word for "firm up" or "strengthen."

express dispensation A permission granted by the Church releasing a person from following a canonical requirement, such as a certain impediment to a valid marriage.

SECTION ASSESSMENT

NOTE TAKING

Use the table you created to help you answer the following questions.

1. What is the difference between a mixed marriage and a marriage with disparity of cult?
2. Why do couples entering into a mixed marriage or a marriage with disparity of cult need special permission or dispensation to marry?
3. How is the role of the bishop different in a mixed marriage than in a marriage with disparity of cult?

COMPREHENSION

4. What challenges do special marriage situations present to the Catholic spouse?
5. What conditions do couples preparing for a mixed marriage or a marriage with disparity of cult discuss with the priest?

VOCABULARY

6. What is the meaning of *express dispensation*?

REFLECTION

7. Think of someone you know (perhaps yourself) who is a child of a mixed marriage or a marriage with disparity of cult. Write about three things the Catholic parent did to promote the child's faith. How did the non-Catholic parent offer his or her support?

Section Summaries

Focus Question

How does a Catholic couple prepare for and celebrate the Sacrament of Matrimony, and what are its effects?

Complete one of the following:

Write or record a short vignette that depicts some of the positive characteristics of family life that contribute to a child's remote preparation for marriage. Examples: a child witnesses parents holding hands; parents and child pray together; parents model service to those in need within and outside of the immediate family. The examples should be shared in narrative form.

Carefully read paragraphs 1625–1632 of the *Catechism of the Catholic Church*. Explain what the Church means by "to be free." Also, define *true consent* in your own words. Answer in a one-page report.

Research the meaning and history of *marriage banns*. What is their purpose? How are marriage banns handled in the Church today? How were they typically handled in the recent past? Answer in a one-page report.

INTRODUCTION
Marriage Is a Sacred Covenant

Marriage is a sacred covenant between the man and woman and between the couple and God in which the couple pledges to a lifelong, faithful, and fruitful love. A Catholic marriage takes place publicly in a church. Sacramental marriage differs from natural marriage in that it participates in the New Covenant of Christ, and is thus a sign to the world of God's love. Sacramental marriages are celebrated between the baptized in a liturgical setting.

Read Part II, Chapter 1, "Fostering the Nobility of Marriage and the Family," from *Gaudium et Spes* (47–52). Answer: What is the significance of the Second Vatican Council document's use of the word *covenant* rather than *contract* regarding marriage?

SECTION 1

Preparation for the Sacrament of Matrimony

Marriage preparation is of prime importance to the Church. It is the Church's responsibility to prepare couples well for marriage. Remote preparation begins in the home during childhood and includes developing good friendships, practicing your faith, and seeking out healthy examples of marriage. Proximate preparation involves a couple seeking marriage in the Church meeting with a priest, learning about the Sacrament of Matrimony, preparing for the possibility of children, learning about good communication, and preparing spiritually for the sacrament. Immediate preparation focuses in a special way on the planning of the nuptial Mass with the priest.

Is it possible to love a spouse forever? Read how Pope Francis responded to this question in his February 14, 2014, address in St. Peter's Square (Address to Engaged Couples Preparing for Marriage). Summarize his response in two well-organized paragraphs.

SECTION 2

The Order of Celebrating Matrimony

When a baptized man and a baptized woman come to be married in the Church, their marriage is based on their free and mutual consent given through the exchange of vows by the spouses using an approved formula. In order to fruitfully receive the graces of the Sacrament of Matrimony, spouses should be properly disposed. The normal celebration of a wedding between two baptized Catholics is in a church within the celebration of a nuptial Mass.

Read the abridged form of the pastoral letter by the Catholic bishops of the United States titled *Marriage: Love and Life in the Divine Plan* (available on the USCCB website). Search for and write down any sentences that begin with "Marriage is." Then write your own "Marriage is" sentence that incorporates the definitions you read in the pastoral letter.

SECTION 3

Effects of the Sacrament of Matrimony

Marriage is the avenue through which a husband and wife grow together in perfection and holiness while also contributing to the glory of God in their family and the world around them. The Sacrament of Matrimony's main effects are that the couple are united in a permanent bond and that they are promised a lifetime of God's grace.

→ Interview a married couple, husband and wife separately. Ask these questions: What is the grace of the Sacrament of Matrimony? What is a grace in your marriage? Write down and compare their responses.

SECTION 4

Mixed Marriage and Marriage with Disparity of Cult

The Church encourages Catholics to marry one another; however, marriage between a Catholic and a non-Catholic is not "an insurmountable obstacle." In a mixed marriage one person is a baptized Catholic while the other is a baptized non-Catholic of another Christian community. A marriage with disparity of cult is a marriage between a baptized Catholic and a nonbaptized person, and it requires even greater care by the Church and between the couple. Each requires special permission and preparation.

→ Read 1 Corinthians 7:14. What does the passage say about holiness in marriage between a Christian and a non-Christian spouse? Write a one-paragraph response.

Chapter Assignments

Choose and complete at least one of the following three assignments assessing your understanding of the material in this chapter.

1. Celebrating the Witness of a Loving Marriage

Create a collage, scrapbook, video, or slide presentation celebrating the witness of a long and successful Christian marriage. Plan as if you will present your final presentation to the couple as an anniversary gift. Some things that you might include in the presentation are newspaper stories marking the wedding and anniversaries; quotations from the couple, their children, and their friends; photos of items and stories of interest that help to mark the years of their marriage; quotations on marriage from Scripture and Church documents; wedding photos; and other family photos. Include a written one-page report that introduces the couple, tells why you chose them, and offers your own opinion on why theirs has been a long, successful, and loving marriage.

2. Contracts vs. Covenants

Work in a group of three to create two role plays that distinguish between a contract relationship and a covenant relationship. For example, a contract relationship might depict a consumer negotiating to buy a car from a salesperson. A covenant relationship could show God promising to make Abraham the father of all nations (see Genesis 17:4–8). The two role plays must utilize only two people in your group. The third person should film the video and upload it onto a viewable platform approved by your teacher. All three people are responsible for developing of the ideas, writing the scripts, and creating the setting (including props and costumes). The role plays should be between three and five minutes each.

3. Learning from Married Saints

A number of canonized saints were married men and women, including St. Bridget of Sweden (see this Chapter's Faithful Disciple). Sometimes only one member of the married couple was canonized, but other times both the man and woman were canonized together. In 2015, Sts. Louis and Zélie Martin, the parents of St. Thérèse of Lisieux, became the first married couple to be canonized on the same day. Choose four of the saints or saint couples from the list below and write the following for each: (1) life summary; (2) how the saints were holy; and (3) what Catholic married couples today can learn from their example.

- Sts. Joachim and Anne (parents of the Blessed Virgin Mary)
- Sts. Zechariah and Elizabeth
- Sts. Gregory the Elder and Nonna (parents of St. Gregory Nazianzen)
- Sts. Basil the Elder and Macrina (parents of St. Basil the Great and St. Gregory of Nyssa)

- Sts. Aquila and Priscilla (mentioned as friends of St. Paul in Acts 18)
- Sts. Louis and Zélie Martin (parents of St. Thérèse of Lisieux)
- St. Stephen of Hungary
- St. Elizabeth of Hungary
- St. Monica
- St. Frances of Rome
- St. Elizabeth Ann Seton
- St. Edward the Confessor

Faithful Disciple

St. Bridget of Sweden

After Bridget's mother died, her father, Birger Persson, a wealthy Swedish governor and judge, sent his daughter to live with her aunt. At some point during these years Bridget had a very dramatic and clear dream of "the Man of Sorrows," Jesus. In the dream, Bridget asked him who had hurt him so. He answered: "All who despise my love." The image and message of the dream would stay with Bridget for the rest of her life.

St. Bridget of Sweden

In the meantime, life proceeded as normal for a young girl living in the Middle Ages. In 1316, at the age of thirteen, she married Ulf Gudmarsson, who was eighteen. Ulf was from another noble family, and he came to work as a judge like Bridget's father. The couple had eight children, four sons and four daughters. Six of the children survived infancy, a very high percentage for that time. One of their daughters was St. Catherine of Sweden.

Bridget was known for great acts of charity. She was also acquainted with several theologians of the time. From 1341 to 1343 she and her husband made the famous pilgrimage across Spain to Santiago de Compostela in honor of St. James, called the Camino de Santiago (the Way of St. James). While on their trip home, Ulf became very ill. Bridget sat praying by his bed. She had a vision of a bishop appearing to her and consoling her that Ulf would recover and that "God had great things for her to do." He did recover for a time, but in 1344 became sick again. Bridget took her husband to a nearby monastery to have the monks pray for him. Ulf died and was buried on those grounds. Bridget took a small house near the abbey so that she could remain near Ulf's grave and pray for him. She said, "I loved him like my own body."

At age forty-one, widowed, Bridget prayed for guidance. She received a message to found a religious order, mainly for women. She had a vision in which God showed her how the abbey church was to be built, the type of clothing the nuns should wear, and how many priests and deacons she would need as chaplains. The Swedish king Magnus Eriksson donated land to construct the abbey, but around this time Christ appeared to Bridget again and told her to go to Rome for the Holy Year, 1350. The message included the charge to pray for the pope and for peace between France and England. Until her death in 1373, she remained in Rome except to go on pilgrimages to the Holy Land.

Though Bridget did found a religious order, she never witnessed the results of any of the things in her vision. In this way, she could be described as a patroness of failure. The vision of her childhood had returned full circle. Like Jesus, her Master, she, too, was a person of sorrows.

St. Bridget is the patroness of Sweden. In October 1999, Pope John Paul II named her also the patroness of Europe. Her feast day is July 23.

 ## Reading Comprehension

1. In Bridget's dream, who did "the Man of Sorrows" say had hurt him so much?

2. What is the name of Bridget's daughter who became a saint?

3. What pilgrimage did Bridget and Ulf take?

4. Why did Bridget live near her husband's grave?

5. Why might St. Bridget be described as a "person of sorrows," like Jesus?

 ## Writing Task

In describing St. Bridget's marriage to her husband, Ulf, Pope Benedict XVI wrote, "It is often the woman, as happened in the life of St Bridget and Ulf, who with her religious sensitivity, delicacy and gentleness succeeds in persuading her husband to follow a path of faith. I am thinking with gratitude of the many women who, day after day, illuminate their families with their witness of Christian life, in our time too" (General Audience, October 27, 2010). Write about a woman in your own family—perhaps your mother or grandmother—who illuminates your family with Christian faith. Explain how she does so.

Explaining the Faith

Why shouldn't Catholics get married on a beach?

The simple answer is because the wisdom and canon law of the Church dictate that the ordinary place of sacraments is a church, and part of being Catholic is submitting to all the Church teaches. If one calls oneself Catholic, it logically follows that one must follow what the Church dictates. In this case, the ordinary location for a wedding blessed by a priest must be in a church.

However, the Church doesn't have teachings "just because," so here is a look at the more complicated answer. First, you cannot forget that Matrimony is a *sacrament*—before it is a celebration, before it is a social event, before all else, it is a sacrament. And a sacrament is more than just some fancy words and formulated actions that look special. Rather, sacraments are the most profound way to encounter God here on earth. They are the most intense way you receive the graces Christ won for us through his Paschal Mystery.

The ordinary location for sacraments is a church. This makes sense, doesn't it? When you walk into a church, you think *God*. The structure and nature of the church building speak of something beyond you. Of course the nature of God transcends a building, but humans need something concrete to remind them that what they're about to do (participate in a sacrament) is something different from the other moments of the day.

Under "extraordinary" circumstances, sacraments can be celebrated outside a church. The best example of such is a Baptism or an Anointing of the Sick performed in a hospital, often for someone who is too sick to make it to the church. This kind of extraordinary exception truly makes sense.

A common argument for having a wedding on a beach goes like this: "Well, isn't God present at the beach? When I look at the ocean, I think of God. So why can't I get married on the beach?" Take a moment and look at a wedding from a different perspective. On a raw level, the only ones who need to be present for the Sacrament of Matrimony to take place are the man and woman because they are the ministers of the sacrament. If this is true, why do couples invite hundreds of people to their weddings? It is because a wedding is about more than just the man and woman—it is also about the faith community surrounding them. The wedding is for the Church. In this case, "Church" refers to the People of God, the Mystical Body of Christ.

Think about someone attending a wedding on the beach. Consider the "commonness" of a beach. People lay out on a beach in swimsuits; people sip drinks with little umbrellas and eat hot dogs on the beach; people fish from beaches; people go running on beaches. The beach is too commonplace for an event as extraordinary as two immortal souls, through the grace of Christ, being united until death. This is a beautiful, even "Godly" event. Doesn't it follow that such an act should happen in a place that is made for worship of God? Could you imagine baptizing your future baby on the beach? There's just something unsettling about that.

The Church in her wisdom maintains the ordinary location for the Sacrament of Matrimony is a consecrated church. And it's for a good reason: to help her fallen, broken people to remember the extraordinariness of the sacrament.

 ## Further Research

Read paragraphs 1621–1624 of the *Catechism of the Catholic Church*. Explain why it is appropriate for Catholics to be married in a church in light of this statement: "It is therefore fitting that the spouses should seal their consent to give themselves to each other through the offering of their own lives by uniting it to the offering of Christ for his Church made present in the Eucharistic sacrifice" (*CCC*, 1621).

Prayer
Prayer for Self-Giving Love

Love is patient, love is kind. It is not jealous, [love] is not pompous, it is not inflated, it is not rude, it does not seek its own interests, it is not quick-tempered, it does not brood over injury, it does not rejoice over wrongdoing but rejoices with the truth.

It bears all things, believes all things, hopes all things, endures all things.

Love never fails. If there are prophecies, they will be brought to nothing; if tongues, they will cease; if knowledge, it will be brought to nothing. For we know partially and we prophesy partially, but when the perfect comes, the partial will pass away. When I was a child, I used to talk as a child, think as a child, reason as a child; when I became a man, I put aside childish things. At present we see indistinctly, as in a mirror, but then face to face. At present I know partially; then I shall know fully, as I am fully known. So faith, hope, love remain, these three; but the greatest of these is love.

—1 Corinthians 13:4–13

THE CHRISTIAN
FAMILY
IN GOD'S PLAN

A Hidden Cross

When Darrel and Gwen Hageman got married they thought having children would be easy. But after two miscarriages in their first few years of marriage, the Hagemans experienced a long period of infertility. They decided to visit the Pope Paul VI Institute, to hopefully treat their fertility issues; however, more years went by without a pregnancy. For couples struggling with infertility, this path is a very real experience of suffering, a hidden cross that most people don't know about.

After seven years, an occupational therapy patient of Gwen's got her thinking about adoption. As Darrel and Gwen started learning about adoption through an education program with Catholic Charities, they stopped seeing it as an alternative and started thinking of it as something to which God had called them. A birth mother saw their portfolio, met with the Hagemans, and immediately felt drawn to them. Gwen was able to be in the room when the birth mother had their son Lucas. "I have never seen sacrificial love to that depth," she said.

Just a few months later the Hagemans received another call to adopt, this time a little girl. Even though Lucas was still a little baby, they decided to say yes, realizing they may not have another chance to adopt.

But God wasn't through surprising the Hagemans yet. A few years later the Hagemans were shocked to find out they were pregnant with first their son Cole and then again with their son Landon. Both pregnancies were difficult and needed medical intervention. When they found out they were expecting their fifth child, John Paul, Gwen didn't have any complications. Before her pregnancy, Gwen had gone on a retreat where she had a powerful experience of intercessory prayer. "At that retreat, before I even knew about John Paul's existence, I left with a sense of God's unconditional love for me. I felt as if the deep physical and spiritual pain I had was lifted. I really do think God chose to heal me."

FOCUS QUESTION

Why are **CATHOLIC MARRIED COUPLES** called to have **CHILDREN AND RAISE** them in the **CATHOLIC FAITH?**

Chapter Overview

Introduction	Marriage Leads to Family
Section 1	The Nature of the Family: A Community of Life and Love
Section 2	The Gift of Children
Section 3	Responsibilities in the Family
Section 4	The Family as the Domestic Church

INTRODUCTION
Marriage Leads to Family

MAIN IDEA
Family life is rooted in the complementarity of spouses, which is reflected in the love they give their children. This love and communion is an image of the love between the Three Divine Persons of the Trinity.

God does not want humans to be alone, but rather to live in community with others. This essential lesson has been in place since the creation of the first humans (see Genesis 2:18). Modern society might tout individualism, but the Church in her wisdom calls you to authentic experiences of community and connectedness, reminding you that you are made to live with and for others, not just yourself. This is known as *complementarity*. Although sin and weakness are part of the human experience, humans can and should open themselves to loving others and being loved.

Jesus Christ, the Son of God, lived in communion with others. He was born into a human family, the **Holy Family**. Jesus immersed himself in relationships with real people in his family and among his friends, and through them experienced the sufferings, disappointments, joys, and everyday encounters of human relationships. From the human experience of Christ you can see that the most basic and essential form of community is family life.

> **Holy Family** The family of Jesus, Mary, and Joseph in which Jesus was raised and lived until he began his public ministry.

NOTE TAKING

Identifying Main Ideas. As you read this section, complete an outline of the contents like the one here.

I. Definition of complementarity
   A. Example of the Holy Family
   B.
II. Complementarity of man and woman
   A.
   B.
III. Christian family is a communion of persons.

Complementarity is at the core of Pope John Paul II's teachings from the Theology of the Body sermons. In these, the biological and personal complementarity between a man and a woman are intrinsically linked.

The Complementarity of Man and Woman

Family life is rooted in the complementarity man and woman experience when they come together in marriage. On seeing the woman God had created for him, the first man said,

> This one, at last, is bone of my bones
>> and flesh of my flesh;
> This one shall be called "woman,"
>> for out of man this one has been taken. (Gn 2:23)

His words previewed the deep and primordial fulfillment found in the marriage bond. When God made man and woman to be together and complement each other, he desired and brought about the family too.

The family has its own fundamental origin in creation and is based on the total self-gift of marriage. Childrearing extends the grace of the Sacrament of Matrimony to new lives. Remember that the Sacrament of Matrimony is a Sacrament at the Service of Communion. This refers to a man and woman conferring holiness on each other and helping each other on the path to salvation. The same blessing extends to the children of a Christian couple.

Pope John Paul II expressed that "the couple, while giving themselves to one another, give not just themselves but also the reality of children, who are a living reflection of their love, a permanent sign of conjugal unity and . . . of their being a father and a mother" (*Familiaris Consortio*, 14). A child is a unique reflection of the love between a husband and a wife. No other combination of parents could create this child. Through the years, a child will offer the family deep satisfaction and opportunities for intimacy and love. Ask parents and most will tell you that nothing else that they have ever experienced has brought as much satisfaction as begetting new life and raising their children.

A Christian Family Is a Communion of Persons That Models the Trinity

Married couples are called to give a total, unified, and faithful gift of themselves to each other. The Divine Persons of the Blessed Holy Trinity model this type of giving in their own love. The Father and Son exchange a fathomless love for each other, and the Holy Spirit proceeds from this infinite ocean of love. The Divine Persons are bound up together in love for each other so that they are "inseparable in what they are" and "inseparable in what they do" (*CCC*, 267).

The best model for families is the relationship of total self-gift found in the Blessed Trinity. Also, because the Blessed Trinity reveals that authentic love begets more love, authentic married love is fruitful. God loves what he creates, and calls humans into a deeper union with himself by sharing in the act of procreation. Therefore, the natural fruit of married, self-giving love is a new life. The new person, truly unique and equal in dignity to other persons, embodies the love of his or her father and mother. The child is the love between spouses personified.

"A man and woman united in marriage, together with their children, form a family" (*CCC*, 2202). The Christian family is indeed a communion of persons that images the relationship between the Divine Persons of the Blessed Trinity in, for example, these ways:

The three angels in the Holy Trinity *icon by Andrei Rublev symbolize the Father (on the left, in blue and purple), the Son (in the center, in red and white), and the Holy Spirit (on the right, in blue and green).*

- The procreation and education of children is modeled on the Father's work of creation.
- The family shares in the prayer and sacrifice of Christ.
- In company with the Holy Spirit, by its very example of day-to-day living, the family witnesses the Gospel to the world.

God is not a Creator who begets human life and then ignores his creation. In the same way, parents don't just have babies; they love their children, rejoice in their children, and work to build up a community of love in their family. A Christian family has a unique opportunity to concretely witness God's love to others outside the family. This fruitful love of a husband and wife becomes a symbol of the inner life of the Blessed Trinity. Pope Francis wrote, "The couple that loves and begets life is a true, living icon . . . capable of revealing God the Creator and Savior" (*Amoris Laetitia*, 11).

♥ A **Prayer** for **Married Couples**

Write two prayers for a newlywed couple you know or for a newlywed couple at your parish. Choose prayer titles/subjects from among the following, or create one of your own:

- A Prayer to Bless Our Home
- A Prayer for Better Communication
- A Prayer to Welcome a Child
- A Prayer to End a Conflict
- A Prayer to Celebrate an Anniversary
- A Prayer of Thankfulness for Each Other

SECTION ASSESSMENT

NOTE TAKING

Use the outline you completed to help you answer the following questions.

1. What does Jesus' participation in a family teach you about the importance of community?
2. How is family life rooted in the complementarity of spouses?
3. Explain how the love between a husband, a wife, and their children images the love between the Divine Persons of the Trinity.

COMPREHENSION

4. Explain the complementarity both between the Divine Persons of the Blessed Trinity and between a husband and wife.

5. How is the Sacrament of Matrimony a Sacrament at the Service of Communion?

CRITICAL THINKING

6. What does the *Catechism of the Catholic Church* mean when it says that the Persons of the Trinity are "inseparable in what they are" and "inseparable in what they do"?

SECTION 1
The Nature of the Family: A Community of Life and Love

MAIN IDEA
The family is the fundamental building block of society, where people learn best the virtues that will help them to be good members of society. Healthy societies are built on healthy families.

You live in a time when there are many different versions of what a family might look like. Besides families made up of a mother, father, and children, some families have only one parent or contain stepparents, stepsiblings, or half-siblings. Some children are raised by grandparents, adoptive parents, or foster parents. There are also children being raised by two parents of the same gender.

The Church never judges the love parents or families have or the effort they give for their children. Yet, without judgment on particular situations, the Church must do the important work of defining and helping to maintain authentic family life. Individual families are the fundamental building blocks of society, the larger human family. It is vital for the Church to uphold and esteem what the family is meant to be: a community of life and love.

Basic Definition of a Family

Fundamentally, the family is made up of a man, a woman, and their children. Marriage, through the vows the husband and wife make to each other, forms the foundation for the permanency, fidelity, and stability that are so essential to family life. Marriage is the "normal reference point by which the different forms of family relationship are to be evaluated" (*CCC*, 2202).

NOTE TAKING

Summarizing Cited Works. Create a chart like the one here. As you read this section, summarize what each of the following cited works says about the nature of the family.

Citation	What the passage says about the nature of the family
CCC, 2202	
Familiaris Consortio, 17	
CCC, 2207	
Pope John Paul II at Perth	
Familiaris Consortio, 46	

In his apostolic exhortation *Familiaris Consortio*, Pope John Paul II roots the family within the plan of creation, writing:

> The family finds in the plan of God the Creator and Redeemer not only its identity, what it is, but also its mission, what it can and should do. The role that God calls the family to perform in history derives from what the family is. . . . Each family finds within itself a summons that cannot be ignored, and that specifies both its dignity and its responsibility: family, become what you are. (*Familiaris Consortio*, 17)

There are legitimate circumstances in which parents and children might not be biologically related, such as in the case of adoption. Still, the primary mode of understanding the family is through marriage, biological parenthood, and the spiritual bonds formed from those relationships. In every family, the members have equal dignity, as well as certain rights, responsibilities, and duties toward each other.

The Family and Society

Where did you first learn to positively interact with other people? From whom did you learn to be kind, to listen and be respectful of others, and to love? Most people begin learning these necessary lessons very early in life, building upon them year by year within their family. Even babies in the womb become acclimated to social life through the nurturing environment of their mother and the sounds emanating from other family members. A secure family environment is essential for people to develop and grow in mind, body, and soul. The family is the place where all people learn to interact with others.

Society needs healthy, functioning families. A family is where people learn to give selflessly through love, and are trained in the "the foundations for freedom, security, and fraternity" that are so important to society (*CCC*, 2207). In a homily given in Perth, Australia, in 1986, Pope John Paul II noted that married couples who overcome modern pressures of society are able to "exercise more fully that special love and responsibility of the marriage covenant which make them see children as God's special gift to them and to society. As the family goes, so goes the nation, and so goes the whole world in which we live."[1]

Pope John Paul II's words that "as the family goes, so goes the nation" certainly reflect the truth. When family life and the relationships between family members are considered necessary and important and are supported by society, then the rest of the culture thrives. Consider the way you learned to be compassionate toward those who are sick or handicapped through how your own family treated you when you were ill. When a person is in a vulnerable position, you probably react out of an instinct of compassion learned at an early age. These kinds of learned social behaviors allow you to take seriously the Gospel imperative of loving your neighbor as yourself (see Matthew 22:39).

The important role of family life is highlighted by what happens to children who are *not* raised in their earliest years in a stable family. More children in these situations show lasting developmental issues such as "problems forming healthy attachments and deficits in neurological and cognitive abilities and physical growth."[2] When individual families cannot fulfill their responsibilities (e.g., meeting the physical and emotional needs of their children), it is up to other agencies in society to help fill in and meet those needs.

More proactively, society is responsible for supporting and strengthening family life so that individual families can fulfill their own needs. In *Familiaris Consortio*, Pope John Paul II addressed the ideal of mutual support between families

and society by recounting a "charter of family rights." Emphasized were the rights to

- establish a family, have children, and bring them up in keeping with a family's own moral and religious convictions;

- the stability of the marriage bond and the institution of the family;

- profess one's faith, hand it on, and raise one's children in it, with necessary means and institutions;

- protection against threats to security and health, especially with respect to dangers such as drugs, pornography, alcoholism, and the like; and

- form associations with other families and so have representation before civil authorities. (*Familiaris Consortio*, 46)

Participation in an individual family can help to provide you with a Christian perspective on the larger human family. You begin to understand that every person, living and dead, is somehow related to you by origin or descent. This means that everyone you encounter is due your respect. People, whether near or far, are not numbers, statistics, or units; they are "someones" who deserve your attention and love.

FAMILY: BELIEVE IN WHAT YOU ARE

In October 2001, Pope John Paul II held a meeting with families at the Vatican to discuss the family in modern society and to encourage the Christian family to be a light of faith in the world. Read the address by Pope John Paul II to families, "Address at the Prayer Vigil of Families," St. Peter's Square, October 20, 2001. This can be found at the Vatican website, www.vatican.va.

ASSIGNMENT

Address each question in three to five well-written paragraphs.

- What questions does Pope John Paul II propose to reflect on the nature of the family and its role in humanity? Explain how each question is answered.

- What does Pope John Paul II mean by "Family, . . . believe in what you are; believe in your vocation to be a luminous sign of God's love" (3)?

SECTION ASSESSMENT

NOTE TAKING

Use the chart you created to help you answer the following questions.

1. What is the "normal reference point by which the different forms of family relationship are to be evaluated" (*CCC*, 2202)?

2. What do you imagine "freedom, security, and fraternity" have to do with family life?

3. Explain what Pope John Paul II meant by "as the family goes, so goes the nation."

4. What is the main emphasis of the "charter of family rights" outlined by Pope John Paul II?

COMPREHENSION

5. What is the fundamental makeup of a family?

6. What happens when individual families cannot maintain their responsibilities?

CRITICAL THINKING

7. Give an original example of a positive behavior or attitude that is fostered in family life.

The Gift of Children

MAIN IDEA
Children are a gift from God. Married couples are called to practice responsible parenthood and to avoid methods of delaying pregnancy that disregard the dignity of human life.

Because marriage is a covenant, not a contract, married love is about more than an emotional or physical connection between two people. Marriage is the beginning of a family, and the start of a couple's bringing about the good fruit of their union. The Church often calls this fruitfulness in having children *fecundity*: "Fecundity is a gift, an *end of marriage*, for conjugal love naturally tends to be fruitful. A child does not come from outside as something added on to the mutual love of the spouses, but springs from the very heart of that mutual giving, as its fruit and fulfillment" (*CCC*, 2366).

A married couple's decision to be open to the gift of a child is a courageous and loving one. Remember that fruitfulness, along with indissolubility and faithfulness, is integral to marriage. God intended sex between husband and wife to be both for expressing love *and* for the procreation of children. "Sacred Scripture and the Church's traditional practice see in *large families* a sign of God's blessing and the parents' generosity" (*CCC*, 2373). A couple who lovingly embrace God's plan and welcome a child into their family share in an amazing way in God the Father's work of creation.

NOTE TAKING

Understanding Main Concepts. Create a graphic organizer like the one here. In the top rectangle, write a sentence defining the two ends of sex in marriage. In the box on the left, list and briefly define ways these purposes are supported. In the box on the right, list and briefly define ways these purposes are opposed.

-
-
-
-

- **Contraception: alters or prevents fertility**
-
-
-

Pope Paul VI's pivotal 1968 encyclical *Humanae Vitae* (*On Human Life*) addressed the meaning of sexual love and procreation in depth. In it, Pope Paul VI explained that "it is necessary that each and every marriage act remain ordered *per se* to the procreation of human life" (*HV*, 11). In other words, every time a couple come together in sexual intercourse, they should remain open to the *possibility* of a child.

When a Catholic married couple observe this teaching and keep the dual purpose of sexual intercourse, they truly stand out today as Christian witnesses. Why is this so? A scan of today's media reveals that most of popular culture associates sex only with pleasure, emotional connection, and *avoiding* pregnancy. Sexual love is portrayed as a casual act, requiring no commitment. Even in modern marriage, openness to the possibility of new life is often disconnected from sexual love. You might hear:

- "We need time to adjust to being married."
- "Once we have enough money saved for a down payment on a house we will think about starting a family."
- "I want to enjoy my twenties and get established in my job. Maybe when I am thirty we'll start thinking about a family."
- "We already have a boy and a girl. We don't need more children."
- "How can we afford to have children? Have you seen how expensive it is?"

Setting aside that many of these responses are things to consider *before* one gets married, they show a mentality that children are somehow owed to a couple only when they determine it is a good time. While money, homes, and careers are certainly to be taken into consideration, they should not take precedence over the good of a child, who is a *person*. "Children are the supreme gift of marriage" in part because the married couple are cooperating with the love of God the Creator in bringing about new life (*Gaudium et Spes*, 50). God said, "Be fertile and multiply" (Gn 1:28).

Responsible Parenthood

It is important to understand what the Church is and isn't saying about **procreation**. The Church emphasizes the importance of responsible parenthood, which is both open to life and conscientious of circumstances within family life. "Openness to life" is often misunderstood as meaning that Catholic couples must have as many children as possible. This is certainly not Church teaching. Offering her teaching wisdom as a guide, the Church leaves to married couples the careful and prayerful discernment of bringing more children into the world.

Remember that the two ends of the sexual act are (1) unity and (2) the procreation and education of children. The Church underscores that married couples are obligated to give the children they are blessed with the attention and good things necessary to help them thrive as integrated human persons. For just reasons, married couples may plan and space the births of their children. Just reasons may include the physical or emotional health of family members, the inability of one or both parents to care for a child, or in some cases,

procreation The cooperation of a married couple with God to bring about new life through sexual intercourse.

the lack of income and resources to care for a child properly.

There is a wide spectrum of responsible parenthood, based on each family's individual situation. However, responsible parenthood also means willingness to accept a child if a pregnancy does unexpectedly occur. It also means taking a hard and prayerful look at reasons for wishing to delay or limit children. Married couples must put raising children before career advancements, having certain material possessions, or the convenience of a certain number of children. Responsible parenthood means thinking of children not as burdens (the modern mentality) but as blessings and gifts from God. The *Catechism of the Catholic Church* explains: "A particular aspect of [the responsibility parents own] is the *regulation of procreation*. For just reasons, spouses may wish to space the births

of their children. It is their duty to make certain that their desire is not motivated by selfishness but is in conformity with the generosity appropriate to responsible parenthood. Moreover, they should conform their behavior to the objective criteria of morality" (*CCC*, 2368).

Thus, it is morally acceptable for couples to regulate birth only in a way that still respects both the unity created in marital intercourse and the possibility of procreation. Responsible parenthood can include both delaying pregnancy and joyfully welcoming a new life. *Humanae Vitae* teaches that it is "morally permissible to take into account the natural rhythms of human fertility and to have coitus (sexual intercourse) only during the infertile times in order to regulate conception" (*HV*, 16). Remember that authentic human love involves a total gift of self. Couples who practice this

MORE BENEFITS OF
Natural Family Planning

- NFP encourages respect and acceptance of the total human person.
- NFP methods support reproductive health. There are no harmful side effects such as those caused by some forms of contraception.
- NFP can help achieve or avoid pregnancy. Depending on the method, it is 97 to 99 percent effective.
- NFP can help diagnose underlying medical problems.
- NFP methods can strengthen communication and growth in virtue in marriage.
- NFP is good for marriages. Some statistics show that NFP users have only a 5 percent divorce rate, which is drastically lower than the average.[3]
- NFP is environmentally friendly and inexpensive.
- NFP values the child.

method of observing the natural rhythms of fertile and infertile times of a woman's cycle, also called Natural Family Planning (NFP), learn to say with their bodies, "I give myself totally to you, all that I am without reservation. Sincerely. Freely. Forever. And I receive the gift of yourself that you give to me. I bless you. I affirm you. All that you are, without reservation."[4] There are a number of ways to practice NFP, but all are based on having sexual intercourse during times of fertility to increase the chances for pregnancy or practicing abstinence from sexual intercourse during times of observed fertility to delay pregnancy.

Refraining from sex in marriage can be difficult for couples, but again the graces of the Sacrament of Matrimony can help them control their passions rather than being enslaved by them. In general, couples who share in decisions of procreation based on the woman's natural fertility cycle cite several benefits for doing so, including the following:

- improved communication
- the absence of the feelings of being used
- development of nongenital aspects of love and affection
- peace of conscience
- the lack of worry of being exposed to side effects of unnatural methods of preventing pregnancy

The practice of natural methods of regulating procreation strengthens the fidelity of the spouses to one another and promotes a lifelong marriage. Other benefits of Natural Family Planning are noted in the feature "More Benefits of Natural Family Planning."

Anti-Life Practices

Unfortunately, the society around you has a degraded and depleted view of human sexuality that does not fully comprehend the message of self-giving love found in marriage. This has led to the acceptance of contraception, sterilization, abortion, and other anti-life

practices as normal components of sexual love. When sexual love is separated from its unitive and procreative ends, human dignity is often cast aside.

One form of disregard for human dignity is **contraception** and **direct sterilization**. They are the purposeful rejection of the procreative dimension of sexual love. The Church has always taught that any act that intentionally denies procreation is intrinsically evil. Contraception and sterilization change the language of the sexual act so that the couple are no longer being truthful with their bodies, which should express a "total reciprocal self-giving of husband and wife" (*Familiaris Consortio*, 32). NFP, in contrast, respects the purpose of sexual love and the design of the bodies of the husband and wife; it requires periodic continence, it encourages tenderness and open communication between them, and it expresses an authentic gift of self. As a reminder, NFP is *not* "Catholic contraception" since it works within the framework of sexual love to carefully discern the spacing of children.

Direct abortion is the most serious and reprehensible form of rejecting human dignity and the purpose of married love. In the United States alone an estimated 4,500 babies are aborted each day. Direct

---

contraception Various methods of preventing pregnancy that are intended to alter or prevent the body's natural state of fertility. Examples include condoms, "the pill" (artificial hormones that render women infertile as long as they are taken), and the intrauterine device. Use of contraceptions are intrinsically evil and against the teachings of the Church. Some products marketed and sold as contraception, such as Depo-Provera, really function as abortifacients.

direct sterilization A direct or deliberate medical or surgical procedure that leaves a person unable to reproduce.

direct abortion The direct or deliberate and intentional killing of unborn life by means of medical or surgical procedures.

---

abortion refers to the intentional termination of a pregnancy by killing the unborn child, before or after implantation in the mother's uterus. The Church has always opposed abortion, and considers it a grave evil. Anyone who has a direct abortion, counsels or coerces someone to have one, or participates in the practice of abortion places himself or herself in mortal sin. There are several forms of direct abortion, including RU-486 (the morning after pill), suction aspiration, saline abortion, and partial-birth abortion. Implantable chemicals such as Depo-Provera that are marketed as contraceptives also function as *abortifacients* (drugs that cause an abortion). Depo-Provera can thin the lining of the uterus, making it hostile to implantation. In these cases Depo-Provera acts as an abortifacient since it ends the life of a human after conception.

Through fetal monitoring and the use of ultrasounds, doctors now know that babies feel pain at only eight weeks into a pregnancy. Abortion is a brutally painful death. Also, there are physical and psychological dangers for the mothers, such as increased risk for infection, hemorrhaging, scarring, complications in future pregnancies, depression, flashbacks, and insomnia. It is with sorrow that the Church is aware of the many factors that might influence a woman to have an abortion. Women who have had abortions should know that the Church cares for and is concerned for them, and wants to help them be healed. It is also the work of the Church to defend innocent life from conception to natural death. This work includes passing laws that protect women and babies from abortion but also helping those in difficult situations, caring for families at risk, and working to alleviate the circumstances—such as single parenthood, poverty, and abuse—that lead to crisis pregnancies.

The Issue of Infertility

Married couples who struggle to have children or are infertile suffer greatly. The Book of Genesis records Abraham speaking boldly to God of his deep desire to father a child: "Lord GOD, what can you give me, if I die childless?" (Gn 15:2). The Church has great compassion for couples dealing with **infertility** and encourages scientific research into the causes of infertility. The Church also supports helping married couples to conceive children through medical methods that respect the unitive and procreative methods of married love.

> **infertility** The inability on the part of a male or female to achieve pregnancy.

There are a number of legitimate means of helping couples who struggle to achieve pregnancy. For example, there are surgeries that repair damage to the reproductive organs and certain prescription drugs that assist hormonal production. Using NFP (especially with the assistance of an NFP-trained medical doctor) tracks reproductive rhythms to enhance the chances of achieving pregnancy.

There are also morally illicit methods to treat infertility that separate the act of marital intercourse from procreation. The Church opposes such methods as **in vitro fertilization (IVF)**, **sperm or egg donation**, and **surrogacy**, because they separate the good of marital intercourse from its two ends of unity and procreation.

Remember that married love is based on the respect and self-giving love of human persons, which

---

in vitro fertilization The achievement of pregnancy without sexual intercourse through collecting eggs from a mother and fertilizing them with sperm outside of the womb.

sperm or egg donation The giving of sperm or eggs from a donor to a person who is not a sexual partner for the purpose of achieving pregnancy.

surrogacy A prearranged legal contract in which a woman carries another person or person's child.

---

extends to every member of the family, children included. The *Catechism of the Catholic Church* teaches:

> A child is not something *owed* to one, but is a *gift*. The "supreme gift of marriage" is a human person. A child may not be considered a piece of property, an idea to which an alleged "right to a child" would lead. . . . The child possesses genuine rights: the right "to be the fruit of the specific act of the conjugal love of his parents," and "the right to be respected as a person from the moment of his conception." (*CCC*, 2378, quoting *Donum Vitae*, II, 8)

Some couples may try every legitimate means to have a child and yet remain infertile. These couples carry a difficult cross; yet, like all suffering, it can be united to Christ's sacrifice on the Cross. United with Jesus, these couples' sacrifices and prayers can be a source of "spiritual fecundity" (*CCC*, 2379). They can express their life-giving love and generosity through other means: foster care, adoption, and giving of their time in various forms of service to those in need. Authentic love between spouses, even those who are in infertile, always expresses itself in generous love.

Name: _____   Surname: _____

Cycle day

Date

Day of the week

Intercourse

Andy and Michelle:
NFP Helps One Couple Struggling with
Infertility

As part of their marriage preparation, Andy and Michelle began learning NFP. Michelle says that this was their first warning about their future struggles. Michelle's menstrual cycles were not within the normal range. A doctor recommended medication, which helped but only masked the issues Michelle continued to have.

After their marriage, the couple became pregnant with their oldest son, Ira. Unfortunately, after Ira, they grieved over the miscarriages of several babies and knew things were not right with Michelle's body. In between complications, Andy and Michelle welcomed their daughter, Ruby, into their family. Yet Michelle was still struggling with irregular cycles.

They found little help through local doctors, who knew very little about the causes of infertility. "The doctors would dismiss looking into the causes," says Michelle. "They just wanted to put me on some medication or suggest in vitro." The couple were tired of medication that did not help her problems and knew that in vitro went against their morals and Church teaching. "All of the research is targeted toward in vitro fertilization," says Michelle. "There is very little money or time being spent on helping women to heal."

A friend recommended the Pope Paul VI Institute for the Study of Human Reproduction (now the Saint Paul VI Institue) in Omaha, Nebraska. Andy says they were very excited after learning about the institute, which conducts research and works with couples to heal and help restore reproductive health. "We wanted more children, sure," says Andy. "But we also went to the institute for the sake of her health."

At the Pope Paul VI Institute Andy and Michelle met with Dr. Thomas Hilgers, the founder. "Dr. Hilgers and the institute were the first place that worked to figure out why we were miscarrying," says Michelle. "We learned what was going wrong, and worked to find a treatment." Common, moral treatments recommended by the institute include surgery to overcome tubal blockages in the male or female or a procedure known as lower tubal ovum transfer, which transfers the woman's eggs beyond the tubal blockage so that

sexual intercourse within marriage can result in pregnancy. The treatment for Michelle ended up being surgery.

Michelle and Andy welcomed their third child, Able, into their family after the surgery, and Michelle says she is feeling whole again. "You don't have to have your body not functioning properly for years," she says. "Seek out a doctor who knows NFP and respects the dignity of women and the family through a holistic approach." Michelle notes that there are a growing number of doctors across the country trained in NFP.

SECTION ASSESSMENT

NOTE TAKING
Use the graphic organizer you created to help you complete these items.

1. How does NFP support the two ends of sexual intercourse in marriage?

2. Explain how contraception, direct abortion, in vitro fertilization, and surrogacy violate the two ends of sexual intercourse in marriage.

COMPREHENSION

3. Name three elements of responsible parenthood.

4. Explain why the Church says that children and fecundity are a gift to married couples.

5. Explain how responsible parenthood includes both the unitive and procreative aspects of sexual love.

6. Name some of the benefits of NFP.

REFLECTION

7. Name three good reasons not to postpone having children after getting married.

CRITICAL THINKING

8. What are three ways the Church defends marriage and innocent life from conception until natural death?

SECTION 3
Responsibilities in the Family

MAIN IDEA
Parents are the primary educators of their children, especially in the faith. Children are called to honor and respect their parents and love their siblings.

Responsible parenthood extends beyond making wise moral decisions about family planning. Obviously, once a child is born, the real work begins! Through the graces of the Sacrament of Matrimony, parents and their children strive together for holiness. The gift of family life comes with certain responsibilities for each of the members. These are addressed in the Fourth Commandment—honor your mother and father—and its accompanying requirements for both parents and children.

Duties of Parents

With procreation comes the corresponding obligation for parents to educate children. Parents are always charged with this task before anyone else—relatives, teachers, peers, or media. *Education* here refers to a completely integrated training as a human person but most especially morally and spiritually. This begins when parents create a home "where tenderness, forgiveness, respect, fidelity, and disinterested service are the rule," the best place "for *education in the virtues*"

NOTE TAKING

Concept Webs. As you read, make two concept webs like the ones here. In one, list duties of parents. In the other, list duties of children. Give at least three examples for each concept.

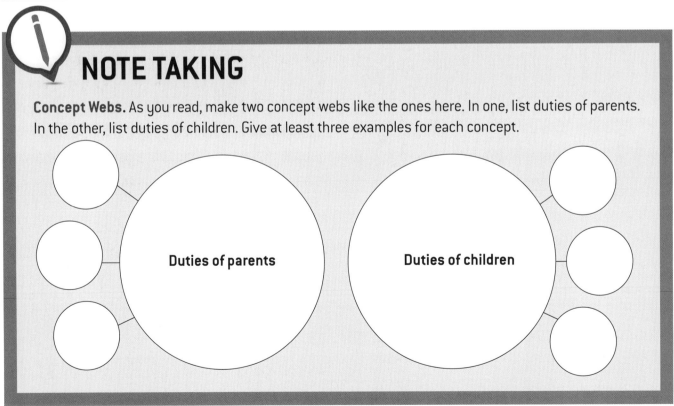

Duties of parents

Duties of children

Vincent van Gogh's famous 1890 painting First Steps *captures an intimate family moment that is universal for all times and places.*

(*CCC*, 2223). The following subsections list important ways for parents to fulfill this obligation.

Modeling Behaviors

Parents create a loving home by modeling right relationships, wisdom, the virtues, and a strong prayer life themselves. It would be difficult for a child to learn the lessons of loyalty and honesty from parents who had been unfaithful to each other. More positively, parents who show respect for each other are more likely to have the lesson of respect resonate with their children. For example, when Mom lets Dad choose the evening's activities or when Dad takes on putting the children to bed after Mom has had a difficult day, children see the harmony created by parents who show consideration for each other. Also, husbands and wives who say "please" and "thank you" to each other and to their children are more likely to hear the same respect in return.

Sharing Family Time

Another way parents can intentionally create a loving, welcoming atmosphere in their home is by setting aside time that is specifically just family time. In a world in which each family member often has multiple activities that create a busy schedule, parents must stress the primacy of family life over all the other demands on their time. Making time to attend Sunday (or Saturday evening) Mass together as a family is one way of doing this. Another is by making sure that the family shares a meal together each day. A recent national study showed a link between regular family meals, academic success, psychological health, and lower alcohol and substance abuse in teens among families who regularly ate meals together.[5] When parents intentionally plan their schedules around family life—making time to read, talk, work, and play together—instead of letting their activities dictate how much time they have together, everyone thrives.

Disciplining Children

Although you may not imagine yourself ever having to discipline a child, if you become a parent, this will be another responsibility. Discipline refers to providing the necessary structure to teach children how to live peacefully and to accept personal responsibility. Discipline helps the family function better. Often discipline is needed to help establish the connection between good and bad behaviors and their consequences, which helps children develop, mature, and be able to discern between virtue and vice as they get older. Sometimes parents must even lead by example by acknowledging their own failings to their children. Parents who apologize to their children for losing their temper and yelling teach them to admit when they have done something wrong and ask for forgiveness out of love and humility.

Evangelizing Children

The most essential role of parents, however, is the "responsibility and privilege of *evangelizing their children*" (*CCC*, 2225). This ideally happens from birth, when parents bring their child to receive the Sacrament of Baptism. Parents should foster a familiarity with and love of the faith through teaching about the faith, praying with their children, taking them to Mass and the sacraments, modeling the virtues, speaking about how God has worked in their own lives, and above all praying for their children's holiness and their future vocations.

Duties of Children

The Book of Sirach teaches children:

> With your whole heart honor your father;
>   your mother's birth pangs do not forget.
> Remember, of these parents you were born;
>   what can you give them for all they gave you? (Sir 7:27–28)

Out of gratitude for all their parents have done and also out of obedience to the Fourth Commandment, children are called to honor and respect their parents. Your parents, though they are not flawless, have nevertheless most likely strived and worked for what is best for you for your whole life. They desire what is best for you. They have learned much already from their own experiences that you

have not, and they often seek to help you avoid painful, sinful, or dangerous experiences yourself.

Though it can be difficult, you have much control over the peace in your home through how you honor and respect your parents and others in authority. Think about the tension and instability it creates in the home when a child chooses to argue, lie, or disrespect a parent. These actions affect more than just the two or three people directly involved as they spread to the entire household and give a bad example. It is true that you are becoming more and more capable of making adult decisions, many of which your parents probably already let you make. Still, you are called to obedience to your parents while you live at home. There are many ways you can show obedience: helping around the house with chores, choosing not to argue with a parent, using kind and respectful language, and making wise and moral decisions that honor your parents.

Mutual respect in families extends to relationships between siblings, which create harmony in family life. Under the Fourth Commandment, children also owe gratitude, respect, and obedience to grandparents, godparents, and other family members, as well as teachers, pastors, and the catechists who have taught them about the faith.

Obedience to parents is due for as long as a child lives at home; however, children should continue to show respect for their parents even as adults living outside the home. When you become an adult, you will realize the wisdom that your parents have, and hopefully you will seek it out. Adult children also have the duty to give their parents "material and moral support in old age and in times of illness, loneliness, or distress" (*CCC*, 2218).

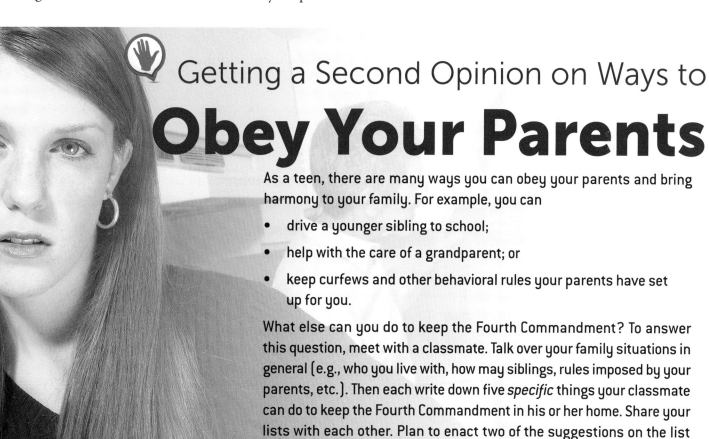

Getting a Second Opinion on Ways to
Obey Your Parents

As a teen, there are many ways you can obey your parents and bring harmony to your family. For example, you can

- drive a younger sibling to school;
- help with the care of a grandparent; or
- keep curfews and other behavioral rules your parents have set up for you.

What else can you do to keep the Fourth Commandment? To answer this question, meet with a classmate. Talk over your family situations in general (e.g., who you live with, how may siblings, rules imposed by your parents, etc.). Then each write down five *specific* things your classmate can do to keep the Fourth Commandment in his or her home. Share your lists with each other. Plan to enact two of the suggestions on the list your classmate made for you within the next week. When the week is completed, write a one-page summary of how well you completed each item. Staple the list prepared by your classmate to your paper.

SECTION ASSESSMENT

NOTE TAKING

Use the concept webs you made to help you answer the following questions.

1. As a primary duty of parents, what does *education* refer to?

2. What is the most essential role of parents?

3. Name some ways children follow the Fourth Commandment to honor and respect their parents.

4. What are the responsibilities of adult children to their parents?

COMPREHENSION

5. What do studies show are the results of shared family meals?

6. What does *discipline* refer to in family life?

7. How long is obedience due from a child to his or her parents?

8. What are some primary ways parents *evangelize* their children?

REFLECTION

9. What are other ways you could better live out the Fourth Commandment in your family?

SECTION 4
The Family as the Domestic Church

MAIN IDEA

The Christian family is called to be a place where members grow in love, virtue, wisdom, and holiness. The Church calls the family the *domestic church*.

By choosing for his Son to be born and raised in a human family, God the Father signified the importance of the family in nurturing the life of the Church. Jesus kept the Fourth Commandment in his obedience to Joseph and Mary while also obeying the will of his Father in heaven. It was in the Holy Family that Jesus shared the same type of family life as most children do. And it was within the safety and love of his family that Jesus "advanced [in] wisdom and age and favor before God and man" (Lk 2:52).

From the beginning of Christianity, the Church was present in the family. In the Acts of the Apostles and in St. Paul's Letter to the Romans, there is mention of Christians meeting in family homes to celebrate the Eucharist, and presbyters (priests) and other ministers received their vocations from family life. The Second Vatican Council emphasized the family as the domestic church: "From the wedlock of Christians there comes the family, in which new citizens of human society are born, who by the grace of the Holy Spirit received in baptism are made children of God, thus perpetuating the People of God through the centuries. The family is,

NOTE TAKING

Understanding a Key Concept. As you read this section, design a graphic like the one here that lists words and phrases associated with *domestic church*.

Word

Word

WORDS

DOMESTIC CHURCH

Words Word

Words

Word

so to speak, the domestic church. In it parents should, by their word and example, be the first preachers of the faith to their children" (*Lumen Gentium*, 11).

Within the family, all members carry out what the *Catechism of the Catholic Church* calls the **common priesthood** by receiving the sacraments, praying and giving thanks, striving to live holy lives, and practicing sacrificial love and charity toward each other. The *Catechism* goes on to say, "Thus the home is the first school of Christian life and 'a school for human enrichment.' Here one learns endurance and the joy of work, fraternal love, generous—even repeated—forgiveness, and above all divine worship in prayer and the offering of one's life" (*CCC*, 1657, quoting *Lumen Gentium*, 10).

Families are also the source of vocations to the priesthood and consecrated life. Most priests and religious would list their own families as a source of their religious vocation. The encouragement children receive from parents to be open to religious life or ordination is certainly one help to cultivating a vocation. Also, the daily examples of faith, hope, and love lived out in family life keep open those possibilities.

Growing in Faith in the Christian Family

The Christian family is indeed a child's first experience of belonging to the Church. It is the parents' primary responsibility to provide an environment where God's loving presence is easily experienced and faith in Jesus Christ is proudly professed. Other members of the family—grandparents, godparents, aunts, and uncles—can contribute to a child's religious upbringing, but it is parents who have the primary responsibility. Concretely, this

> **common priesthood** The priesthood of the faithful. Christ has made the Church a "kingdom of priests" who share in his priesthood through the Sacraments of Baptism and Confirmation.

means that parents should teach their children prayers, form their consciences, encourage virtuous behavior, and promote the teachings of the Church. Often, these lessons are not taught deliberately but rather arise out of normal family situations. For example, parents can encourage the Beatitude of "Blessed are the peacemakers, for they will be called children of God" (Mt 5:9) by facilitating peaceful resolutions to situations when siblings bicker.

Children also contribute to their parent's growth in holiness. St. Teresa of Calcutta once told the story of a little girl of six or seven whom she picked up off the street and took to Shishu Bhavin, a children's home. She gave the girl a bath, nice clothes, and food, but that same evening the girl ran away. The little girl was brought to Shishu Bhavin a number of times, receiving clean clothes and food, but then always running away. Finally, Mother Teresa sent a sister to follow the girl. The sister found the girl with her mother and her sister sitting under a tree. The mother was cooking a meal from food scraps she found in the street. Mother Teresa explained: "And then we understood why the child ran away. The mother loved that child. And the child loved the mother. They were so beautiful to each other. The child said, 'bari jabo'—it was her home. Her mother was her home" (*Words to Love By*).

Faith, hope, and love experienced and shared in a Christian family cannot be duplicated in any other setting. As children grow, parents have the responsibility to educate them in accord with the faith to the best of their ability. This is often done well in Catholic schools. The United States Catholic Bishops teach that "Catholic schools afford the fullest and best opportunity to realize the threefold purpose of Christian education among children."[6] First, Catholic schools can forge a deeper relationship between school and family. Second, they can easily facilitate students' participation in the liturgy and the sacraments. And, third, they can provide a favorable environment for teaching the Catholic faith. The right to choose a school for their children is a fundamental right of parents.

Ways for **Families** to **Encourage** Religious Vocations

When parents affirm the value of religious and priestly vocations, they allow their children the openness to explore these vocations as a real possibility. There are several things parents and families can do to encourage religious vocations, including:

- Practicing a life of prayer. Children raised in families where prayer is naturally part of their life and conversation with God is encouraged will be able to easily take their discernment of a vocation to prayer.

- Participating and fostering a love for the sacraments, especially the Sacrament of the Eucharist and the Sacrament of Penance. When families regularly partake in the sacraments, they not only open themselves to grace but also understand the importance of faith in relation to other competing interests.

- Telling how, as parents, they view their marriage and their roles as mother and father as a God-given vocation.

ASSIGNMENT

Write a one- to two-page report on the life of a contemporary saint who was a priest or in a religious order. Include as many of the following details in the report as possible:

- the saint's name and order he or she was in (or founded, if applicable)

- the years of the saint's life

- where the saint lived

- how his or her family influenced his or her vocation

- some of the influential words or deeds of the saint

- the charism and/or apostolate of the saint and his or her religious community

- when the saint was canonized

- Befriending priests, religious sisters, and religious brothers. Families can make time in a social setting to listen to the stories of their calling, vocation, and ministry.
- Sharing stories of saints.
- Describing the priesthood and religious life in positive ways, such as finding God's path to freedom and happiness. Stories that portray religious life as dramatic, freeing, and exciting—a radical acceptance of Jesus' call to discipleship—appeal to a young person's sense of adventure and altruism.

- Inviting friends of teenage children into the house for an open discussion about their plans for the future, including college, career, and vocational plans. Parents can encourage and commend each person for the unique plan God has for them.
- Taking a group of teens to visit a seminary or religious house. Parents can arrange for a tour or participate in a sponsored retreat there.
- Cultivating habits of service to the poor, sick, elderly, and children. Families can encourage teens to explore the types of service they are drawn toward and to share material possessions and the gift of self.

School of Vocations

As a child grows, he or she should become more attuned, through prayer and the sacramental life, to his or her own unique vocation. Children have the right to listen to God and choose their own vocation and profession, not one someone else has chosen for them. However, it is wise for children to listen to their parents' good counsel in these matters since their parents know them so intimately. In the end, parents should welcome and respect with joy and thanksgiving God's vocational call to their children, whatever it may be, and encourage their children to follow God's lead. The *Catechism of the Catholic Church* teaches, "[Parents] must be convinced that the first vocation of the Christian is to *follow Jesus*. . . . Becoming a disciple of Jesus means accepting the invitation to belong to *God's family*, to live in conformity with His way of life" (*CCC*, 2232–2233).

When Jerry and Bernadette Strand attended Mass, prayed night after night, modeled virtuous living, and conversed about their faith as their children grew up, they did not necessarily do so because they wanted a son to become a priest. Yet it was because his parents prioritized the faith and had a spiritual life at home

that their oldest son, Luke, felt called to the priesthood. What is more surprising is that, because Jerry and Bernadette encouraged Luke's vocation, soon their sons Jacob and Vincent also responded to their own calls to the priesthood. The Strands now have three sons ordained as priests.[7] Being open and honest about living out the faith is the best gift they gave to their sons.

Participating in the domestic church of the family reminds you that you are part of a larger Christian family. In *Familiaris Consortio* Pope John Paul II emphasized that "no one is without a family in this world: the Church is a home and family for everyone, especially those who 'labor and are heavy laden'" (*FC*, 85).

SECTION ASSESSMENT

NOTE TAKING

Use the graphic you designed to help you complete the following items.

1. Write a definition of *domestic church* in your own words.

2. Name two words you most associate with the domestic church.

3. How do the two words you chose express your definition of the domestic church?

COMPREHENSION

4. What does the *Catechism of the Catholic Church* teach that one learns in the home, "the first school of Christian life" (*CCC*, 1657)?

5. What are three things parents should do to promote their children's growth in faith and openness to a religious vocation?

6. How can children contribute to their parents' growth in holiness?

7. What are some things Jerry and Bernadette Strand did that facilitated their sons' priestly vocations?

8. What did Pope John Paul II, in *Familiaris Consortio*, remind people in regard to having a family?

CRITICAL THINKING

9. What did Pope John Paul II mean when he wrote that "no one is without a family in this world"? How does the Church fulfill these words? How can you help in this task?

10. What are three practical ways not mentioned in the section for parents to help their children discern their vocation?

Section Summaries

Focus Question

Why are Catholic married couples called to have children and raise them in the Catholic faith?

Complete one of the following:

→ Read paragraphs 1652–1654 of the *Catechism of the Catholic Church*. Write one paragraph that summarizes what is meant by "openness to fertility."

→ Prayerfully read Psalm 127. What does this psalm say about the house that puts God first? What analogy does it use for the gift of sons?

→ Explain how the Fourth Commandment is the basis for the duty of parents to their children, and children to their parents. For reference, see paragraphs 2214–2233 of the *Catechism of the Catholic Church*.

INTRODUCTION

Marriage Leads to Family

Family life is rooted in the complementarity of man and woman, based on the total self-gift of marriage. The Divine Persons of the Blessed Trinity model the type of love people should strive for in the relationships between the husband and wife and between parents and their children. Authentic married love is fruitful. Parents love their children and work to build a community of love in their families.

→ St. Augustine wrote in his work *De Trinitate* (*On the Trinity*): "If you see charity, you see the Trinity. The Father is unreservedly infinite donation, the Son is active receiving, and the Spirit is the perfect unity of the one who gives and the one who receives. They are three: the Lover, the Beloved, Love." Write a reflection on how the terms *Lover*, *Beloved*, and *Love* can be used to describe relationships within the human family.

SECTION 1

The Nature of the Family: A Community of Life and Love

The Church must do the important work of proclaiming what the family is meant to be: a community of life and love, founded on marriage. A secure family environment is essential for people to develop and grow healthy in mind, body, and soul. Pope John Paul II said that "as the family goes, so goes the nation." The family is where people learn to give selflessly through love and where they are trained in the foundations for freedom, security, and fraternity. When family life and the relationships between its members are considered necessary and important and are supported by society, then the rest of the culture thrives.

> Read these Gospel passages: Matthew 5:13–16; Matthew 7:21, 24–25; Matthew 19:3–6; Matthew 22:35–40; John 2:1–11; John 15:9–12; John 15:13–16; and John 17:20–23. Choose two passages from the Gospel of Matthew and two passages from the Gospel of John, and write two sentences on each explaining what they mean in light of marriage and family life.

SECTION 2

The Gift of Children

The decision of a married couple to be open to life is a courageous and loving one that shares in the Father's work of creation. In modern society, sexual intercourse is falsely thought of as a casual act that requires no commitment. The Church emphasizes the importance of responsible parenthood, which is both open to life and conscientious of circumstances within family life. For just reasons, married couples may plan and space the birth of their children through means that respect the unitive and procreative ends of sexual intercourse. The anti-life practices of contraception, sterilization, and abortion do not respect these ends or human dignity and are intrinsically evil. Those who struggle to have children or are infertile suffer greatly. The Church supports married couples trying to conceive children by encouraging methods that respect the dignity of the human person and the two ends of sexual love.

> Name some practical issues and decisions that might arise as Catholic parents strive to follow the definition of responsible parenthood.

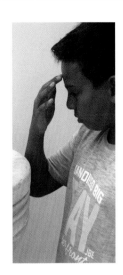

SECTION 3

Responsibilities in the Family

Corresponding to the call to procreation is the parental obligation to educate their children. Education is an integrated task to form the whole human person, especially morally and spiritually. The most essential role of parents is the evangelization of their children. Out of gratitude and obedience, children are called to honor and respect their parents.

→ Share an early lesson you learned about your Christian faith. Who taught you? What did the person teach you? What else do you remember about the occasion? Write your remembrances in a three-paragraph reflection.

SECTION 4

The Family as the Domestic Church

The family is the domestic church, in which all members live out their common priesthood in several ways, especially by receiving the sacraments. It is the parents' responsibility to provide an environment where God's loving presence is experienced and faith in Jesus Christ is professed. Parents should welcome and respect God's vocational call to their children, whatever it may be, and encourage their children to follow it.

→ Of the ways listed in the feature "Ways for Families to Encourage Religous Vocations," which way do you think is most important? Write three paragraphs naming and explaining your choice.

Chapter Assignments

Choose and complete at least one of the following three assignments assessing your understanding of the material in this chapter.

1. Examining Primary Sources: *Familiaris Consortio*

Read the following paragraphs from the papal encyclical *Familiaris Consortio*. You can access the encyclical at www.vatican.va. Using complete sentences, write your answers to each of the following questions.

- Paragraph 3: What is the only way the hopes people have in marriage and family life can be fulfilled?

- Paragraph 4: What does the Church understand to be an "inescapable requirement of the work of evangelization" regarding family life? What makes this work challenging today?

- Paragraph 13: What does the marriage of a baptized man and baptized woman become a symbol of? How are spouses a reminder of Jesus' sacrifice on the Cross? How is marriage a real symbol of the event of salvation?

- Paragraph 14: What is parental love called to become? What are some opportunities for service if a couple face sterility?

- Paragraph 15: How do Christian marriage and the Christian family build up the Church?

- Paragraph 30: How is an anti-life attitude born from the anxieties and tensions of the world?

- Paragraph 32: What does it mean to say that couples who turn to contraception act as "arbiters" of God's plan?

- Paragraph 38: To what did St. Thomas Aquinas compare the dignity and vocation of marriage?

Finish with a one-paragraph synopsis of *Familiaris Consortio*, including its date of publication and one quotation from an outside source on its importance to the Church and the world.

2. Video: Positive Characteristics of Family Life

Family life parallels the sacramental life of the Church. The family is the domestic church. For example, families welcome and initiate new members with customs and rules. The Church welcomes and initiates new members. Families share meals of unity. The Church celebrates the Eucharist, a sacrificial meal of unity. Family members occasionally argue and fight with one another and then say, "I'm sorry," and forgive. The Sacrament of Penance leads to reconciliation. Family members care for one another when members are sick or dying. The Church does the same in the Sacrament of the Anointing of the Sick. And, as explained in Section 4 of this Chapter, vocations are fostered in family life.

Using these examples, create a three-minute video that depicts some positive aspects of family life. The video can be of ritual celebrations like birthdays, holidays, sacraments, or reunions. Create a voiceover for the video that offers an explanation of the event taking place and why it is important to your family.

Share the video in an online platform with your teacher. If you are able to share the video with the class, you can play the video without sound and share your voiceover narration live.

3. A Mock Email Exchange on Artificial Contraception

Research more about why the Catholic Church teaches that married couples should not use artificial contraception. More information can be found at www.usccb.org (search "Love and Sexuality"). Then, pretend you are emailing a friend who does not see anything wrong with artificial contraception. Explain the Church's teaching about artificial contraception clearly over a series of two or three emails. You must also include the friend's counterargument.

This assignment requires you to be able to understand a contrary perspective. By the conclusion of the email exchange, you should summarize for the friend the truth of the Church's teaching about the goodness of being open to life within marriage.

Faithful Disciple

St. Elizabeth Ann Seton

An incomplete family life as a child and as a wife was part of the impetus for St. Elizabeth Ann Seton, the first native-born American saint, to found a religious congregation of women whose ministry primarily involved educating and caring for poor children.

St. Elizabeth Ann Seton

Elizabeth Bayley was born near New York City in 1774, two years before the beginning of the American Revolution, into a wealthy family. The family settled on Staten Island. Her father was a doctor. Her maternal grandfather was the pastor of St. Andrew's Episcopal Church on Staten Island. Elizabeth was baptized and raised as an Episcopalian.

Tragedy first struck Elizabeth at the age of three, when her mother died. Dr. Bayley remarried to Charlotte Barclay, and the couple had five children. Their stepmother loved and cared for Elizabeth and her older sister, Mary Magdalene, but when the marriage broke up, Charlotte rejected the two girls. They were sent to live with relatives because their father was in London, England, doing medical studies. Elizabeth's journals reveal that this was a period of darkness for her, as she felt she had lost two mothers in childhood.

At age nineteen, Elizabeth married William Seton, a wealthy businessman in the import and export trade. The Setons belonged to Trinity Episcopal Church in New York City, a congregation filled with socially prominent members. The Setons had a happy marriage and were the parents of five children, three girls and two boys.

The Setons' idyllic life began to crumble when William's father died and they were given charge of William's six younger siblings. William's business began to deteriorate around this time; conflicts between England and France made the shipping business volatile. Then William became deathly ill with tuberculosis. Taking one last chance to save his life, he, Elizabeth, and their eldest daughter, Anna Maria, traveled to Italy, where the climate was warmer. But William's health worsened, and he died in Italy on December 27, 1803. While there, William's Italian business partners received Elizabeth warmly. Elizabeth was interested in and impressed by their Catholic faith. When she returned to New York, she took instruction in Catholicism and was received into the Catholic Church in 1805.

As was customary for many widows of the time, Elizabeth started an academy for young girls as a way to support her own children. However, when the parents of her students found out she was a Catholic, they removed their children from the school. Elizabeth was considering a move to Canada when she met a visiting priest who was president of St. Mary's College in Emmitsburg, Maryland. He asked her to open a similar academy in Emmitsburg to meet the needs of the Catholic children living nearby.

In 1810, Elizabeth established the St. Joseph's Academy and Free School in Emmitsburg. It was the first free Catholic school in America, the beginning of the parochial school system. Elizabeth also founded a religious community of sisters, known at first as the Sisters of Charity of St. Joseph's, to care for the children of the poor. Elizabeth, as foundress, was called "Mother Seton." Bylaws were written into the congregation's charter to allow Elizabeth to always be able to support and care for her own children. Mother Seton had a deep devotion to the Bible, the Eucharist, and the Blessed Mother. Having lost two mothers at an early age, she deeply appreciated the motherly love and guidance of Mary. She also appreciated being a mother to her now extended family of religious sisters and the children they taught and cared for.

Elizabeth Ann Seton died in 1821 at the age of forty-six from the effects of tuberculosis, the same illness that caused the death of her husband. She was beatified in 1963 by Pope John XXIII, who said of her, "In a house that was very small, but with ample space for charity, she sowed a seed in America which by Divine Grace grew into a large tree." Pope Paul VI canonized St. Elizabeth Ann Seton on September 14, 1975, the first American-born saint. She is the patron saint of Catholic schools.

Reading Comprehension

1. Why did Elizabeth feel she had lost two mothers in childhood?

2. What piqued Elizabeth's interest in the Catholic Church?

3. Why was Elizabeth's first attempt at opening an academy in New York City unsuccessful?

4. What special bylaws did the Sisters of Charity of St. Joseph's add to the congregation's charter to benefit Mother Seton?

Writing Task

Of the following descriptions, which do you think best describes St. Elizabeth Ann Seton's legacy: convert to Catholicism; wife and mother who became a saint; first American saint; or founder of the American parochial school system? Explain your answer.

Explaining the Faith

Can a marriage be valid if one or both of the spouses do not want to have children?

From what you have already read about marriage, you know that the essential promises and benefits of marriage, which are consented to during the exchange of vows, are indissolubility, faithfulness, and fruitfulness. This means that spouses who exchange consent are agreeing to be married to each other until death separates them, to be faithful to each other, and to be open to having children.

Therefore, a marriage is *not* valid if one or both spouses do not want to have children. This is because fruitfulness, or openness to procreating and raising children, is one of the vows made. If either spouse were to recite their vows but were internally determined that they would never be open to having children, it would negate their vows. In other words, the spouse or spouses are giving false consent, since they do not actually intend to keep the vow of fruitfulness.

There are certain nuances to the question, such as if one or both spouses were determined not to have children at the time of their marriage or if they decided later that they did not want to have children, in which case the marriage might be valid. Still, fruitfulness is an essential element to the Sacrament of Matrimony. The resolve to never have children would be a serious sin in that it denies the total gift of self which is essential to marriage.

 ## Further Research

What are good reasons for a married couple to have children? Cite a quotation from paragraph 50 of *Gaudium et Spes* (found at www.vatican.va) in your answer.

Prayer
Prayer to the Holy Family

Heavenly Father, you have given us the model of life in the Holy Family of Nazareth. Help us, O Loving Father, to make our family another Nazareth where love, peace, and joy reign. May it be deeply contemplative, intensely Eucharistic, and revived with joy.

Help us to stay together in joy and sorrow in family prayer. Teach us to see Jesus in the members of our families, especially in their distressing disguise. May the Eucharistic heart of Jesus make our hearts humble like his and help us to carry out our family duties in a holy way. May we love one another as God loves each one of us, more and more each day, and forgive each other's faults as you forgive our sins. Help us, O Loving Father, to take whatever you give and give whatever you take with a big smile.

Immaculate Heart of Mary, pray for us. St. Joseph, pray for us. Amen.

CHALLENGES TO MARRIAGE AND FAMILY LIFE

5

The Phrase That Saved a Marriage

Only the rare couple will not find marriage to be difficult at times. Rick Evans and his wife, Keri, were not that rare couple. The Evanses, parents to five children, seemed to struggle in their differences from the beginning of their marriage. There were many arguments.

Rick often traveled for work, but the fighting continued over the phone and long distances, which led to their both being "perpetually defensive." After a particularly passionate fight, Rick turned to God right there in his hotel room. "I don't know if you could call it prayer—maybe shouting at God isn't prayer, maybe it is—but whatever I was engaged in I'll never forget it," says Rick. "Deep down I knew that Keri was a good person. And I was a good person. So why couldn't we get along? Why had I married someone so different than me? Why wouldn't *she* change?" In the depths of his sorrow, a phrase came to him by inspiration: "You can't change her, Rick. You can only change yourself." Rick began to pray constantly for the grace to change himself.

Home from his trip, Rick began to ask Keri, "How can I make your day better?" At first the question made Keri defensive, so she gave Rick menial tasks such as cleaning the kitchen or garage to get him away from her. After two weeks, Keri finally responded back by initiating a moment of apology and the first real connection the couple had experienced in a very long time.

Rick asked, "What can I do to make your day better?" every day for more than a month. He also continued to pray as the walls of defense and hurt began to fall. "We didn't solve all of our problems then, but the nature of our fights changed. To have a partner in life is a remarkable gift. I've learned that the institution of marriage can help heal us of our most unlovable parts. And we all have unlovable parts."[1]

FOCUS QUESTION

How do the **GRACES** of the **SACRAMENT OF MATRIMONY** help couples face the **CHALLENGES** that come with **MARRIAGE AND FAMILY LIFE**?

Chapter Overview

INTRODUCTION
Upholding God's Plan for Marriage

MAIN IDEA
The institutions of marriage and family life are facing a number of unique challenges in society. Many of these issues spring from flawed ideologies.

Marriage and family life are the seed of individual and societal stability and flourishing. Yet today, marriage has become a topic of great debate both in society and in the Church. It is no longer assumed that most people will eventually get married and have children. The *Catechism of the Catholic Church* notes that, due to sin, the union between a man and a woman "has always been threatened by discord, a spirit of domination, infidelity, jealousy, and conflicts that can escalate into hatred and separation. This discord can manifest itself more or less acutely, and can be more or less overcome according to the circumstances of cultures, eras, and individuals, but it does seem to have a universal character" (*CCC*, 1606).

You have learned that marriage, while involving very personal feelings between the spouses, is not merely a private matter. Marriage is a public institution that has a large impact on the couple, their children, their extended family and friends, and society. Upholding God's plan for marriage is in everyone's interest. However, a number of challenges face marriage and family life today. These include the following:

- A loss of mutual dependence of spouses due to the exaggeration of the independence of spouses

- The acceptance of no-fault divorce and remarriage

- Cohabitation and de facto unions

- The wide acceptance of homosexual unions

NOTE TAKING

Summarizing Details. Create a graphic organizer like the one here. Below the heading "SIN," highlight five threats to modern marriage you gleaned from reading this section.

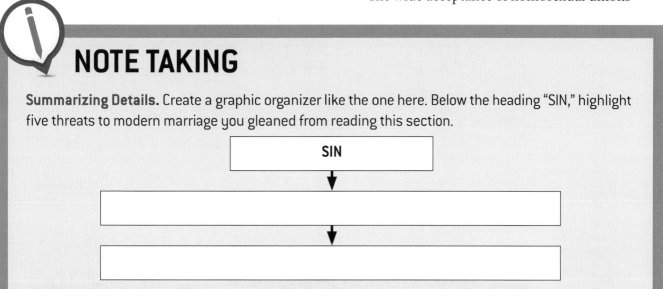

- The impact of the media and challenges to traditional marriage by the law

- Financial burdens on spouses

- Loss of understanding of the dignity of life and willingness to accept children as a gift from God

- Increase in mixed marriages

- Sexual license leading to greater use of contraceptives and abortion

While many of these challenges are not new, they have increased greatly in the past few generations. Consider that 59 percent of people in their twenties were married in 1960, compared to 20 percent in 2011.

According to the US Census Bureau, as marriage has declined, **cohabitation** has become more widespread, nearly doubling since 1990. The divorce rate for first marriages in the United States is between 42 and 45 percent. A more recent study found that the percentage of children born to unmarried women has risen dramatically over the past half century, from 5 percent in 1960 to 40 percent in 2017.[2]

> **cohabitation** The occasion of an unmarried man and unmarried woman living together in the same home and having a sexual relationship.

Understanding the Challenges

The reasons for the rise in challenges to marriage are complicated, but a sense that marriage restricts personal freedom, also known as **individualism**, has played a major role in the decline of healthy, lasting marriages. Pope Benedict XVI offered this opinion:

> Today, to many young people and even to some who are not so young, definitiveness appears as a constriction, a limitation of freedom. And what they want first of all is freedom. They are afraid that in the end they might not succeed. They see so many failed marriages. They fear that this juridical form, as they understand it, will be an external weight that will extinguish love. (Meeting with Priests of Diocese of Albano, August 31, 2006)

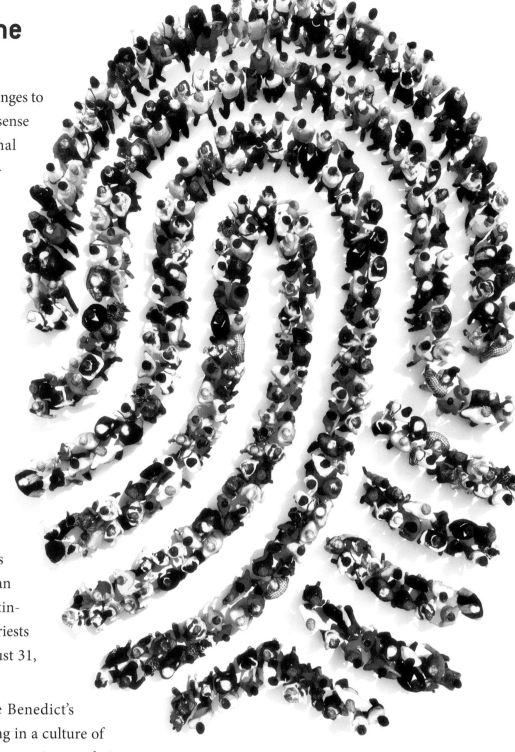

Pope Francis echoed Pope Benedict's words, noting that "we are living in a culture of the provisional. . . . The idea of commitments being temporary occurs everywhere."[3] The *Catechism of the Catholic Church* encourages you and all Catholics not to lose hope, but to seek out God's healing and mercy because "without his help man and woman cannot achieve the union of their lives for which God created them 'in the beginning'" (*CCC,* 1608). This chapter focuses on a number of challenges to marriage in light of marriage as an indissoluble and faithful union between a man and a woman.

> **individualism** The philosophy that places the private interests of each person above the common good of society. It is often practiced by sacrificing social values and norms to the personal desires of individuals.

What Has Happened since 1968?

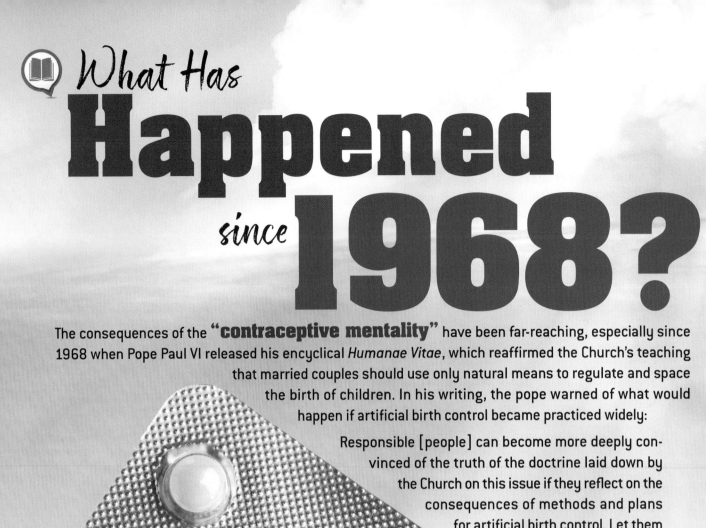

The consequences of the **"contraceptive mentality"** have been far-reaching, especially since 1968 when Pope Paul VI released his encyclical *Humanae Vitae*, which reaffirmed the Church's teaching that married couples should use only natural means to regulate and space the birth of children. In his writing, the pope warned of what would happen if artificial birth control became practiced widely:

Responsible [people] can become more deeply convinced of the truth of the doctrine laid down by the Church on this issue if they reflect on the consequences of methods and plans for artificial birth control. Let them first consider how easily this course of action could open wide the way for marital infidelity and a general lowering of moral standards. Not much

ASSIGNMENT

Write a one- to two-page position paper on the "contraceptive mentality" explaining its effects on women. In the paper, cite up-to-date statistics to support your claims.

experience is needed to be fully aware of human weakness and to understand that human beings—and especially the young, who are so exposed to temptation—need incentives to keep the moral law, and it is an evil thing to make it easy for them to break that law. Another effect that gives great cause for alarm is that a man who grows accustomed to the use of contraceptive methods may forget the reverence due to a woman, and, disregarding her physical and emotional equilibrium, reduce her to being a mere instrument for the satisfaction of his own desires, no longer considering her as his partner whom he should surround with care and affection.

Finally, careful consideration should be given to the danger of this power passing into the hands of those public authorities who care little for the precepts of the moral law. Who will blame a government which in its attempt to resolve the problems affecting an entire country resorts to the same measures as are regarded as lawful by married people in the solution of a particular family difficulty? Who will prevent public authorities from favoring those contraceptive methods which they consider more effective? Should they regard this as necessary, they may even impose their use on everyone. It could well happen, therefore, that when people, either individually or in family or social life, experience the inherent difficulties of the divine law and are determined to avoid them, they may give into the hands of public authorities the power to intervene in the most personal and intimate responsibility of husband and wife. (*Humanae Vitae*, 17)

What has happened since 1968? Unfortunately, Pope Paul VI's predictions about the results of a contraceptive mentality have come true in many cases. Here are some of the results:

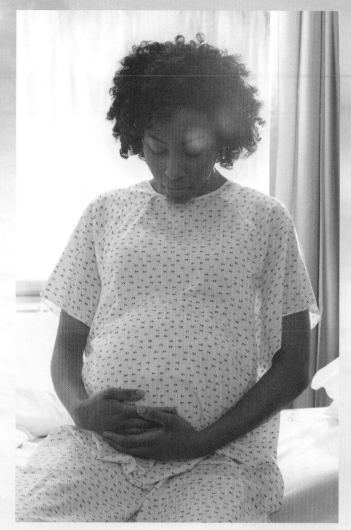

- The rates of abortion, sexually transmitted diseases, out-of-wedlock births, and divorce have risen dramatically.

- Sexual exploitation and sexual abuse of women occur at unprecedented levels.

- Population control policies are now a part of nearly every foreign aid discussion between developing and developed nations. The reception and implementation of contraception, abortion, and sterilization tools by developing nations is now a requisite for reception of foreign aid in dollars.

- The defining element of a woman's identity—her potential for bearing new life—has been redefined as a liability. Her new identity is as a person with the freedom to choose to end prenatal life if she wishes, while ironically the man bears no responsibility.[4]

SECTION ASSESSMENT

NOTE TAKING

Use the graphic organizer you created to help you answer the following questions.

1. What does the *Catechism of the Catholic Church* say about the nature of sin and marital unity?

2. Of all the issues mentioned in this section, which do you feel is the greatest threat to marriage? Explain.

VOCABULARY

3. Define *individualism*.

COMPREHENSION

4. What have some of our recent popes said about why the challenges to marriage and family life have increased greatly in recent generations?

CRITICAL THINKING

5. How have you witnessed what Pope Francis described as "a culture of the provisional" regarding marriage? Give at least three examples.

SECTION 1
Marriage Is until Death

MAIN IDEA
God created marriage to be for life. While a civil divorce cannot end a sacramental marriage, the Church can examine the facts of a marriage to decide whether there was an essential requirement missing that prevented the marriage from being valid.

When some Pharisees came to test Jesus and asked him whether it was lawful for a man to divorce his wife, Jesus' response reiterated God's original intention for marriage: "Have you not read that from the beginning the Creator 'made them male and female' and said, 'For this reason a man shall leave his father and mother and be joined to his wife, and the two shall become one flesh?' So they are no longer two, but one flesh. Therefore, what God has joined together, no human being must separate" (Mt 19:4–6).

The Catholic Church, in fidelity to the words of Christ, must uphold the teaching that marriage is indissoluble. A valid marriage between baptized Christians cannot be dissolved for any reason other than death. While there are many variables in each case of **civil divorce**, it is important to understand the effect of divorce on the institution of marriage, the spouses, the children, and society:

- Divorce injures the covenant of indissolubility to which the spouses consented.

- Divorce injures the meaning of the Sacrament of Matrimony. It weakens the sign of love that

> **civil divorce** The dissolution of a marriage contract by the legal system. It does not free a person from a valid marriage.

NOTE TAKING

Understanding Main Concepts. Create a chart like the one here. As you read this section, summarize Church teaching on each topic.

Topic	What the Church teaches
Divorce	
Divorce and remarriage	
Annulment	

marriage should provide to society, and divorce often gives scandal.

- Divorce gravely harms the spouses and their children. Children of separated parents struggle from the hurt of divorce into their adult lives, often perpetuating it in their own relationships. This in turn carries instability into society.

There are cases in which the Church deems it permissible for a separation or even a civil divorce to take place, such as the need to ensure the rights and care of children, some instances of adultery, and cases in which a spouse or children are in danger. In cases of separation, the Church encourages reconciliation, while also recognizing that it is not always possible or safe.

A civil divorce does not, however, end a sacramental marriage. In the eyes of the Church, the husband and wife do not cease being spouses. Though a person in such a situation experiences great sadness, he or she can find comfort and grace within the Church. A divorced or separated Catholic in good standing remains a member of the Church and should continue to receive the graces and sacraments of the Church. Within the Church the person can find the courage and support to live faithfully to his or her marriage though the spouses are separated.

In the United States the ease of **unilateral divorce** (also called "no-fault" divorce) often makes it easier for couples to choose divorce than to try to resolve marital problems. Since unilateral divorce was widely adopted in the late 1960s, the divorce rate has gone up dramatically. More and more couples use the ease of divorce as a final solution to marital problems rather than attempting to work them out, even though studies

> **unilateral divorce** A divorce in which one spouse contracts the divorce without the consent of the other spouse.

have shown that a majority of couples who think about divorce but ultimately stay together will describe themselves as "happily married" five years later.[5] Sometimes one spouse is willing to work on the marriage while the other is not. In some situations, one spouse pursues a civil divorce without the consent of the other spouse. The Church recognizes that there is a great difference in culpability between a spouse who tried to keep a marriage together and one who did not.

The Question of Divorce and Remarriage

A further difficulty with divorce is the question of those who remarry solely based on a civil divorce. Those who do so put themselves in an objective state of sin by choosing to no longer honor the vows of their existing sacramental marriages. Their remarriages, which are invalid, are a source of scandal to others and weaken the institution of marriage. Though they cannot receive the sacraments nor serve as a sponsor for Baptism and Confirmation, Catholics who are divorced and remarried are not fully separated from the Church. They are encouraged to "listen to the Word of God, to attend the Sacrifice of the Mass, to

persevere in prayer, to contribute to works of charity and to community efforts in favor of justice, to bring up their children in the Christian faith, to cultivate the spirit and practice of penance and this implore, day by day, God's grace" (*Familiaris Consortio*, 84).

Of particular care and concern are the children born to new marriages. The Church hopes that parents will seek out the sacraments and religious education for their children. Doing so is one way for parents to regain their own path to Christ through the Church.

As long as the new couple continues in an invalid remarriage, they are barred from receiving the sacraments. Situations revolving around invalid marriages vary widely. Typically, if the couple chooses to repent, first through the Sacrament of Penance, and the marriage is declared null and void by a Church tribunal, the individuals are welcomed back to full communion with the Church.

Annulment

Sadly, recent statistics show that 28 percent of Catholic marriages end in divorce, lower than the overall rate of nearly 50 percent but enough to involve about eleven million Catholic divorced men and women living in the United States.[6] The state considers marriage a contract, and obtaining a divorce ends that contract. The Church, however, always sees marriage as a sacramental covenant. Thus, while the legal contract of a marriage might have ended with divorce, in the eyes of God and the Church, a marriage is presumed valid unless otherwise proven. An **annulment**, or declaration of nullity, states that a marriage thought to be valid according to Church law actually fell short of an essential requirement.

> **annulment** A declaration by the Church that a sacramental marriage was invalid, that it never existed validly from the beginning; also called a *declaration of nullity*.

Remember, the backbone of a valid marriage is the *free consent of both parties to the vows of indissolubility, faithfulness, and being open to children*. Therefore, to exchange proper consent, both parties must understand what marriage is all about and must be mentally and emotionally capable of agreeing to it.

In declaring a marriage annulled, the Church asserts that at the time of the Sacrament of Matrimony, when the couple declared their consent, at least one element of a valid marriage was lacking, and thus the marriage is invalid. For example, someone who marries but has no intention of being permanently faithful to his or her spouse violates the promises of fidelity and indissolubility. Evidence of this lack of intention will usually arise when the person is unfaithful to his or her partner shortly after the wedding. Or a person of childbearing age could marry but intend not to have children; this, too, would render a marriage invalid. An annulment does not deny that a relationship existed but rather declares that an essential element for a valid marriage was missing. An annulment also does not mean that children born from the union are illegitimate, since the parents were presumed to be married.

Once an annulment is declared, the Church will permit a marriage with another person, as long as the grounds for nullity from the first (invalid) marriage are no longer there. The following are some of the common grounds for nullity:

- *Insufficient use of reason.* One or both parties did not know what was happening during the wedding due to insanity, mental illness, or lack of consciousness.

- *Error about the quality of the person.* One or both parties intended to marry someone who either possessed or did not possess a certain quality; for example, one person was already married or was an atheist or had a criminal past but the other party did not know.

- *Future conditions.* One or both parties attached conditions to the marriage; for example, "I will marry you if you will complete your education after the marriage."

- *Force.* One or both parties married because of physical or mental force that they could not resist.

- *Misunderstanding of marital sacramental dignity.* One or both parties believed that marriage is not a sacred relationship but only a civil arrangement.

It is important to know that the annulment process is not concerned with behavior after the wedding day. If there were no grounds for invalidity on the wedding day, then the marriage is an indissoluble bond regardless of what might have happened later. For example, a husband might be unfaithful to his wife, but if his intent on the day of the wedding was to be faithful, the infidelity will not factor into an annulment.

Anyone who is divorced must obtain an annulment in order to be married in the Church. There are several steps to the process, including collecting a report about the previous marriage, obtaining witness statements, and talking to the former spouse. These are submitted to the diocesan marriage tribunal. After the evaluation of facts, the tribunal makes a judgment on the validity of the marriage, with verification of the ruling by a neighboring diocese.

Support for **Troubled Marriages:** # Retrouvaille

The Church does not abandon a couple to the challenges of marriage after their wedding. There are a number of Church-sponsored programs designed to strengthen and repair marriages. One such program is named Retrouvaille, which is a French word meaning "rediscovery," to help couples, including those who are separated or divorced, successfully overcome problems in their marriages. The program consists of a weekend experience, followed by six to twelve sessions; it provides tools and a space to rediscover each other, communicate, and begin living together in a positive way.

During the weekend experience, a team of couples and a priest gives a series of presentations encouraging methods of renewed communication for the couples to examine their relationships. Couples have a chance to reflect individually on the presentation and then discuss together privately what they have heard. The weekend is not advertised as a cure-all but is designed to begin the process of marriage renewal. The post-weekend sessions are perhaps more crucial. These sessions use the techniques presented during the weekend to communicate, work through, and heal marriage problems.

ASSIGNMENT

Write a prayer for couples in troubled marriages.

SECTION ASSESSMENT

NOTE TAKING

Use the chart you created to help you answer the following questions.

1. How is the Church's teaching on divorce based on Jesus' words?

2. What does the Church teach about divorce and remarriage?

3. How does annulment differ from divorce?

COMPREHENSION

4. Describe some of the effects of divorce on the family and society.

5. What are circumstances under which the Church may permit a civil divorce?

6. How does a divorce affect a Catholic's membership in the Church?

7. What are Catholics who are divorced and remarried without an annulment encouraged to do to remain connected with the Church?

VOCABULARY

8. What happened after *unilateral divorce* became common in the late 1960s?

CRITICAL THINKING

9. Some have falsely referred to an annulment as a "Catholic divorce." Explain why this is not so.

10. Using the list of the common grounds for nullity in this section, describe a situation that would be grounds for an annulment.

SECTION 2

Marriage Is between One Man and One Woman

MAIN IDEA

Persons with homosexual inclinations should be treated with respect and care. At the same time, the Church must proclaim the truth that married and sexual love is based on sexual complementarity for the unity of spouses and for procreation.

"Love is love," proclaims a slogan supporting the redefinition of marriage to include same-sex partners. The implication is clear: marriage is about love, so any two people who love each other should be free to be married. Such an idea strikes a chord today, as it attempts to hold up the universal ideals of love and freedom. Love and freedom are certainly foundational to marriage. However, love and freedom are subject to the truth about God's design of the nature of marriage and of the human person made up of body and soul. To understand Church teaching on the sanctity of marriage as it relates to same-sex unions, you must understand what the Church teaches about homosexuality.

Homosexuality

The issue of homosexuality and same-sex unions is one that should be approached with compassion and care. The *Catechism of the Catholic Church* explains that "[persons with deep-seated homosexual tendencies] must be accepted with respect, compassion, and sensitivity. Every sign of unjust discrimination in their regard should be avoided. These persons are called to fulfill God's will in their lives and . . . to unite to the sacrifice of the Lord's Cross the difficulties they may encounter" (*CCC*, 2358).

NOTE TAKING

Concept Web. Create a concept web like the one here. In the smaller circles, list four supporting details, gleaned from this section, about what the Church teaches concerning homosexuality.

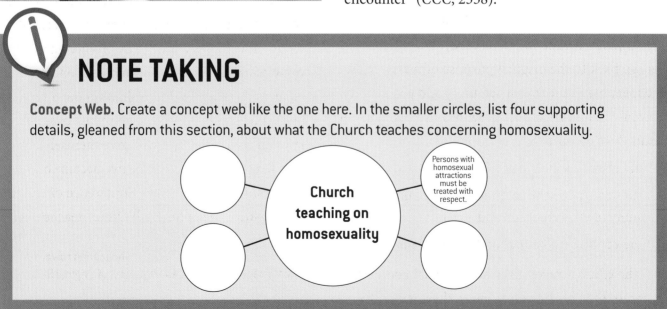

Church teaching on homosexuality

Persons with homosexual attractions must be treated with respect.

194   **Your Christian Vocation**

Persons with homosexual attraction are called to love and be loved, as every person is. Recall the definitions of different types of love from Chapter 2. Modern culture would have you believe that the highest expression of love is sexual love, *eros*. Yet it is *philia*, friendship love, and *agape*, self-giving love, that are really the two highest types of love. These types of loves can create deep, lasting, and fulfilling friendships and connections for the person with homosexual attraction.

Society urges you to believe that to love someone, you must accept and approve every decision that person makes without question. Yet as a Christian, you know this isn't true. You would not idly sit by while a friend destroyed his or her health and life through drug use. True love wills the deep and lasting good of the other person. This means that you act with that person's ultimate end in mind—that they are created for eternal happiness in heaven.

This type of love can sometimes lead to difficult choices, perhaps to having to say no to something because of a greater yes to striving for virtues such as chastity. With homosexuality, the greater yes is the truth and meaning of sexual love, always within the context of marriage. Homosexual acts are a false representation of married love. The Church says that "homosexual acts are intrinsically disordered" (*CCC*, 2357, quoting *Persona Humana*, 8). The reasons for this go back to the original purpose of marriage and the meaning of the sexual act: unity and procreation. Homosexual acts do not share in these two ends of sexual love because they

- are closed to the gift of life;
- do not lead to the intended bodily and spiritual unity of the sexual act; and
- are contrary to natural bodily complementarity.

The Church recognizes homosexual acts as disordered, but this does not mean that persons with homosexual desires are disordered persons. The Church loves and accepts them as made in the image and likeness of God. Those people who act hatefully toward them not only act badly; they act against what the Catholic Church teaches.

One way you can model a Christian mindset is by refusing to reduce persons with same-sex attraction to the labels of "homosexual," "lesbian," or "gay." Such language attempts to define a person solely by his or her sexual tendencies, refusing to see the individual person as an integrated whole. Pope Francis noted what is wrong with this type of labeling when he stated that "people should not be defined only by their sexual tendencies: let us not forget that God loves all his creatures and we are destined to receive his infinite love."[7]

Like all people, those with same-sex attraction struggle with **concupiscence**, which may include lust after someone of the same sex, as someone with heterosexual inclinations might struggle with lust after the opposite sex. Everyone faces the same challenge to work against temptations toward sin and live chastely in his or her state of life.

Same-Sex Unions

The sexual differences between men and women are essential to marriage. Complementarity is the starting point for understanding why protecting and promoting marriage as the union between one man and woman isn't arbitrary discrimination but a teaching of authentic truth. Only through sexual complementarity can a husband and wife give themselves completely to each other so that "the two become one flesh" (Gn 2:24). The United States Conference of Catholic Bishops video "Made for Each Other" teaches, "Only

> **concupiscence** The tendency or inclination toward sin every person experiences as a result of Original Sin.

a man and a woman—at every level of their identity: biological, physiological, emotional, social, spiritual—are capable of authentically speaking the language of married love, that is the language of total self-gift, open to the gift of the other and the gift of life."[8]

When the Church resists attempts in society to redefine marriage, she does so in service to truth, justice, love, and authentic freedom, not to keep people unhappy. It is not hateful to say that an immoral action is sinful, when it is said with charity. Rather, it is a sign of compassion to desire that people turn away from sin that harms them and society.

The Church recognizes that attempts to redefine marriage to include same-sex couples, or any other attempts to redefine marriage, empty marriage of its meaning and do so to the detriment of the family and society. The question is therefore not about denying individual rights but about promoting the good of individuals and of the whole of society.

SUPPORT FOR PERSONS WITH
Same-Sex Attraction

The Church has several ministries for all types of people with same-sex attraction or other sexual issues. These ministries first encourage such persons to move beyond a label and find their deepest identity in God who has called them son or daughter. One such ministry, *Courage*, has five goals: chastity, prayer, fellowship, support, and good role models. More information about these ministries can be found at the United States Conference of Catholic Bishops' website (www.usccb.org) under "Issues and Action/Homosexuality."

SECTION ASSESSMENT

NOTE TAKING

Use the concept web you created to help you answer the following questions.

1. What does the Church teach about how persons with same-sex attraction should be treated?

2. Explain how a person with homosexual inclinations may express the highest form of love.

3. Why are homosexual acts intrinsically disordered?

COMPREHENSION

4. Why does the Church resist attempts to redefine marriage?

5. What are people with homosexual and heterosexual inclinations called to do when faced with lustful temptations?

6. Explain the importance of complementarity in defining marriage.

VOCABULARY

7. What does *concupiscence* have to do with lustful temptations?

REFLECTION

8. Describe a way you could treat someone as Pope Francis describes: "not . . . defined only by their sexual tendencies."

SECTION 3
Marriage Is a Unique Relationship

MAIN IDEA
The Church is particularly concerned about cohabitation because it is so common today and because it causes unhappiness for individuals and families. It is a false imitation of the commitment to marriage.

In the United States today, about 60 percent of all marriages are now preceded by the couple's cohabiting, or living together and engaging in sexual relations. A recent snapshot of the average cohabiting household shows the following:

- Persons with lower levels of religious participation and education are more likely to cohabit.

- Those who had parents who divorced or had a previous marriage are more likely to cohabit.

- The average cohabiting household stays together just over one year.

- Approximately one in four children are born into cohabiting households.

- Children with cohabiting parents are more likely to experience a family breakup, live in poverty, suffer abuse, and have negative psychological and educational outcomes.[9]

Many couples mistakenly believe that cohabitation will lower their later risk of divorce or help them to know if they are compatible before marriage. Other reasons often cited by couples for living together outside of marriage include convenience, financial savings, a sense of security, or to take the relationship to "the next level." However, any perceived advantages are dramatically negated by severe risks (see "Counterpoint to Cohabitation," later in

NOTE TAKING

Listing Evidence. Make a list of reasons the Church disapproves of cohabitation, de facto unions, and common law marriage.

What the Church teaches about cohabitation:

1. It goes against God's plan for marriage by implying a fidelity that does not exist.
2.
3.
4.

this section. According to a multitude of studies, cohabiting puts the relationship at higher risk for breakup and divorce after marriage.[10] And all of the benefits listed for cohabitation can be gained through a noncohabiting relationship.

The Church is particularly concerned about cohabitation because it is so common today and because it causes unhappiness for individuals and families. First, it goes against God's plan for marriage because it implies a fidelity and level of commitment that the couple do not yet have, as these are possible only in marriage. Second, a sexual relationship outside of marriage is a false imitation of the expression of unity and openness to life found in a married sexual relationship; sexual love "demands a total and definitive gift of persons" (*CCC*, 2391) in the Sacrament of Matrimony. Lastly, cohabitation works against the heart's deepest desires for stability, trust, and complete union.

The Church welcomes couples who cohabit to be married but initiates a serious discussion on the dangers presented by living together. The couple are often strongly encouraged to stop cohabiting as a sign of their belief in the Sacrament of Matrimony and as a pledge of their desire to do what is best for their future marriage.

Cons of Cohabitation

- The experience of cohabitation *changes the attitudes about commitment and permanence* and makes couples more open to divorce.
- Cohabitors have *more conflict over money* after they marry than noncohabitors do.
- *Domestic violence is a more common problem* with cohabitors than with married persons, and this pattern will carry over to a subsequent marriage relationship.
- Cohabitors who marry are *less effective at conflict resolution* than those who did not cohabit.
- *Using sex as a controlling factor* can be a negative pattern which cohabiting couples can bring to their subsequent marriage.

Source: USCCB

Counterpoint to
COHABITATION

The Church wants to safeguard the happiness of individuals and couples. Knowing that cohabitation increases a couple's chance of divorce, the Church regards cohabitation as a particular danger to them and the institution of marriage. Couples who live together often do not clearly evaluate the reasons they have for cohabiting. Here are responses to common reasons a couple might use to justify living together before marriage.

REASON 1: "It's more convenient for us."

Cohabiting because of convenience is poor preparation for married life, which at times is inconvenient and demanding. Research shows that couples who live together before marriage tend to

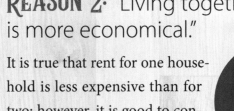

prefer "change" and open-ended lifestyles, neither of which are good for the permanency of marriage. Once they do marry, couples who first cohabited often "experience superficial communication and uncommitted decision-making" due to a lack of good relationship skill development while cohabiting.[11]

REASON 2: "Living together is more economical."

It is true that rent for one household is less expensive than for two; however, it is good to consider the *practical* and *spiritual* implications of this mentality. Practically speaking, couples who cohabit often run into the issue of "his" and "her" money, which can lead to frustration and disagreements that carry over into attitudes about money in marriage. Living together for economic reasons is dangerously overpragmatic in that it ignores the deeper spiritual good of waiting for the stable and committed relationship of marriage. Money is important, but short-term savings are less important than investing in a solid foundation for a lifetime relationship.

REASON 3: "We want to see if we are compatible before we get married."

Research bears witness to the fact that couples who live together communicate significantly less well and are less satisfied when they do marry. Couples who live together before marriage are much more likely to divorce than those who don't because they have "practiced" by living in nonbinding commitment. Those who live together before marriage report an over-reliance on sexual relations and "less emphasis on conversation and other ways of communication—ways that ultimately lead to a more fulfilling sexual union after marriage."[12] Cohabitation is not a beneficial shortcut to the natural development of a relationship found in a chaste dating and engaged relationship.

Long-Term Cohabitation

Cohabitation is also sometimes referred to as **de facto union** or **common law marriage**. Both of these designations usually indicate a couple have lived together for an extended amount of time. Because of the duration, some additional legal rights and responsibilities sometimes go into effect in these types of arrangements, including financial obligations for a partner and children. However, aside from the troubling social and spiritual implications of de facto unions and common law marriages, it is often unclear what the legal rights of such couples are. Unfortunately, according to the Vatican's Pontifical Council for the Family, these unions "do not imply marital rights and duties, and they do not presume to have the stability that is based on the marriage bond. They are characterized by their strong assertion to not take on any ties. The constant instability that comes from the possibility of terminating the cohabitation is consequently a characteristic of de facto unions" (*Family, Marriage and "De Facto" Unions*).

De facto unions and common law marriages also act against the nature of marriage and the sexual act by imitating something that they are not. Because they are built on shaky foundations, they often fail. The facts about such unions, as well as shorter-term cohabitation, only reinforce that the Church has a couple's best interest in mind when she says that a couple should begin living together only after making a total and definitive gift of themselves in marriage. There is no good way to shortcut God's design for marriage without damaging the relationship and those touched by it.

> **de facto union** The occasion of an unmarried couple living together, usually for an extended amount of time.
>
> **common law marriage** The occasion of a man and woman living together for a prolonged time and holding themselves to be married but having not been formally married in the Church or through the legal system.

SECTION ASSESSMENT

NOTE TAKING

Use the list you made of reasons the Church disapproves of cohabitation to help you answer the following questions.

1. How do cohabitation, de facto unions, and common law marriages act against the nature of marriage?

2. What are some misconceptions about cohabitation and its effect on marriage? How does the Church contradict these misconceptions?

COMPREHENSION

3. Why is the Church particularly concerned about cohabitation?

4. What might a cohabiting couple be encouraged to do before being married in the Church?

VOCABULARY

5. What are common characteristics of *de facto unions* and *common law marriages*?

CRITICAL THINKING

6. De facto unions are often "characterized by their strong assertion to not take on any ties." Explain what this means and why such an attitude is detrimental to a relationship and future marriage.

SECTION 4
Marriage Is Faithful

MAIN IDEA
The marriage bond is made to be perpetual and exclusive. A Christian marriage can never be dissolved.

NOTE TAKING

Identifying Main Ideas. As you read this section, complete an outline of the contents in a format like the one here, filling in more details.

I. Marriage is faithful
   A. Effects of marriage
      1.
      2.
   B. Perpetual nature of marriage
      1.
      2.
II. Personal changes that affect marriage
   A. Physical changes
   B.

Marriage by its very nature is faithful. Spouses vow to be true to each other for life. The *Code of Canon Law* describes the effects of marriages in this way: "From a valid marriage arises a bond between the spouses that by its very nature is perpetual and exclusive; . . . the spouses are strengthened and, as it were, consecrated for their duties and dignity of their state by a special sacrament" (*CCC*, 1638, quoting Canon 1134). Recall that the bond forged in the Sacrament of Matrimony is covenantal in nature; it is binding because it has been initiated by God. This bond is unique and different from other bonds you may be used to in life (e.g., a "lifetime warranty" on a product you purchase). Because it is from God, the Christian marriage bond is *perpetual*. This means that it will continue without interruption until the death of one spouse. It is also *exclusive*. The bond of unity is between two married people; their faithfulness is to one another. No one else may come between them.

Marriage by its very nature is lifelong. It can never be dissolved. True love lasts. As the Song of Songs states, "Deep waters cannot quench love, nor rivers sweep it away" (8:7). Fidelity means faithfulness to obligations. In marriage, fidelity refers to the faithfulness to the vows promised between husband and wife. Being faithful isn't always easy; it takes strength and determination to persevere and make marriage a lifelong commitment.

Personal Changes That Affect Marriage

It is inevitable that a man and woman will experience physical, emotional, and spiritual changes during the course of married life. On a superficial level, their outward appearance will change. When you marry someone for life, it's wise to be aware that the person across from you on your wedding day may look significantly different as the years progress.

More seriously, some people experience devastating *physical* changes even when they are very young. One married woman in her early thirties with two young children was overwhelmed by an undiagnosed neurological condition that caused her unspeakably painful migraine headaches. As the condition worsened and appeared more often, the side effects included vomiting and passing out to a state of semiconsciousness. The husband and the young children had their lives put on hold as she battled this illness. The husband had to pass up a job promotion to spend more time caring for both his wife and children. Yet the man looked on the situation as positively as possible: "My wife is the one suffering. Not me or my children. We are learning first-hand about compassion and love." Still, it was not what either spouse expected when they were first married.

People change *emotionally*, too. In a marriage, the responsibilities associated with supporting a household, raising children, and cultivating a deeper love with a spouse require both the husband and wife to pay special attention to the changing emotional needs of their spouse and themselves. Sometimes the sheer busyness of days keeps husbands and wives from connecting emotionally. If this goes on, the spouses may find that their relationship has grown cold and distant and that one or both of them may feel depressed. To remain emotionally engaged, a couple must make a commitment to do things such as,

- make each other feel special;

- listen to each other's needs;

- do things to make the other happy;

- appreciate the other's virtues;

- recall with fondness their shared past; and

- look forward to their future together.

Spiritual changes also occur over the course of a marriage. Typically, at the time of parenthood, married

couples grow the practice of the faith they learned as children. Parents seek to have their children baptized and later enrolled in formal religious education. Personally, as the spouses mature, they seek a deeper faith that discovers meaning in religious worship and symbols that previously may have been practiced only by rote. However, the spouses must recognize that the other person may be at a different place spiritually. Also, life events—both joyful and tragic—affect people in different ways. What is important is that neither the husband nor the wife leave the other behind or let the other remain alienated spiritually while he or she moves forward.

There will always be tensions between wanting a relationship of novelty and wanting one of predictability. A married couple must understand that external forces beyond their control will impact their relationship. In marriage, a couple learn to work together through the primary tensions and external forces to maintain a healthy relationship.

FACING EXTERNAL THREATS IN MARRIAGE

There are several external factors that can affect married life. Imagine how a relationship between a husband and wife would be impacted by each of the following situations. Write one or two detailed paragraphs in response to the question(s) accompanying each situation.

CAREER CHANGE/JOB RELOCATION

Given changes in the economy, there are times in a marriage when a spouse may face the loss of a job. An offer of new employment may require the family to move away from extended family and long-established friendships. Sometimes this type of decision crops up when the children are in crucial years of school or one spouse is in the midst of caring for an ill parent.

- When are times that career choices must come first in married life? When are times when other family considerations should take precedence over career?

CONFLICTS WITH CHILDREN

When children reach adolescence and begin to assert their independence, parents may have different ideas on how to address issues that arise. If the parents disagree, the teen may play one parent against another. This can cause a serious rift in the parents' relationship.

- Describe a particular family incident in which a conflict with a teenager can negatively impact the relationship of a husband and wife.

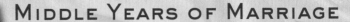

MIDDLE YEARS OF MARRIAGE

There are many events and issues that can lead to disruption in the middle years of marriage. When children leave the house for college, career, and/or marriage, the couple experience "empty nest" syndrome: the husband and wife are alone with each other for the first time in many years. Also, one or both partners may experience a so-called "mid-life crisis," in which the realization sets in that the dreams of youth will not be fulfilled. This may lead to boredom, depression, or, oppositely, the tossing aside of routines for new adventures. Negatively, a spouse may give up on marriage and be lured to **adultery**, which undermines the covenant of marriage and breaks the Sixth Commandment. Even a one-time affair rocks the trust and stability of the marriage, because it harms the total self-gift of married love. Infidelity is not simply a betrayal of physical love; it goes to the innermost being of a person's ability to totally love and trust the spouse.

- What are ways couples can stay focused on each other during the child-rearing years to avoid being caught by surprise when they are empty nesters?

RETIREMENT

The retirement years are not as well defined as they once were. In the past, age sixty-five was a definite time of retirement. At that point, the couple likely had raised their children, paid off their mortgage debt, and accumulated enough pension and Social Security for their remaining years, on average to their early seventies. Today, many adult children return home to live with their parents. More and more grandparents are required to give part- or full-time care to grandchildren. And with today's higher cost of living and variances in pensions and Social Security, many people must work more years than ever before. Life expectancy today is at an all-time high of 78.2 years. And even those couples with traditional retirements may face problems—for example, getting used to being around each other for the majority of their waking hours.

- What are some practical suggestions for couples to manage the stresses of retirement?

> **adultery** Marital infidelity, or sexual relations between a married person and someone other than his or her spouse. Adultery is a sin against the Sixth Commandment (see *CCC*, Glossary).

Help for PORNOGRAPHY ADDICTION

The accessibility, affordability, and anonymity of pornography, especially on the internet, have made it an increasingly destructive force in society today. Those who say that pornography is "not hurting anyone" are sadly mistaken. In marriage, pornography can be devastating. It destroys the intimacy and trust of the spouses, leads to communication obstacles, interferes with the viewer's ability to create and sustain personal interaction with their spouse and children, and harms the viewer's attitude toward sexual intimacy within the marriage. Pornography viewing can often be experienced as marital infidelity by the other spouse.

The *Catechism of the Catholic Church* calls pornography a "grave offense" because it perverts the sexual act, injures the dignity of all involved, and immerses those involved in a "fantasy world" (*CCC*, 2354). The Church's teaching on the harm and sinfulness of pornography is grounded in the affirmation of the dignity of the human person and the gift of human sexuality and marriage in God's plan.

Deliberately viewing pornography is a sin against chastity. Sexual intimacy and the pleasure derived from it are gifts from God and should remain personal and private, enjoyed within the sacred bond of marriage alone. The human body should not be unveiled or treated in a way that objectifies it sexually and reduces it to an erotic stimulant. Jesus is clear in his teaching that sexual immorality is not only a matter of one's actions but also a matter of one's heart (see Matthew 5:28).

ASSIGNMENT

Develop a plan now for avoiding the sin of pornography. Read the section "To Young People" in the United States Conference of Catholic Bishops' statement *Create in Me a Clean Heart: A Pastoral Response to Pornography* (www.usccb.org). Make a list of seven responses to pornography based on the sentences in the section that contain the following verbs:

1. Show
2. Reject
3. Reject
4. Refuse
5. Choose
6. Seek
7. Ask

Sacramental Grace in Marriage

You live in a time when it can be difficult to have a happy and holy marriage. Yet Christ has promised that "where sin increase[s], grace overflow[s] all the more" (Rom 5:20). Couples celebrating the Sacrament of Matrimony with the proper disposition are promised all of the grace they need in order to live out their vocation and be a sign of Christ's love to the world.

Jesus Christ has not left husbands and wives on their own. He is constantly present with them in their marriage. He loves them and is faithful to them, as he wishes them to do for each other. The *Catechism of the Catholic Church* teaches:

> Christ dwells with [Christian spouses], gives them the strength to take up their crosses and so follow him, to rise again after they have fallen, to forgive one another, to bear one another's burdens, to "be subject to one another out of reverence for Christ," and to love one another with supernatural, tender, and fruitful love." (*CCC*, 1642, quoting Ephesians 5:21)

In the journey of married life, a couple take on this "supernatural" dimension for each other, for their children, and as a witness to the world. By recognizing and embracing the sacramental grace of their marriage, the couple live out the true meaning of a sacrament. Husbands and wives cooperate with and perfect the gift of sanctifying grace by participating in the other sacraments, especially the Eucharist, by praying, by constantly remembering the noble state of married life, and by reminding themselves that their lives witness Christ for each other and their children and that their life as a couple is a sign of Christ to the world.

SECTION ASSESSMENT

NOTE TAKING

Use the outline you completed to help you answer the following questions.

1. What does it mean to say that a marriage is perpetual and exclusive?
2. What are three types of personal changes that occur in married life?

COMPREHENSION

3. How do couples grow in the practice of their faith when they become parents?
4. Name two things a married couple can do to remain emotionally engaged with each other.
5. What is "empty nest" syndrome?
6. How does Romans 5:20 reflect Christ's promise to married couples?

CRITICAL THINKING

7. Write a step-by-step "recipe" for married couples to help them recognize and keep Christ in their marriage.

Section Summaries

Focus Question

How do the graces of the Sacrament of Matrimony help couples face the challenges that come with marriage and family life?

Complete one of the following:

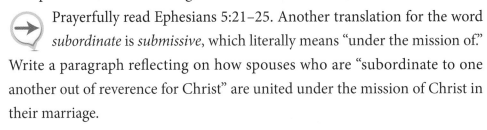

Prayerfully read Ephesians 5:21–25. Another translation for the word *subordinate* is *submissive*, which literally means "under the mission of." Write a paragraph reflecting on how spouses who are "subordinate to one another out of reverence for Christ" are united under the mission of Christ in their marriage.

Imagine that you will be married in fifteen years. Share some effective choices you could make now, in five years, and in ten years that would help you navigate some of the challenges of married life mentioned in this chapter.

Read and summarize paragraphs 1641–1642 of the *Catechism of the Catholic Church*. Explain what the "grace proper to the sacrament of Matrimony" is intended to do.

INTRODUCTION
Upholding God's Plan for Marriage

Because of sin, the union between a man and a woman has always been threatened by discord. Yet there are a number of particular challenges today that are facing marriage and family life. Among the reasons for the increase in challenges today are individualism and an inability to make lasting commitments. The increase in cohabitation is another prime factor. Upholding God's plan for marriage is in everyone's interest.

What do you perceive to be the greatest challenges to marriage in today's society? Cite evidence in a three-paragraph response.

SECTION 1
Marriage Is until Death

The Catholic Church upholds the teaching that marriage is indissoluble. Divorce weakens the sign of love that marriage should be, gives scandal, harms the spouses and their children, and carries instability into society. A civil divorce does not end a sacramental marriage. Spouses who divorce and remarry have removed themselves from receiving the sacraments. An annulment is not a "Catholic divorce." An annulment of a sacramental marriage does not deny that a relationship existed but rather says that an essential element for a valid marriage was missing or there was an impediment to a valid marriage.

➡️ Read about some of the common grounds for declaring a marriage null found in the *Code of Canon Law* under Book IV, Part I, Title VII, Chapter III, "Specific Diriment Impediments" (www.vatican.va). Choose one impediment that you don't understand. Research it, and write one paragraph explaining its meaning.

SECTION 2
Marriage Is between One Man and One Woman

The sexual differences between men and women are essential to marriage. Attempts to redefine marriage to include same-sex couples empty marriage of its meaning and do so to the detriment of the family and society. On a larger scale, the issue of homosexuality should be approached with compassion and care. The Church says that "homosexual acts are intrinsically disordered" because they cannot express a total unitive and procreative gift of self. This does not mean that persons with homosexual desires are disordered persons. The Church accepts persons with homosexual attraction with respect, compassion, and sensitivity.

➡️ Imagine that a close friend tells you he or she experiences same-sex attraction. Write a thoughtful, nonjudgmental letter to your friend in which you express your care and acceptance of him or her as a child of God, explain what the Church teaches, and provide some examples of how he or she can find support.

SECTION 3

Marriage Is a Unique Relationship

Many couples believe that cohabitation will lower their risk of divorce or help them to know if they are compatible. The Church is concerned about cohabitation because it is so prevalent, causes unhappiness, and is a false imitation of married love. De facto unions and common law marriages are names for cohabitation that generally exist for a great length of time. They are legally ambiguous, do not imply marital rights and duties, and do not provide the stability of marriage.

→ Write some reasons other than those listed in the section that a couple might choose to cohabit, and answer them in defense of the Church's teaching on marriage and premarital sexual relationships.

SECTION 4

Marriage Is Faithful

Christian marriage is a lifelong commitment. The bond between a married couple is perpetual and exclusive. There are several personal changes that affect marriage, including physical, emotional, and spiritual changes of one or both partners. External changes (e.g., career changes, conflicts with children, mid-life crises, and retirements) may also impact married life. The graces of the Sacrament of Matrimony help married couples overcome the many challenges against the unity and indissolubility of their marriage.

→ Browse a list of marriage enrichment programs at the United States Conference of Catholic Bishops' website on marriage (foryourmarriage. org). Briefly summarize in three to five written paragraphs two of the programs you find most interesting.

Chapter Assignments

Choose and complete at least one of the three assignments assessing your understanding of the material in this chapter.

1. Research and Report

 Choose *one* of the following topics, and research relevant information to support its position:

- Married couples who follow the teachings of *Humanae Vitae* have happier and more satisfying marriages.

- The benefits and blessings of a large family strongly outweigh its challenges.

- Because of Christ and the founding of the Church, women are given more esteem and value in married life than ever before.

- Divorced Catholics have served the Church well in ministry.

Write a five-hundred-word paper supporting one of these positions. Cite specific evidence and examples to support your claims.

2. Novena for Married Couples

Create a novena for married couples. *Novena* comes from the Latin word for "nine"; it is a prayer that takes place over nine days. Use the following sample day and answers as your template for designing the remaining eight days of your "Novena for Married Couples":

Day 1

- *Copy a Scripture passage on marriage:* Home and possessions are an inheritance from parents, but a prudent wife is from the LORD (Prv 19:14).

- *Write a two-sentence reflection on the passage:* Common sense, wisdom, and prudence are marks of family life. Domestic happiness depends on these gifts that spouses share with each other much more than on any material possessions that they might acquire.

- *Choose and name a married saint. Write a prayer to this saint on behalf of healthy marriages:* St. Monica (332–387)

St. Monica, you suffered through the debilitating effects of emotional abuse in your marriage, only to witness the conversions of your husband and your son, St. Augustine. Pray for married couples to persevere in faith that they too might be unified in seeking the Lord. We ask this in Christ's name. Amen.

3. Finding Solutions to the Challenges of Married Life

Interview seven to ten married people (individually, not as couples). Ask each person to name four of the greatest challenges married couples face in today's culture. Create a chart or graphic organizer to list each of the challenges they name. In an accompanying column or space, offer your own comments (at least two paragraphs per comment) on the challenges mentioned and on possible solutions in light of the Church's teaching on marriage you learned in Chapters 3, 4, and 5.

Faithful Disciple

Servant of God Catherine de Hueck Doherty

Catherine Kolyschkine was born at the turn of the twentieth century in Russia. She was raised in the Russian Orthodox Church. When Catherine was fifteen, she married Baron Boris de Hueck.

World War I and the Russian Revolution changed Catherine's life. Most of Catherine's family was killed at the hands of the Bolsheviks. Catherine and Boris escaped to England, and then, in 1921, to Canada, where their son, George, was born. Along the way, Catherine had converted and become a Roman Catholic.

Though safe in Canada, Catherine and Boris were now at the lowest end of poverty. Boris was sick and unable to work. Catherine took whatever job she could find to support her family. In the meantime, Boris began a series of extramarital affairs. The couple became estranged, and Catherine eventually had the marriage annulled.

Eddie Doherty and Servant of God Catherine de Hueck Doherty

One of Catherine's talents was as a lecturer. She was discovered by a Canadian lecture bureau, and she soon began to travel on its behalf around North America. Catherine became wealthy again and was able to support her son in the fashion that she had known growing up.

But Catherine was also restless. The Russian Revolution, the war, and the breakup of her marriage had left deep marks on her. She could not resign herself to simply returning to a life of comfort. Jesus' words to the rich young man—"If you wish to be perfect, go, sell what you have and give to [the] poor, and you will have treasure in heaven" (Mt 19:21)—were never far from Catherine's thoughts.

In 1930, Catherine took up Jesus' challenge. With the blessing of the archbishop of Toronto, she sold all of her possessions, provided for her son, and then went to live in the worst slums of the city, with a desire only to console the poor people who lived there. Eventually other men and women came to work with Catherine. They established a "Friendship House" where they lived simply, modeling the life of St.

Francis of Assisi. They begged for food and clothing and shared everything they acquired with the poor. They also began a newspaper—*The Social Forum*—which was based on the social teachings of the Church.

Catherine's work was misunderstood by many, and eventually the Friendship House in Toronto, and the second one she founded in Harlem, ended in failure. But another part of Catherine's life was on the rebound. A famous American journalist, Eddie Doherty, was assigned to do a newspaper story on Catherine's apostolate. While reporting, he fell in love with Catherine. They were married in 1943. Four years later, Catherine and Eddie moved to Combermere, a small village north of Toronto where the bishop had invited them to come and continue their work. Catherine and Eddie were not sure what direction their lives would take in this out-of-the-way place. But on their arrival in Combermere, they planted a small apple orchard. For some reason, they knew this place would be their home.

A new community was founded in Combermere called the Madonna House. Eventually it would grow to nearly two hundred members, including several priests. In 1954, the community connected itself more formally with the Church, and its members took vows of poverty, chastity, and obedience. Catherine and Eddie even took vows of chastity and lived celibate lives from that time on. Eddie was ordained a priest in the Melkite Greek Catholic Church in 1969.

Eddie Doherty died in 1975. Catherine de Hueck Doherty died on December 14, 1985, after a long illness. She left behind a spiritual family of hundreds of members and many foundations for helping the poor. Her devotion to the poor led Pope John Paul II to open the cause for her canonization in 2000. Catherine has been given the title "Servant of God," the first step toward being declared a saint.

 ## Reading Comprehension

1. How did Catherine recoup her monetary wealth after losing it upon her relocation to Canada?

2. Which words of Jesus inspired Catherine to look beyond living a life of comfort?

3. How did Catherine meet Eddie Doherty?

4. What was the main work of the Friendship House and Madonna House?

 ## Writing Task

Catherine de Hueck Doherty said, "One side of the cross is empty. That is where we belong." What does this quotation mean? Name two ways Catherine lived the meaning of this quotation. Share a way you might live the meaning of this quotation in the future.

Explaining the Faith

Just as people fall in love, they also fall out of love. Isn't a failed marriage just a regular part of life?

Failed marriages may be a regular part of life, but they happen because of fallen human nature, not falling in and out of love. You know from Scripture that at creation God intended marriage and family life to build up human community. From the beginning, marriage was meant to last for life, and Jesus affirmed this plan. Jesus also did something new. He raised marriage up to the level of a sacrament, as a sign of God's love in the world. And how does God love? His love is an unending and unbreakable promise. Since marriage is an image of God's unending love, spouses should not break their promises either.

Married love might begin with a man and a woman falling in love, but any good marriage will also require an ongoing commitment of the mind and the will. In other words, deep and lasting love involves not just emotions, which can come and go, but also the dedication and promise that even when spouses don't feel in love, they are committed to remaining in a marriage. Marriages stay healthy, happy, and rooted in profound love because the couple have faced hard times and adversity together. They do this first and foremost by together relying on the grace from the Sacrament of Matrimony to carry them during the times when the feeling of love might be difficult.

 ## Further Research

Read paragraphs 1646–1648 of the *Catechism of the Catholic Church*. Explain what is meant by "Love seeks to be definitive; it cannot be an arrangement 'until further notice'" (*CCC*, 1646). What do you think would happen to married love if the vow of indissolubility were not made?

Prayer

If I Am Called Down That Path

Heavenly Father,

Thank you for this time in your presence.

I have learned about the unbreakable and sacred bond of marriage.

Help me to begin to determine if I am called to married life.

Help protect me from temptations against chastity.

Teach me to be a loyal friend.

Allow me to be enlightened as I form new friendships with people of the opposite sex.

Make me strong enough to keep the lifelong commitments of marriage
    if I am called down that path.

And continue to offer your Holy Spirit to those married couples who are dear to me:
    especially my parents, my grandparents, and others who have shared the graces of
    the Sacrament of Matrimony with me.

Remain with me always.

I make this prayer in the name of your Son, Jesus Christ, our Lord.

Amen.

THE
VOCATION
TO HOLY ORDERS

A PRIEST Who Offers HOPE

Fr. Anthony Baetzold, C.F.R., a priest of the Community of Franciscan Friars of the Renewal, grew up as the youngest of four children in upstate New York. Born David Baetzold, he was a cradle Catholic and attended Mass every Sunday. Fr. Anthony says that his faith was mostly lived externally, in that he had no real personal engagement with God. He describes his teenage years as marked by a "practical atheism," in which he never outright denied God but rather lived his life as if there was no God.

This continued into college at Pennsylvania State University, when at twenty-one years old, he had what he describes as "a dramatic encounter" with God. "That's when everything changed for me. I just began to be open to the whole faith journey with the Lord," Fr. Anthony recalls.

After attending more school and working for a few years, during a visit to New York City, Fr. Anthony discovered the Community of Franciscan Friars of the Renewal, also known as the CFRs. This was a new order begun in 1987 by eight Capuchin friars looking for personal and communal renewal within the Church. They lived the life of St. Francis of Assisi in a way that attracted Fr. Anthony.

He joined the CFRs soon after this and spent about five years in religious formation before taking his final vows with the community. During this time, his name changed from David to Anthony, to symbolize his new life as a religious. Four years later, he was ordained to the priesthood. He described his ordination day at St. Patrick's Cathedral in New York City as the best day of his life. "Finally, my vocation was completed in a very real way," he says. "It's an incredible experience, because God does something in your life on that day that is unexplainable."

FOCUS QUESTION

How did **CHRIST INSTITUTE** the **MINISTERIAL PRIESTHOOD?**

Chapter Overview

Introduction	Priesthood Is for the Church
Section 1	Priesthood in the Economy of Salvation
Section 2	Bishops: The Episcopate
Section 3	Priests: The Presbyterate
Section 4	Deacons: The Diaconate

INTRODUCTION
Priesthood Is for the Church

MAIN IDEA
The ministerial priesthood was instituted by Christ at the Last Supper and passed on through apostolic succession. The ministerial priesthood exists for you, as a member of the Church.

NOTE TAKING

Sentence Summaries. Write sentences summarizing the content in this section. Use all of these terms at least once.

- essential
- Last Supper
- Eucharist
- Apostles
- apostolic succession
- bishops
- presbyters
- deacons

This chapter and Chapter 7 examine the vocation to the **ministerial priesthood**. This may seem unrelated to your own path, as most young Catholics probably will not be called to the ordained priesthood. Nevertheless, a study of the Sacrament of Holy Orders and the corresponding primary vocation is absolutely crucial for all Catholics. This is because the priesthood is for *you*. Without priests, there would be no access to the Mass and the Eucharist. Without priests, you would not be able to receive the mercy of God made tangible in the Sacrament of Penance.

Would you even know the Gospel without priests? St. Paul said, "How can they call on him in whom they have not believed? And how can they believe in him of whom they have not heard? And how can they hear without someone to preach?" (Rom 10:14). In other words, everyone needs someone to evangelize them. The *Catechism of the Catholic Church* teaches, "No one—no individual and no community—can proclaim the Gospel to himself" (*CCC*, 875).

Think about how you began your life in the Church and progressed in your faith. You were most likely baptized by your parish priest. Maybe he even gave you your First Holy Communion. You have received the Eucharist and encountered the Gospel from a priest. Every threshold moment in your faith and your growth as a person has been accompanied by the ministry of a priest. Priests are essential to the life of the Church. And since you are part of the Church, priests are vital to your life.

> **ministerial priesthood** The priesthood of Christ, consisting of priests and bishops, received in the Sacrament of Holy Orders. Its purpose is to serve the common priesthood by building up and guiding the Church in the name of Christ.

The Institution of the Priesthood

Christ instituted the priesthood of the Church at the Last Supper at the same time he instituted the Eucharist. This is not coincidental: the priesthood and the Eucharist are intimately, inseparably connected. Christ offered himself in the forms of bread and wine to his Apostles and said, "Do this in memory of me" (Lk 22:19). With these words, he commanded that his very presence be continued through the Apostles.

Christ's institution of the ministry of the priesthood at the Last Supper opened the door for everyone to receive the graces of the Paschal Mystery in the Eucharist—the very presence of Christ himself, Body, Blood, soul, and divinity. At the Eucharist, priests "exercise in a supreme degree their sacred office . . . , acting in the person of Christ and proclaiming his mystery" (*CCC*, 1566). At the Eucharist, Christ's great sacrifice that redeemed the world is made present, strengthening and uniting the Church.

The Sacrament of Holy Orders is, and has been from the earliest days of the Church, exercised in three degrees: in the ordination of the *episcopate* (the order of bishops or episcopal order), the *presbyterate* (the order of priests or presbyteral order), and the *diaconate* (the order of deacons or diaconal order). The ministerial priesthood, which serves the common priesthood of all the faithful, consists of bishops and priests. Only bishops share in the full priesthood of Christ. Priests—the coworkers of the bishop—share in the priesthood of the bishop. The bishop and priest have other roles in the Church—including the preaching of the Gospel and governance of the Church—but none is more important than their role in celebrating the Eucharist. Christ identifies himself so much with the ministerial priesthood that bishops and priests are able to say on his behalf, "This is my body. This is my blood." The third degree of the Sacrament of Holy Orders is the diaconate. Deacons assist bishops and priests in their ministries.

Development of the Three Orders

The Twelve Apostles, symbolic of the twelve tribes of Israel, were those who shared in Jesus' life in a way that was unique among his other disciples. Jesus chose the Twelve *Apostles* (a word that means "one sent") to be his emissaries or ambassadors to the world. Through the Apostles, Christ continues his own mission: "As the Father has sent me, so I send you" (Jn 20:21). The public ministry of the Apostles began at Pentecost with the coming of the Holy Spirit. When the Apostles were welcomed in their ministry, those who received them were actually receiving Christ. An ancient Church tradition expressed: "The Church from the Apostles, the Apostles from Christ, Christ from God."[1]

The Apostles continued the celebration of the Eucharist and guided the Christian communities by helping to settle any disputes that arose. By the end of the first century, the Church had expanded throughout the entire Roman Empire into virtually every province. Eventually the provinces were administratively divided into large units called a *diocese*, from a Greek word meaning "administration." By the fourth century, a diocese described a geographical district under the jurisdiction of a bishop. Each of these dioceses had a bishop who had received his authority and sacred power through the laying on of hands from one of the Apostles or from a bishop who had been ordained by one of the Apostles. These bishops in turn laid hands on other bishops and the presbyters who would assist them, and so on to this day. The connection of the Apostles to the bishops (and to priests, to the degree that they share in the office of the bishop) is called **apostolic succession**.

> **apostolic succession** The handing on of the Apostles' preaching and authority directly from the Apostles to the bishops through the laying on of hands. Apostolic succession continues to this day.

The first bishops were responsible for overseeing religious and moral life, ensuring that those in need were cared for, and safeguarding Church doctrine. As the local churches multiplied, presbyters were given the responsibility of pastoral care for these local churches. The First Letter of Peter states that presbyters (priests) should care for the Church in imitation of Christ, the "chief Shepherd": "Tend the flock of God in your midst. . . . Do not lord it over those assigned to you, but be examples to the flock. And when the chief Shepherd is revealed, you will receive the unfading crown of glory" (1 Pt 5:2–4). Deacons aided the bishops and priests by ministering to the poor and to widows, serving at Eucharist, and preaching God's Word.

The Catholic Church is an apostolic Church. Through the power of the Holy Spirit, the Church guards and hands on the teachings of the Apostles. The Church continues to be taught, made holy, and guided by the successors of the Apostles—the bishops (assisted by the priests) in union with the pope. This fulfills a command (see, for example, John 21:15–19) of Christ that extends to the end of time.

SECTION ASSESSMENT

NOTE TAKING

Use the sentences you wrote to help you answer the following questions.

1. When did Christ institute the Eucharist and the priesthood?
2. Why is the priesthood essential for all Catholics?
3. Who shares in the ministerial priesthood of Christ?
4. What were the first bishops responsible for?
5. What were the priests responsible for as the number of local churches multiplied?
6. How did deacons aid bishops and priests?

REFLECTION

7. Write one paragraph telling about a priest who has been influential in your life.

Priesthood in the Economy of Salvation

MAIN IDEA
Christ is the ultimate High Priest, whose sacrifice was definitive. All baptized persons share in his priesthood, either through the common priesthood or through the ministerial priesthood.

The priesthood originates in the Old Testament. The people of Israel were God's Chosen People, "a kingdom of priests, a holy nation" (Ex 19:6). One of the twelve tribes of Israel, the tribe of Levi, was set apart specifically for leadership in liturgical service.

It was the Levites' responsibility to act on behalf of the community in offering gifts and sacrifices to God. For example, if an Israelite man and his son brought one of their prized sheep into the Temple grounds, they themselves would carry the sheep to a special place to cut the animal's throat and catch the animal's blood in a basin. When the sheep was dead, the father and son would carry it to the **altar of holocausts**, where a priest would meet them. After pouring the blood on the altar, the priest would place each part of the sheep, including its head and feet, on the coals, where it would be consumed by the fire. The priests offered these sacrifices on behalf of the Israelite people.

As circumstances changed over time, priests took on other roles besides offering sacrifices. When the Israelites were in exile in Babylon, there were no sacrifices because the people were apart from the Temple. The priests emerged during this time as teachers and leaders. They led regular sessions of study and prayer. They also

> **altar of holocausts** In the Old Testament, a small mound of stones upon which the flesh of sacrificed animals could be burned. The word *holocaust* means "sacrifice."

NOTE TAKING

Identifying Main Ideas. As you read this section, complete an outline of its contents. The outline here is a sample. You should fill in more details.

I. Priesthood in the Old
  Testament
   A. Role of Levites
    1.
   B. Who was Melchizedek?

II. Christ is the High Priest
   A. Connections with the Old
     Testament
    1.
   B.

III. Sharing in Christ's priesthood
   A. Common priesthood of
     the faithful
    1.

"Everything that the priesthood of the Old Covenant prefigured finds its fulfillment in Christ Jesus, the 'one mediator between God and men'" (CCC, 1544, quoting Hebrews 5:10).

Christ Is the High Priest

In the New Testament, the Letter to the Hebrews describes Jesus as "high priest forever according to the order of Melchizedek" (Heb 6:20). By his sacrifice on the Cross, a single offering, Jesus merited all the grace for the salvation of humankind. Christ is the ultimate High Priest. In what may have been a primitive Christian creed in the First Letter to Timothy, Christ is described as the "one mediator between God and the human race" (1 Tm 2:5). He is the one High Priest who can offer the only perfect sacrifice. Note, also, that the Letter to the Hebrews offers glimpses into how Christ perfectly fulfills the role of High Priest:

- Jesus, in the humanity that he assumed, responded fully and freely to God's call; he is the Son of God (see Hebrews 5:5).

- Jesus is the perfect mediator because he is truly human as well as truly divine and thus can sympathize with human weakness (see Hebrews 4:15).

- Unlike the Jewish priests who offered incomplete sacrifices every day, Jesus had only to offer one, perfect sacrifice (see Hebrews 10:14).

- Jewish priests offered the blood of animals; Jesus offered his own blood (see Hebrews 9:11–12).

- Jesus' sacrifice atoned for all sins and established a New Covenant (see Hebrews 9:15).

- Jewish priests entered the man-made sanctuary and visited God alone; Jesus entered the sanctuary of heaven, where God is, and enabled all to enter with him (see Hebrews 9:24).

- Jesus now intercedes for people as the eternal priest, and he will come again (see Hebrews 9:27–28).

rewrote and organized large portions of the Scriptures during this time of captivity. When the Israelites were finally released and permitted to return to Jerusalem, the priests resumed their role of offering sacrifices but continued on as teachers and leaders as well.

The role of priests in the Old Covenant was important, yet their continual sacrifices could not make up for the separation between God and humankind that sin had wrought. Nonetheless, the priesthood of the Old Covenant did prefigure the high priesthood of Jesus Christ, the God-made-man who would save the world from sin. Melchizedek was an Old Testament priest who explicitly prefigured Christ. He is identified in Genesis 14:18 as "king of Salem" and "a priest of God Most High" who brought the gifts of bread and wine to Abram prior to the establishment of the covenant with Abram and his renaming as Abraham.

The bloody sacrifice of Christ on the Cross, made present in the unbloody sacrifice of the Eucharist, is unique because it accomplished once and for all what the previous sacrifices failed to do: **redemption** of the world.

Sharing in Christ's One Priesthood

All the baptized are called to participate in the one priesthood of Christ. The common priesthood of the faithful is received at Baptism and deepened by Confirmation. The ministerial or hierarchical priesthood is received by bishops and priests through the Sacrament of Holy Orders.

The Common Priesthood of the Faithful

Jesus Christ, the High Priest and mediator, is the head of the Body of Christ, the Church. Just as all the Israelites were "a kingdom of priests" (Ex 19:6), so too do Catholics, through the Sacraments of Baptism and Confirmation, become members of a priestly people. At your Baptism you became a member of Christ's Body, sharing in the one priesthood of Christ to bring God's presence to others: "You are 'a chosen race, a royal priesthood, a holy nation, a people of his own, so that you may announce the praises' of him who called you out of darkness into his wonderful light" (1 Pt 2:9).

The common priesthood is lived through the graces received at Baptism. It is "a life of faith, hope, and charity, a life according to the Spirit" (*CCC*, 1547). There are similarities between the common priesthood

> **redemption** A word that literally means "ransom"; the act of Christ in which he paid the price of his own sacrificial Death on the Cross to ransom, or set free, the world from the slavery of sin.

and the ministerial priesthood. For example, one of the characteristics of the ministerial priesthood is that priests offer Christ's sacrifice; they are the mediators between God and humans. Similarly, all the baptized are called to offer their lives as a "living sacrifice" (Rom 12:1). Also, ordained priests are a type of bridge between God and humans, and those in the common priesthood are to be bridges bringing God's presence to others.

More specifically, you participate in the common priesthood and share in the priesthood of Christ when you

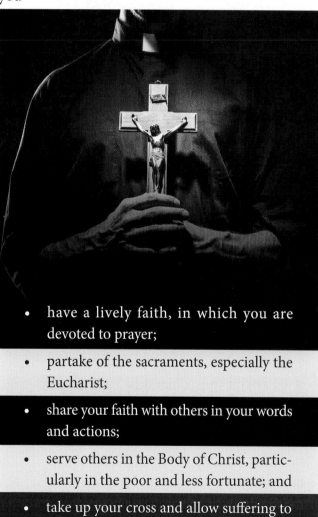

- have a lively faith, in which you are devoted to prayer;
- partake of the sacraments, especially the Eucharist;
- share your faith with others in your words and actions;
- serve others in the Body of Christ, particularly in the poor and less fortunate; and
- take up your cross and allow suffering to sanctify you.

As St. Paul's Letter to the Colossians advises: "And whatever you do, in word or in deed, do everything in the name of the Lord Jesus, giving thanks to God the Father through him" (Col 3:17).

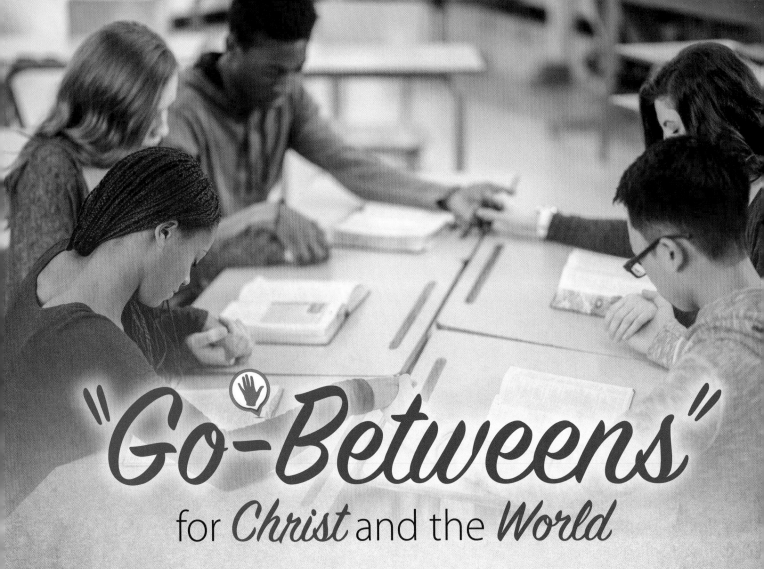

"Go-Betweens"
for *Christ* and the *World*

Baptized Christians share in the priesthood of Christ, serving as "go-betweens" bringing God's love to others. On your own or with a group of classmates, enact one of the following priestly deeds. When you have finished, write a one-page reflection summarizing your experience.

- *Share Christ's message.* Organize a Scripture study during your lunch break or after school. At your meeting, study a Scripture passage with some peers. Discuss its meaning. Plan ways you and those at the meeting can put the passage into practice.

- *Build up the community.* Bridge differences and hurt feelings within your school or peer group. Reconcile with anyone you have hurt and offer forgiveness to anyone who has hurt you. On a schoolwide basis, discover peer groups or individuals in conflict, and reflect on ways to bring everyone closer together.

- *Serve others.* Reflect on the servant leadership modeled by Christ. How can you serve others who are the "least" rather than those who are in power? Determine several possibilities, and put one of the ideas into practice.

- *Worship.* Share in Christ's priesthood by offering your prayer and worship to God the Father. Let the Spirit pray through you. With a friend, attend a weekday Mass. After Mass, talk over the meaning of the Scripture readings for the day. Discuss and act on a way you can put the message of the readings into practice.

The Ministerial Priesthood

The ministerial priesthood also shares in the one priesthood of Christ. Just as there is one redemptive sacrifice of Christ, made present in the Eucharist, so too is there one priesthood of Christ "made present through the ministerial priesthood without diminishing the uniqueness of Christ's priesthood: 'Only Christ is the true priest, the others being only his ministers'" (*CCC*, 1545, quoting St. Thomas Aquinas). While the common priesthood and the ministerial priesthood are related to and serve each other, they are distinctly different.

Whereas those in the common priesthood are concerned with the unfolding of baptismal grace in their own lives, the ministerial priesthood is directed toward unfolding the baptismal grace of all Christians. At the service of the common priesthood, the ministerial priesthood is the medium through which Christ unceasingly builds up and leads his Church.

All Christians are called to be "other Christs" to those around them. However, those called to the ministerial priesthood have an even more specific role. They are to be *in persona Christi Capitis*, which is Latin for "in the person of Christ the Head." They are other Christs in the way Christ is head of the Body: they direct and serve the rest of the Body, particularly in the administration of the sacraments. This is why the ministerial priesthood has its own specific sacrament, the Sacrament of Holy Orders.

A good example of this relationship is shown during the Mass. The Second Vatican Council taught that "the faithful, in virtue of their royal priesthood, join in the offering of the Eucharist" (*Lumen Gentium*, 10). However, it is only the ordained priest who, "acting in the person of Christ, . . . makes present the Eucharistic Sacrifice, and offers it to God in the name of all the people" (*Lumen Gentium*, 10). This is why only the ordained priest says the Eucharistic Prayer aloud while offering the faithful sacrifice with and on behalf of all the baptized.

Prayer for Priests and Bishops

In the *Roman Missal* instruction for the Holy Thursday Chrism Mass (the annual Mass the bishop of a diocese celebrates with his priests at which all the sacred oils are blessed), there is the suggestion that in his homily the bishop "speaks to the people and to his priests about priestly anointing, urging the priests to be faithful in their office and calling on them to renew publicly their priestly promises." After this renewal of promises, the bishop addresses the people in these words:

As for you, dearest sons and daughters,

pray for your priests,

that the Lord may pour out his gifts abundantly upon them,

and keep them faithful as ministers of Christ, the High Priest,

so that they may lead you to him,

who is the source of salvation.

And pray also for me,

that I may be faithful to the apostolic office

entrusted to me in my lowliness

and that in your midst I may be made day by day

a living and more perfect image of Christ,

the Priest, the Good Shepherd,

the Teacher and the Servant of all.

May the Lord keep us all in his charity

and lead all of us,

shepherds and flock,

to eternal life.

The people respond to each section of the prayer with "Christ, hear us. Christ, graciously hear us."

ASSIGNMENT

Do both of the following:

- Write a prayer for priests and bishops in your diocese. Mention three specific needs of your local church and her ordained ministers.

- Write a prayer for an increase of vocations to the ministerial priesthood. Include in your prayer the names of candidates for ordination in your diocese.

SECTION ASSESSMENT

NOTE TAKING

Use the outline you completed to help you answer the following questions.

1. How were the Levites different from the other tribes of Israel?

2. Who was Melchizedek? What is his significance for understanding the priesthood?

3. Why is Christ alone the one High Priest?

4. What are the three characteristics of the ministerial priesthood?

COMPREHENSION

5. Name three ways the Letter to the Hebrews describes Christ as the unique High Priest.

6. How was Christ's sacrifice different from those in the Old Testament?

7. How do Catholics participate in the common priesthood of the faithful and share in the priesthood of Christ?

CRITICAL THINKING

8. How does the common priesthood differ from the ministerial priesthood?

REFLECTION

9. Write a paragraph about someone you know who models the servant leadership of Christ.

SECTION 2
Bishops: The Episcopate

MAIN IDEA

Bishops are successors to the Apostles. Their role is to teach, sanctify, and govern. The pope, the bishop of Rome, holds a role of primacy within the Church.

Key to understanding the role of bishops, also known as the order of the episcopate, is apostolic succession. A bishop can only be ordained by another bishop, who could only have been ordained by another bishop, and so forth. This line goes all the way back to the Apostles. Bishops are chosen by the pope from among priests.

Bishops have the *fullness* of Holy Orders. The word *bishop* comes from the Greek *episkopos*, which means "overseer." Bishops are the spiritual leaders of the Church; like the Apostles, they continue Christ's mission of salvation. Most are the head of a diocese, a geographic area that comprises many parishes. More accurately, a bishop is the pastor of his diocese. *Pastor* is a Latin word meaning "shepherd." The image of the shepherd is present throughout Scripture and Tradition. Above all, Jesus is the "good shepherd" who "lays down his life for the sheep" (Jn 10:11) and even goes after one who has gone astray (see Luke 15:4–7). Some of the most ancient images of Christ are of the Good Shepherd.

Thus, it is no coincidence that bishops, acting *in persona Christi Capitis*, are considered the shepherds

NOTE TAKING

Identifying Details. Create a chart like this one to keep track of details about the three main points in this section. Make sure to reference the pope and the college of bishops in one or more of these categories.

How a bishop teaches	How a bishop sanctifies	How a bishop governs
• Guards Revelation	• Leads people into worship of God	• Leads his diocese
•	•	•
•	•	•
•	•	•
•	•	•
	•	

of their dioceses. The language from the First Letter of Peter reflects this: "Tend the flock of God in your midst, [overseeing] not by constraint but willingly, as God would have it" (1 Pt 5:2). A bishop has many duties and obligations and a full schedule; however, all of these are in service of his role as *shepherd*. He is foremost the pastor of his people. He is to love them with the love of Christ. He is to give his life for his people, as Christ gave his.

Every bishop has a special staff, called a *crozier*. It is purposely shaped like a shepherd's crook: the hook at one end symbolizes bringing the stray sheep back into the flock, and the pointed finial at the other end symbolizes goading a reluctant sheep.

In his role as shepherd, a bishop has three main duties: to teach, to sanctify, and to govern. Although priests and deacons aid him in these roles, it is the bishop who has the final authority within his diocese to administer these duties.

Teaching

Bishops have as their principal task the proclamation of the Gospel. They are to lead new disciples to Christ as "teachers endowed with the authority of Christ, who preach to the people committed to them" (*Lumen Gentium*, 25). They must guard the treasury of Revelation—that is, Scripture and Tradition—and defend it vigilantly against "any errors that threaten their flock" (*Lumen Gentium*, 25). A bishop is in charge of supervising evangelization and catechesis in all their forms within his diocese.

Archbishop Wilton Gregory of the Archdiocese of Atlanta proclaimed in a homily for the ordination of fellow bishop Luis Zarama that every bishop must use his zeal and talents to proclaim and defend the Deposit of Faith, yet "each bishop has to do so according to his own style and skill," saying:

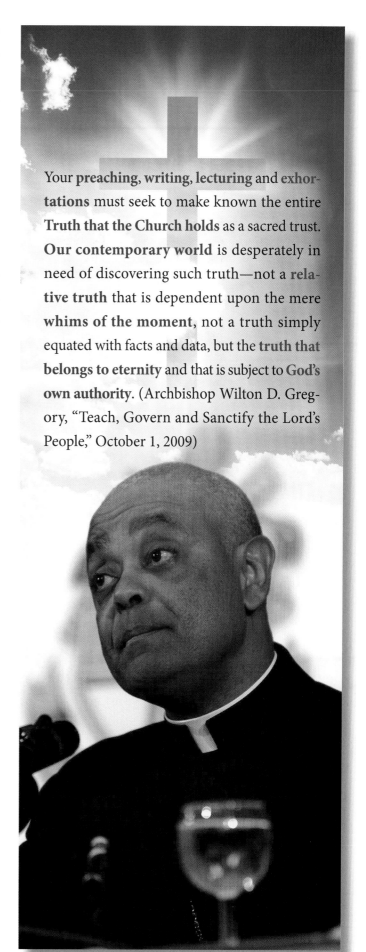

Your **preaching, writing, lecturing** and **exhortations** must seek to make known the entire **Truth that the Church holds** as a sacred trust. **Our contemporary world** is desperately in need of discovering such truth—not a **relative truth** that is dependent upon the mere **whims of the moment,** not a truth simply equated with facts and data, but the **truth that belongs to eternity** and that is subject to **God's own authority.** (Archbishop Wilton D. Gregory, "Teach, Govern and Sanctify the Lord's People," October 1, 2009)

Bishop Neal Buckon celebrates Mass at Twin Peaks Chapel on Travis Air Force Base in California.

A bishop teaches on three levels within the Church: in his own diocese; on a national level with a conference of bishops from his own country; and on an international level, when collaborating with the pope and other bishops from around the world as the college of bishops. (The teaching office of the worldwide body of bishops is known as the Magisterium.)

Sanctifying

The spiritual welfare of his people is a bishop's sacred trust. His teaching should always be directed toward leading his people into worship of God. This is primarily manifested in the offering of the Eucharist, "the utmost and the central means of sanctifying the Lord's flock."[2] The duty of sanctification necessarily begins in a bishop's own life, as he is an example for his flock. His personal relationship with the Lord should lead him to bring others into communion with Christ. He is called to work tirelessly to enliven in his people a desire for holiness and sanctity.

The duty of a bishop to sanctify is fulfilled as he administers the sacraments. Only a validly ordained bishop can administer all of the sacraments. Only a validly ordained bishop may confer the three degrees of the Sacrament of Holy Orders. Bishops are the ordinary ministers of the Sacrament of Confirmation, though they may delegate these duties to priests in certain situations. (Without the express delegation of a bishop, liturgical law permits priests to give the Sacrament of Confirmation when celebrating the Rite of Christian Initiation of Adults and when a Christian is in danger of death.)

St. Polycarp, the bishop of Smyrna, was martyred in the mid-second century. On the day of his death he was recorded saying of Jesus, "Eighty and six years I have served him, and he has done me no wrong."

Governing

A bishop is the authoritative leader for the Catholic Church within his diocese. This is symbolized by the *cathedra*, the special chair in the cathedral of the diocese that is meant only for him. The Second Vatican Council stated that

> bishops, as vicars and ambassadors of Christ, govern the particular churches entrusted to them by their counsel, exhortations, example, and even by their authority and sacred power, which indeed they use only for the edification of their flock in truth and holiness, remembering that he who is greater should become as the lesser and he who is the chief become as the servant. (*Lumen Gentium*, 27)

A bishop is to govern and lead as Christ did: by laying down his life for his people. "Let the greatest among you be as the youngest, and the leader as the servant" (Lk 22:26). Any authority a bishop has comes from Jesus himself. It is more than just commanding others to do what he wants; instead, his governance is always aimed at drawing people into the truth of Christ.

A bishop also has other practical roles within his diocese, such as

- guiding and assigning the clergy;
- overseeing matters of canon law;
- managing financial matters;
- granting a seal (called an *imprimatur*) that says certain theological books are free from doctrinal error;
- consecrating the oil of the sick (for the Sacrament of the Anointing of the Sick), the oil of the catechumens (for those preparing to be baptized), and sacred chrism (for Baptism, Confirmation, and Holy Orders); and
- making a visit—called the *ad limina [apostolorum]* ("to the threshold [of the Apostles]") visit—every five years to meet the pope in person.

A bishop's responsibilities are countless. However, at the heart of all these duties is his position as pastor for his people.

The Bishop of Rome

The pope, or Supreme Pontiff, is central to the Church's hierarchical structure. The word *pope* comes from the Greek word for "papa" or "father," which is why the pope is often referred to as the Holy Father. The pope is the successor to St. Peter, meaning that he can trace his lineage directly back to Peter, to whom Christ himself gave his authority: "And so I say to you, you are Peter, and upon this rock I will build my church, and the gates of the netherworld shall not prevail against it" (Mt 16:18). As the bishop of Rome—the place where St. Peter was bishop and was martyred—the pope has **primacy** of authority over the whole Church. Another ancient title for the pope is "Servant of the Servants of God."

One of the most important charisms the Holy Father possesses is that of **infallibility**. Guided by the Holy Spirit and by virtue of his office as supreme pastor, the pope speaks infallibly when "he proclaims by a definitive act a doctrine pertaining to faith or morals" (*CCC*, 891, quoting *Lumen Gentium,* 25). The pope may also speak a teaching on faith or morals *ex cathedra*, or "from the throne," because he is speaking from the authority of the chair of St. Peter. If a pope proclaims a doctrine infallibly, he cannot be in error.

That said, not everything a pope says and writes is infallible. In fact, while popes may offer many teachings about the faith that are without error, only rarely does a pope make a statement ex cathedra. The most recent occurrence was Pope Pius XII's ex cathedra

Pope Francis

declaration of the dogma of the Blessed Mother's Assumption into heaven in 1950. Catholics owe their assent and obedience of faith to infallible statements of the pope and bishops. Catholics must listen to and obey the pope, even when he is not speaking explicitly ex cathedra. Most of the time the pope is explaining already-defined doctrines of faith in a way that is applicable and pertinent to the present day.

Also, it's important to recognize here that while a pope's pronouncement of an ex cathedra statement is rare, infallible teaching is not rare at all and it can be offered through both the extraordinary Magisterium and ordinary Magisterium. An infallible teaching of the extraordinary Magisterium includes both a pope's ex cathedra statements and the pronouncement of an **ecumenical council**. The second way—through the

> **primacy** The authority of the bishop of Rome—the pope—over the entire universal Church.
>
> **infallibility** "The gift of the Holy Spirit to the Church whereby the pastors of the Church, the pope and bishops in union with him, can definitively proclaim a doctrine of faith or morals for the belief of the faithful. This gift is related to the inability of the whole body of the faithful to err in matters of faith and morals" (*CCC*, Glossary).

> **ecumenical council** An assembly of representatives from the entire Church for consultation on Church matters. There have been twenty-one ecumenical councils. The first was the First Council of Nicaea (325). The most recent was the Second Vatican Council (1962–1965).

ordinary Magisterium—is even more common. This includes the teachings of popes through documents, letters, and papal encyclicals while always drawing on the consistent and constant Church teaching of the past.

The College of Bishops

A bishop is assigned the pastoral care of his own local church, a diocese, but he also bears responsibility with all of the bishops for the care of the universal Church. Foremost, bishops are to act in communion with the Holy Father. All of the bishops together, along with the pope, are called the college of bishops; when they operate together, they are said to be acting in **collegiality**. When collaborating collegially with other bishops and the pope, bishops also teach on a worldwide level as part of the Magisterium. It is the task of the Magisterium to preserve the truth first taught by Christ and handed down through apostolic succession.

The college of bishops has no authority on its own except in union with the pope. An example of the Magisterium acting collegially is in an ecumenical council. It is the function of the pope to convoke a council, preside over it, and confirm its decisions. Bishops also act collegially insofar as individual bishops represent the teachings of the universal Church in their own dioceses.

The college of bishops shares in the gift of infallibility when, guided by the Holy Spirit and in union with the pope, they teach about or protect Revelation in matters of faith and morals, such as at an ecumenical council. The most recent ecumenical council was the Second Vatican Council, convened by Pope John XXIII. It was held in Rome from 1962 to 1965.

> **collegiality** The participation of each of the worldwide bishops, with the pope as their head, in a "college" that takes responsibility for both their local diocesan churches and also the Church as a whole.

Special Places and Titles Associated with

BISHOPS

Every Catholic parish is part of a greater diocese, which is a certain territory headed by a particular bishop. Archdioceses are simply larger dioceses. A few dioceses, along with an archdiocese, come together to be called an ecclesiastical province; in that context, the archdiocese is sometimes called the "metropolitan see." For example, the Archdiocese of Chicago is the metropolitan see for the Province of Chicago, which includes the archdiocese itself and the other dioceses in Illinois: Belleville, Joliet, Peoria, Rockford, and Springfield. An archbishop is also sometimes referred to as the "metropolitan bishop," which means he has the full authority of bishop within his own archdiocese and some limited, supervisory influence over the other dioceses in the province.

Special terms related to the role of bishop are described below. All of these roles and terms are directed to the salvation of souls, which is the ultimate task of bishops.

CARDINAL. A title given to certain bishops and archbishops (and sometimes priests) by the pope. Cardinals are often archbishops of the largest archdioceses in their nations. The word *cardinal* comes from the Latin *cardo* for "hinge" or "pivot," as cardinals originally were priests in "pivotal" churches in Rome who assisted the bishop. Cardinals are a key administrative link in assisting the pope; they have been called "Princes of the Church," and they have the exclusive role of electing a new pope.

ARCHBISHOP. The bishop of an archdiocese. Archbishops are responsible for particular tasks and obligations in a province. There is no further degree of Holy Orders when a bishop becomes an archbishop.

ORDINARY or **LOCAL ORDINARY.** Typically another name for a diocesan bishop. He is the pastoral and legal head and representative of his diocese. A superior of a religious order may also be known as an ordinary.

AUXILIARY BISHOP. A bishop who assists the ordinary. An auxiliary bishop is often assigned when the diocese is large in area or population or there is a special pastoral need such as many different spoken languages in the diocese.

COADJUTOR BISHOP. A bishop who also assists the ordinary; unlike an auxiliary bishop, a coadjutor bishop has the right to succeed the ordinary when he retires, resigns, or dies. (The mandatory retirement age for an ordinary is seventy-five.)

TITULAR BISHOP. A bishop who is not an ordinary of an active diocese but rather an ordinary of a historical diocese that is no longer in existence, such as in areas of the world where there are not a great number of Christians.

BISHOP EMERITUS. The title given to a bishop who is no longer the active leader of a diocese. This is usually due to advanced illness or age.

SECTION ASSESSMENT

NOTE TAKING

Use the chart you created to help you answer the following questions.

1. As part of their teaching duty, what must bishops guard and defend?
2. What do the sacraments have to do with a bishop's sanctifying duty?
3. To what is a bishop's governance always aimed?

COMPREHENSION

4. What do the two ends of a crozier symbolize?
5. Name three practical roles of governance a bishop takes within his diocese.
6. Who is the bishop of Rome? Why does the bishop of Rome have primacy?
7. When was the last time a pope spoke ex cathedra? What dogma did he define?
8. What is the college of bishops?

VOCABULARY

9. Define *infallibility*.
10. How is an *ecumenical council* an example of *collegiality*?

REFLECTION

11. Name a priest you know with the leadership qualities that would make him a good bishop. Explain why you thought of him.
12. Recall the occasion when you had the closest contact with your local bishop.

SECTION 3
Priests: The Presbyterate

MAIN IDEA
Imaging Christ to make him visible, a priest lays down his life for his Bride, the Church. His primary ministries are to proclaim the Word of God and celebrate the sacraments.

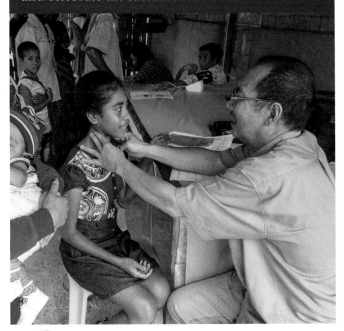

When you think about the priests in your life, perhaps your current parish priest comes to mind. Possibly you think of the priest who baptized you or even a priest at your high school. Or maybe you picture a missionary priest in a far-off country who recently visited your parish or school. Regardless of who comes to mind when you imagine a priest, you are likely to also think about what a priest *does*: things such as saying Mass, hearing confessions, feeding the poor, preparing homilies, teaching, and so forth.

While all of these things priests do are extremely important, the priestly order, or presbyterate, is more about *who priests are* than about *what priests do*—their duties and responsibilities. As you learned in Section 1, a priest offers sacrifice and is a mediator between humans and God. Ministerial priests hold these roles because they share in the one priesthood of Christ, who made the perfect sacrifice and is the one mediator between God and humans. They truly act *in persona Christi Capitis*, most especially in the Mass. In doing so, priests act and speak on behalf of their congregations.

A Latin title for priests is *alter Christus*, or "another Christ." A priest is called to be the servant of all, just

NOTE TAKING

Identifying Main Ideas. Create a two-column chart like the one here to help you organize your answers to the following questions.

What is more important than what a priest does?	
How is a priest "wedded" to the Church?	
How are priests ministers of the Word?	
How are priests ministers of the sacraments?	
What are the two types of priests?	

as Christ was. A priest is to lay down his life, to unite his own sacrifice to that of Christ's, "who by love made himself the least and the servant of all" (*CCC*, 1551). This sacrifice happens most profoundly when he offers the sacrifice of the Mass, but a priest is actually called to sacrifice his entire life. During the Rite of Ordination for priests, the ordaining bishop says to the newly ordained priest, "Know what you are doing, and imitate the mystery you celebrate; model your life on the mystery of the Lord's cross."

Pope Benedict XVI explained in further detail the priest's call to service:

> As an *alter Christus*, the priest is profoundly united to the Word of the Father who, in becoming incarnate took the form of a servant, he became a servant (Phil 2:5–11). The priest is a servant of Christ, in the sense that his existence, configured to Christ ontologically, acquires an essentially relational character: he is *in* Christ, *for* Christ and *with* Christ, at the service of humankind. (General Audience, June 24, 2009)

Note that Pope Benedict XVI uses the term *ontologically*. It comes from the word *ontological*, which means "related to one's very being or existence." When a man is ordained a priest, *his very self* is transformed. A man does not merely work as a priest but rather he *is* a priest. And, indeed, he will be a priest forever, even in heaven.

How a Priest Is Wedded to the Church

Recall that the heart of every vocation is the invitation to be a gift to others, which is known as the law of self-giving (see Chapter 1, Section 4, under "Law of Self-Giving"). This understanding fits the Sacrament of Holy Orders well, for it, like the Sacrament of Holy Matrimony, is a Sacrament at the Service of Communion. This means that because a priest's life is so united to Christ's, he imitates in an exceptional way the radical gift of self that Christ demonstrated for his Church.

Christ's love for the Church is described in Scripture as the love a bridegroom has for his bride. The Old Testament established the image of Christ as the Bridegroom and the Church as the Bride (see

Hosea 2:21–25). The bridal image also appears in the New Testament. John the Baptist named Jesus as the Bridegroom, "the one who has the bride" (Jn 3:29). St. Paul compared the intimate love Christ has for the Church with the strong mutual love found in marriage: "Husbands, love your wives, even as Christ loved the church and handed himself over for her to sanctify her, cleansing her by the bath of water with the word, that he might present to himself the church in splendor, without spot or wrinkle or any such thing, that she might be holy and without blemish" (Eph 5:25–27).

The Church completes the mission of Christ on earth. The Church is called the Bride of Christ because Christ has entered a covenant with the Church similar to that of a man and woman in marriage. Headed by Christ the Bridegroom, his Bride, the Church, is the dwelling place of the Holy Spirit. Since a priest is *in persona Christi Capitis*, he too is "wedded" to the Church. Just as a husband gives himself completely to his wife, so too does a priest give himself totally to the Church. Some priests even choose to wear a simple wedding band to signify this relationship.

What a Priest Does

Although *who a priest is* will always be the essential starting point for understanding priesthood, it is also crucial to understand *what a priest does* in the Church. Foremost, a priest is a coworker with his bishop. Although subordinate to the bishop, he joins in the bishop's duty to teach, sanctify, and govern. When a priest is ordained, he makes a promise of obedience to his local bishop. As the bishop's representative, a priest has no authority apart from his bishop. A priest functions in several other ways, described in the following subsections.

Parish priests frequently direct sessions to prepare engaged couples who want to marry in the Church.

Minister of the Word of God

Priests fulfill the command of Christ to "go into the whole world and proclaim the gospel to every creature" (Mk 16:15). Priests are ministers of the Word of God. The word *minister* means "servant." Priests serve the truth of Christ and his Church by helping others to understand the Word of God and live it in their own lives. His homilies during Mass, chiefly the Sunday Mass, are the primary setting in which a priest proclaims and explains Scripture. A main purpose of a Sunday homily is to elaborate on a theme running between the Gospel and the first and second readings.

A priest will pray and reflect upon the readings and Gospel during the week leading up to Sunday. He will also consider the particular liturgical season, such as

Advent or Lent. His homily should connect the theme of the Scripture readings to current events in the parish and in the worldwide Church.

Minister of the Sacraments

Priests are ministers (servants) of the sacraments. Their whole mission is liturgical. The very heart of their priestly life is centered on the eucharistic sacrifice. The renowned archbishop Fulton Sheen once said, "Each morning we priests hold in our hands the Christ who shed blood from his veins, tears from his eyes and sweat from his body to sanctify us. How we should be on fire with that love, that we may enkindle it in others!"[3]

Priests are also the proper ministers of the Sacraments of Baptism, Penance, and the Anointing of the Sick, and they serve as the Church's witness at the Sacrament of Matrimony. Liturgical law also permits priests to celebrate the Sacrament of Confirmation after the Baptism of adults and for those in danger of death.

Also part of the liturgy of the Church is the **Liturgy of the Hours,** or the Divine Office, which consists of Psalms, readings from other Scripture passages and the spiritual masters, and songs. The Liturgy of the Hours is prayed at certain times or "hours" of the day. All priests and religious are required to pray certain parts of the Divine Office every day, and the laity are encouraged to pray it too. The Liturgy of the Hours is "like an extension of the Eucharistic celebration" (*CCC*, 1178). The priest prays the daily Divine Office in the name of the whole Church and for the whole world. You might think of it this way: the Mass is the diamond in the day of a priest, and the Divine Office is the gold ring within which the diamond is set.

> **Liturgy of the Hours** The official daily prayer of the Church, also called the Divine Office. It is a set of prayers for certain times of the day that carries out St. Paul's command to "pray without ceasing" (1 Thes 5:17).

Other Actions of the Priest

No one day of a priest looks just like another, other than that each day includes the celebration of Mass, praying the Liturgy of the Hours, and personal prayer. Although the role of priests is primarily liturgical, in that they are to meet the spiritual needs of people under their care, that does not mean they neglect the physical and emotional needs of the people.

There is no way to compile a comprehensive list of the activities of a priest, but here are some examples of common tasks of a parish priest:

- visiting the sick in their homes or in the hospital
- teaching children in a parish school or religious education program
- working with various parish committees to plan practical matters of the parish

- helping people get ready for the sacraments, such as by preparing a couple for marriage or helping catechize those to be baptized

- offering spiritual direction

In imitation of Christ, priests also have a special obligation toward the poor, especially those within their parish. "Poor" refers to those in physical poverty (lacking basic necessities) but also to those who are emotionally or spiritually poor (e.g., lonely or struggling in their faith).

Types of Priests

There are two general categories of priests: diocesan priests and religious priests (priests who are in a religious order; some religious communities are *clerical*, meaning they include priests). A diocesan priest is obedient to his bishop; a religious priest is obedient both to his **religious superior** and to the bishop of his diocese. More information on each category of priest follows.

Diocesan Priests

Diocesan priests are bound to a particular geographic area. Most often, diocesan priests are assigned to a particular parish. The lead priest at a parish is called a *pastor*, and the priests who assist him are called *parochial vicars*. A parish priest is present in the daily lives of his parishioners; he is to share in both the joys and the sadness that accompany everyday life. In his role as parish priest, he is privy to the deeper and often hidden stories of both kinds of experiences.

A diocesan priest pledges obedience to his bishop and works to support his bishop's ministry. Part of this promise involves the obligation to accept assignments at the bishop's service. While most bishops have a personnel board or council made up of other priests to help them determine the priests' assignments, the bishop is ultimately responsible for all appointments.

Not all diocesan priests are parish priests. For example, a priest may be a prison chaplain, a hospital chaplain, a school principal, a college or high-school teacher, a diocesan administrator, an author, a retreat director, a vicar general, a director of religious education, or even a full-time student. When assigned to these special duties, a diocesan priest will most often still live "in residence" at a parish. On the weekends and at other times when he is free, he will usually be asked to assist at the parish by celebrating Mass and the other sacraments and perhaps by sharing in a parish-based ministry.

Religious Priests

A religious priest takes vows of poverty, chastity, and obedience and follows the charism of his community. For example, a man may be a Franciscan *and* a priest. As their obedience is both to their religious superior and to the bishop of their diocese, many religious priests have been called on to "share in the care of souls and in the practice of apostolic works under the authority of bishops" just as the diocesan clergy do (*Presbyterorum Ordinis*, 33). There are plenty of religious priests who are also parish priests who serve as pastors or parochial vicars. In other cases, religious priests do not serve in a parish; their ministries are more varied, and they are not bound to one diocese.

Some examples of priestly religious orders are the Augustinians, Jesuits, Franciscans, Holy Cross, and Marists. There are many, many more. You will learn more about the vows and formation of religious priests and the different types of priestly religious communities in Chapter 8.

> **religious superior** The head or leader of a religious community charged with cultivating in the members of the community obedience to God's will, the Church, and the rules of the community.

The Rewards of Being a Parish Priest

All priests are under the patronage of St. Jean-Baptiste-Marie Vianney, a priest who was assigned a parish in the small village of Ars outside of Paris, France, in 1818. The village had only forty houses but four taverns. It was a farming community where people worked on Sunday and did not often go to church.

Fr. John Vianney embraced the people in the community, at first offering them primarily material support. He gave away all of his clothing and much of the furniture in the **rectory** to the poor and ate only two potatoes per day, explaining "some devils can only be cast out by prayer and fasting."

St. John Vianney was pastor in Ars during the years after the French Revolution, and there were many young orphan girls wandering the streets as prostitutes. To combat this problem, St. John Vianney founded an orphanage across the road from the parish church. He would spend the noon hour at the orphanage offering catechetical instruction to the girls.

But what St. John Vianney became best known for in Ars and well beyond was the advice and counsel he offered people who came to him for the Sacrament of Penance. During the last ten years of his life, he spent sixteen to eighteen hours per day in the confessional. In 1855, more than twenty thousand pilgrims came to Ars for St. John Vianney to hear their confessions. He would hear up to three hundred confessions per day, sometimes being able to tell what sins were being withheld by the penitent. St. John Vianney's life was his parish. He said of his parishioners at Ars, "My God, grant me the conversion of my parish. I am willing to suffer all my life whatsoever it may please you to lay upon me.

rectory The house in which a pastor and other parish priests live.

Yes, even for a hundred years I am prepared to endure the sharpest pains; only let my people be converted."[4]

St. John Vianney

Today, many dedicated parish priests are still inspired by the example of St. John Vianney. The life of a parish priest is not an easy one. But it is rewarding, with most of the tangible benefits coming from the priest's proximity to the Eucharist and other sacraments, the emphasis on personal prayer, and his special connection with the parishioners. Recent studies of parish priests find that most are very happy, marked by

- an inner sense of peace;

- a relationship with God;

- a strong spiritual life;

- good relationships with laity, fellow clergy, and superiors, as well as religious obedience in relation to his bishop;

- acceptance of celibacy as a lifestyle to which God has called them; and

- having close personal friends.[5]

Msgr. Stephen Rossetti, a sociologist who has studied the priesthood, writes, "A consistent support and challenge for priests comes from the people of God. Their presence is an important way in which God is manifested to us. As we personally connect with the people whom we serve, we are affirmed, supported, challenged, and 'stretched.'"[6]

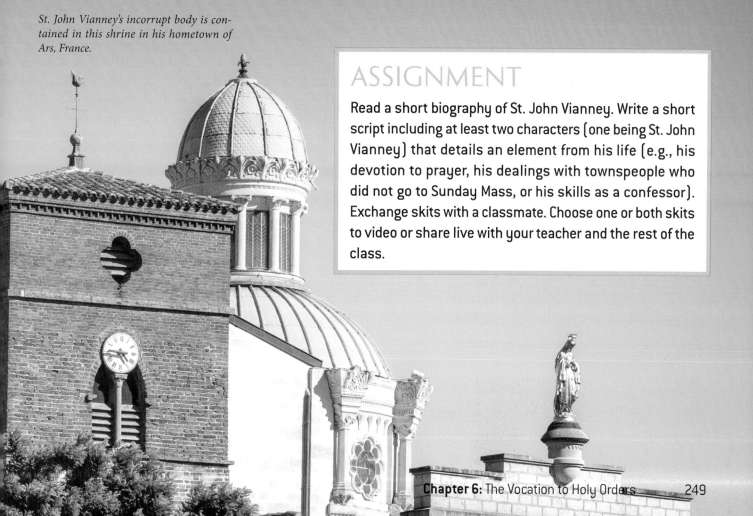

St. John Vianney's incorrupt body is contained in this shrine in his hometown of Ars, France.

ASSIGNMENT

Read a short biography of St. John Vianney. Write a short script including at least two characters (one being St. John Vianney) that details an element from his life (e.g., his devotion to prayer, his dealings with townspeople who did not go to Sunday Mass, or his skills as a confessor). Exchange skits with a classmate. Choose one or both skits to video or share live with your teacher and the rest of the class.

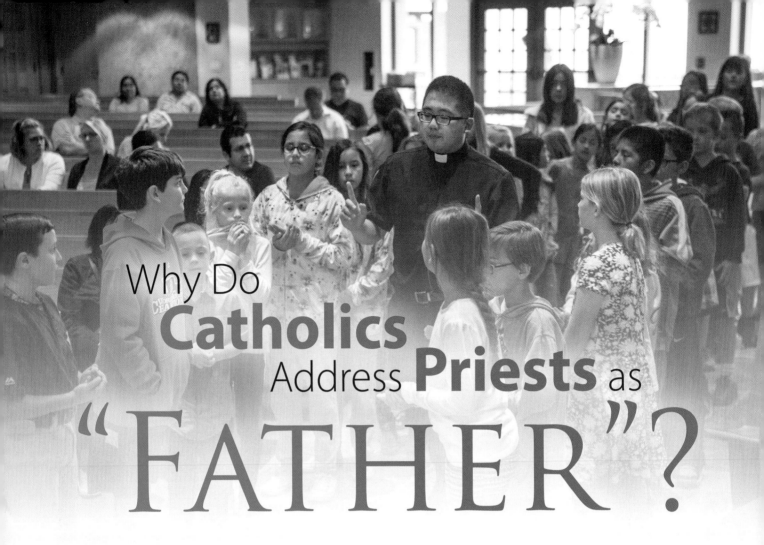

Why Do **Catholics** Address **Priests** as "FATHER"?

The tradition of using the title "Father" for priests is ancient, even going back to apostolic times. St. Paul wrote, "Even if you should have countless guides to Christ, yet you do not have many fathers, for I became your father in Christ Jesus through the gospel" (1 Cor 4:15).

On the surface, it may seem odd to call priests "Father" because most likely none of the priests you have ever met has biological children. (For more information on priestly celibacy, see Chapter 7's "Explaining the Faith.") However, if you look a little deeper, you will find that it is extremely fitting that Catholics call their priests "Father."

Think about what a biological father does: he gives life to his children, and then he provides for their physical and emotional needs, instructing and guiding them into adulthood. The same is true for spiritual fathers, priests. Catholic theologian Scott Hahn writes,

Priests are fathers because they give new life, divine life, through Baptism; but their obligation does not end with the pouring of the water. They go on to nourish the life of their spiritual offspring through the Eucharist. They discipline their "children" through Penance. They instruct through their preaching and teaching. In short, they raise their congregations to full Christian maturity as contributing members of God's household (Eph 2:19). (*Many Are Called*)

A priest has many spiritual sons and daughters. Priests are often with their spiritual children during some of the most dramatic, trying, and joyful times of their lives. Thus, it is immensely appropriate to call a priest "Father."

SECTION ASSESSMENT

NOTE TAKING

Use the chart you created to help you complete the following items.

1. How does a priest act as an *alter Christus*?

2. Explain how a priest is "wedded" to the Church.

3. What is the primary setting in which a priest proclaims and explains the Word of God?

4. Explain the difference between a diocesan priest and a religious priest.

COMPREHENSION

5. What happens ontologically to a priest when he is ordained?

6. Why is the Church called the Bride of Christ?

7. What does it mean to say that priests are ministers of the Word and ministers of the sacraments?

VOCABULARY

8. What does the *Liturgy of the Hours* consist of?

REFLECTION

9. Describe a parish priest you know who has woven his life well into that of the entire faith community.

SECTION 4
Deacons: The Diaconate

MAIN IDEA

The diaconate is the third degree of Holy Orders. There are two types of deacons: permanent and transitional. The diaconate is marked by the call to service, which manifests itself both liturgically and charitably.

Deacons are ordained ministers marked by a character "which cannot be removed and which configures them to Christ, who made himself the 'deacon' or servant of all" (*CCC*, 1570). Church teaching that only a baptized man may receive sacred ordination applies to the ordination of deacons. There is evidence that women in the early Church served as non-ordained deaconesses, the functions of that role corresponding to the need for modesty in the baptismal rites for women and the visiting of widows in their homes. A commission established by Pope Francis in 2016 is studying exactly how women served as deaconesses in the early Church, not about whether women were ever ordained deacons or can be ordained deacons today. Deacons receive the laying on of hands from the bishop in the Sacrament of Holy Orders. The diaconate is at "a lower level of the hierarchy" of Holy Orders (*Lumen Gentium*, 29).

The order of the diaconate was instituted in the early Church by the Apostles to meet a need for assistance in their ministry: "So the Twelve called together the community of the disciples and said, 'It is not right for us to neglect the word of God to serve at table. Brothers, select from among you seven reputable

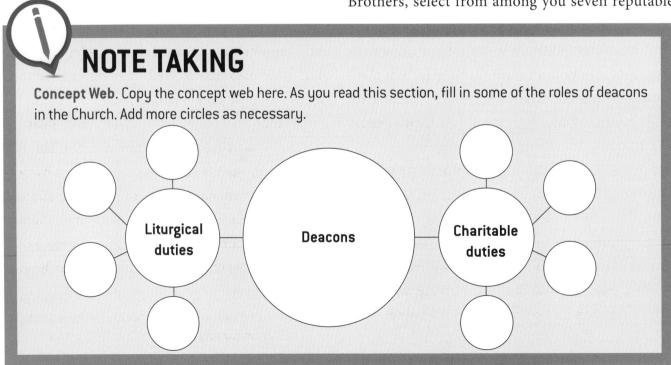

NOTE TAKING

Concept Web. Copy the concept web here. As you read this section, fill in some of the roles of deacons in the Church. Add more circles as necessary.

Liturgical duties — Deacons — Charitable duties

men, filled with the Spirit and wisdom, whom we shall appoint to this task, whereas we shall devote ourselves to prayer and to the ministry of the word'" (Acts 6:1–6). The ministry of these original seven deacons broadened beyond the distribution of food and the serving at the Eucharistic altar to the preaching of the Gospel. One of the deacons, St. Stephen, became the first Christian martyr, stoned to death for his defense of the faith.

Deacons are not "priests lite," nor are they "super laypeople." Instead, they have an order all their own. Being a deacon is not the same as serving as a lector or an altar server at Mass—that is, jobs that are not permanent. Rather, deacons are really ordained ministers who are conformed to Christ in a unique way. Like a priest, a deacon is an ordained minister forever.

Two Types of Deacons: Transitional and Permanent

Although the first deacons mentioned in Scripture held the office in a permanent sense, after a few centuries, the diaconate evolved into a transitional state, a step along the path to priesthood.

These **transitional deacons** still exist today. All Catholic priests are first ordained deacons. This type of diaconate usually lasts about a year and provides a training in priesthood. A man makes the commitment to celibacy required of priests in the Roman Catholic Church at the time of his transitional diaconate ordination. He then continues his final studies to become

> **transitional deacons** Ordained deacons who are only deacons temporarily as a step to becoming priests.

a priest and often serves in a parish to gain experience in the ordained ministry before his priestly ordination. Even after his ordination to the priesthood, the character imprinted on the man at his ordination to the diaconate remains, configuring him to Christ "who made himself 'deacon' or servant of all" (CCC, 1570). Priests and bishops never cease to perform the diaconal service for which they were ordained.

The Second Vatican Council called for a restoration of **permanent deacons** to serve the Latin Church. (The Eastern Churches had always had the permanent diaconate.) The reinstatement of the permanent diaconate "constitutes an important enrichment for the Church's mission" (*CCC*, 1571). The nature and role of permanent deacons is the same as that of transitional deacons; however, they will never become priests. Another difference is that the permanent diaconate can be conferred upon *both* single and married men

> **permanent deacons** Ordained deacons who will permanently remain deacons.

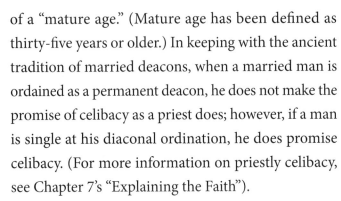

of a "mature age." (Mature age has been defined as thirty-five years or older.) In keeping with the ancient tradition of married deacons, when a married man is ordained as a permanent deacon, he does not make the promise of celibacy as a priest does; however, if a man is single at his diaconal ordination, he does promise celibacy. (For more information on priestly celibacy, see Chapter 7's "Explaining the Faith").

While honoring the gift of celibacy as a special gift for the benefit of the Church, the Church allows in the permanent diaconate for an explicit union of the Sacraments of Holy Orders and Matrimony, and the life and ministries unique to each. Married deacons and their wives are called to give a clear witness to the world of the holiness of marriage and family life. In the United States, there are more than fifteen thousand permanent deacons, more than 90 percent of whom are married.

The Diaconate Is Marked by Service

As with priests, the identity of a deacon—*who a deacon is*—has much more importance than *what he does*; his duties and roles within the Church arise from his identity *as deacon*. The key to understanding this identity lies in the origins of the word *deacon*; it comes from the Greek *diakonia*, which means "service." Therefore, the defining reality of the diaconate is service.

A deacon is a servant because he is conformed to Christ, who came "not to be served, but to serve" (Mt 20:28). Christ himself is the model of the diaconate: his entire ministry and vocation was devoted to service to others. Everyone in the Church is called to be a servant, but deacons embody this role in a sacramental way. Deacons serve the servant Church because they are configured in a particular way to Christ, who is the greatest servant.

Roles of Deacons

A deacon is under obedience to his bishop; he must serve liturgically and charitably how and where his bishop assigns him.

Liturgically, the deacon serves as minister of the Word of God and at the altar. The Second Vatican Council, in restoring the permanent diaconate, established several functions and roles the deacon can perform in liturgy. A deacon may be the ordinary minister of Baptism. A deacon is also able to witness and bless the Sacrament of Matrimony. A deacon can conduct funerals apart from Mass and burial services at the graveside. A deacon may also be the minister of **Benediction**, which includes offering the people a blessing with the true presence of Christ in the monstrance. At Mass, a deacon assists at the altar by bringing the offerings of bread and wine to the priest from the faithful. Through his ordination and connection with the bishop, a deacon is able to read the Gospel and preach a homily. Sharing the Word of God in this manner is one of the deacon's primary roles. Unlike priests, deacons cannot celebrate Mass or administer the Sacraments of Penance, the Anointing of the Sick, and Confirmation. (Note that in the Eastern Churches deacons are not ordinary ministers of Baptism and also cannot witness a marriage.)

In addition to the liturgy, deacons have a particular role in charitable works, connected with their mission of service. This role can manifest itself in a variety of ways. A deacon's charitable works usually begin with the poor within his parish but often extend to the greater community. In his address to the permanent deacons of the United States, Pope John Paul II explained:

> In the midst of the **human condition**, it is a great source of satisfaction to learn that so many **permanent deacons** in the United States are involved in *direct service to the needy*: to the ill, the **abused** and **battered**, the **young and old**, the **dying** and **bereaved**, the **deaf**, **blind**, and **disabled**, those who have known suffering in their marriage, the **homeless**, victims of **substance abuse**, **prisoners**, **refugees**, **street people**, the **rural poor**, the **victims of racial and ethnic discrimination**, and many others. As Christ tells us, "as often as you did it for one of my least brothers, you did it for me." (Meeting with Men Ordained to the Permanent Diaconate, September 19, 1987)

In addition to these liturgical and charitable roles, deacons often serve the catechetical life of their parish, sometimes leading baptismal or marriage preparation sessions. They can be hospital chaplains or have an administrative function in the parish or diocese.

> **Benediction** The rite in which Jesus, in the Blessed Sacrament contained in a monstrance, is exposed to the Adoration of the faithful.

SECTION ASSESSMENT

 NOTE TAKING

Use the concept web you created to help you complete the following items.

1. What can a deacon do liturgically during Mass that a layperson cannot?
2. What groups of people might deacons help through charitable works?

 COMPREHENSION

3. How many original deacons are mentioned in the Acts of the Apostles?
4. Differentiate between a transitional deacon and a permanent deacon.
5. What is the defining characteristic of the diaconate, found in the origins of its name?
6. How does the diaconate differ between the Latin Church and the Eastern Church?

 VOCABULARY

7. Define *Benediction*.

Section Summaries

Focus Question

How did Christ institute the ministerial priesthood?

Complete one of the following:

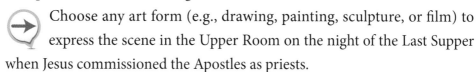

Choose any art form (e.g., drawing, painting, sculpture, or film) to express the scene in the Upper Room on the night of the Last Supper when Jesus commissioned the Apostles as priests.

Read Hebrews 4:14–8:6. Write a list of all the ways this passage defines Jesus as the High Priest.

Describe what happened to each of the Apostles: Simon Peter; Andrew; James, son of Zebedee; John; Philip; Bartholomew; Thomas; Matthew; James, son of Alphaeus; Thaddeus; Simon the Cananean; and Matthias, who replaced Judas. Research online to determine which local church each Apostle served and how it is believed his life ended. Write a one-sentence summary for each Apostle.

INTRODUCTION

Priesthood Is for the Church

The priesthood is for the Church; therefore, it is for you. Jesus established the priesthood at the Last Supper when he also instituted the Eucharist. Without priests, there would be no Eucharist. Apostolic succession is key to Holy Orders. There are three orders: the episcopate, the presbyterate, and the diaconate.

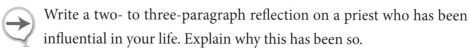

Write a two- to three-paragraph reflection on a priest who has been influential in your life. Explain why this has been so.

SECTION 1

Priesthood in the Economy of Salvation

Priests in the Old Testament offered sacrifices and acted as mediators between people and God. Christ is the ultimate High Priest and the one mediator between God and man who brought about salvation. Every Catholic is baptized into the common priesthood of Christ. It is a life of faith, hope, and charity. There are similarities between the common priesthood and the ministerial priesthood, but ministerial priests share in Christ's priesthood in a unique manner. The ordained priest is directed toward unfolding the baptismal grace of all Christians.

The Old Testament prophets reminded the people of the right interior disposition for offering sacrifices. Write a statement describing what each of these passages says about that disposition: Jeremiah 6:19–20; Amos 5:21–27; and Hosea 6:6.

SECTION 2

Bishops: The Episcopate

As the direct successors to the Apostles, bishops have the fullness of Holy Orders. The main mission of bishops is to teach, sanctify, and govern the Church. The college of bishops, in union with the pope, constitutes the Magisterium. The bishop of Rome, the pope, is the successor to St. Peter and has primacy over the universal Church.

Use a diocesan directory to research the name of the first bishop in your diocese, the name of the bishop who served the longest in your diocese, and the date your current bishop was ordained to both the priesthood and the episcopate.

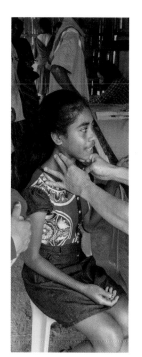

SECTION 3

Priests: The Presbyterate

Priests are marked in a special way in conformity to the priesthood of Christ. In their role as *in persona Christi Capitis*, they are "wedded" to the Church and are to lay down their lives for her. Priests are ministers of the Word and ministers of the sacraments. Though *who a priest is* is always more important than *what a priest does*, the priest's work is essential to the Church. Foremost, a priest is a coworker with his bishop. A priest functions as a minister of the Word of God and a minister of the sacraments. There are two types of priests, diocesan and religious. A diocesan priest is obedient to his bishop. A religious priest is obedient to both his bishop and his religious superior.

➡️ Read paragraph 1564 of the *Catechism of the Catholic Church*. Answer: What are three things priests are consecrated to do through the Sacrament of Holy Orders?

SECTION 4

Deacons: The Diaconate

Deacons are ordained ministers whose primary purpose is that of service, as Christ was servant of all. The order of the diaconate was instituted by the Apostles. There were seven original deacons. One of those deacons, St. Stephen, was the first Christian martyr. The diaconate evolved into a transitional state, a step toward priesthood. The Second Vatican Council called for a restoration of the permanent diaconate. Permanent deacons can be single men or married men. Deacons serve certain liturgical and charitable roles within the Church.

➡️ Read the following passages, and summarize some of the qualities and duties of a deacon in the early Church from them: 1 Timothy 3:8–13; Acts 6:1–4; Acts 7; and Acts 8:4–13.

Chapter Assignments

Choose and complete at least one of the three assignments assessing your understanding of the material in this chapter.

1. Episcopal Coat of Arms

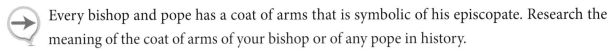 Every bishop and pope has a coat of arms that is symbolic of his episcopate. Research the meaning of the coat of arms of your bishop or of any pope in history.

- Through drawing or painting, artistically recreate the coat of arms. It must be large enough to show the details of the artwork.

- Write a short report that explains the symbolism of the coat of arms.

2. Letter to a Bishop

Write a letter (not an email) to one of the bishops in the United States (see www.usccb.org/dioceses.shtml) requesting information about his personal call to the priesthood; strategies for increasing priestly vocations in his diocese; and what he finds most meaningful about his ministry. Share your email address. Ask the bishop to respond by email or letter. Write a summary of his responses.

3. Restoring the Permanent Diaconate

Work with a partner on this assignment. First, each of you individually read Pope Paul VI's June 18, 1967, papal document *Sacrum Diaconatus Ordinem* (*Restoring the Permanent Diaconate*). This short document has eight parts. Each of you should separately create eight objective questions that can be answered from the content of the document in one or two written sentences. Write your own answers to each question, and then print your questions without the answers on a separate piece of paper. Exchange the questions with your partner and answer each other's questions in full sentences. Using your own answer key, grade each other's papers. Turn in both sets of questions and answers to your teacher.

Faithful Disciple

St. Ignatius of Antioch

Ignatius of Antioch was the second bishop of Antioch, Syria, an important center of Christian activity in the early Church. He was a convert to the faith and a disciple of St. John the Evangelist. A bishop for nearly forty years, he encouraged the faithful by preaching daily and setting an example of fasting and prayer. During his time the Church faced brutal periods of persecution with numerous instances of martyrdom.

However, when the Emperor Trajan rose to power, he did not order the capture of Christians, instead saying they would be executed if they were formally reported by citizens. Ignatius himself may have had an encounter with Trajan in which the bishop publicly proclaimed his faith. In any case, history definitely records that Ignatius was sentenced to death and made to travel from Antioch to Rome by ship, guarded by ten soldiers who treated him cruelly at each stop. Ignatius used the trip to Rome as a chance to witness to the Gospel. At each stop along the way, local Christians, usually accompanied by their bishop, came to hear him preach. He also wrote letters to be taken back to these local churches. Seven of these let-

St. Ignatius of Antioch

ters are preserved today. The common theme in the letters is that Christians should assemble often in prayer, be meek and humble, suffer injuries without protest, and keep in harmony with their bishops and other clergy.

Ignatius saw bishops as symbols of unity and right teaching in the Church. Bishops were the only correct guides to dispel false teaching that had crept into the Church. In his "Letter to the Smyrnaeans," Ignatius wrote, "You must all follow the lead of the bishop, as Jesus Christ followed that of the Father;

follow the presbytery as you would the Apostles; reverence deacons as you would God's Commandment. . . . Where the bishop appears, let the people be, just as where Jesus Christ is, there is the Catholic Church" (chap. 8).

Ignatius eventually reached Rome on December 20, 107. He had already written a letter to the Christians there telling them not to try to prevent his execution. He was first rushed to appear before the emperor at the Colosseum and then off to the Flavian amphitheater, where two lions devoured him. There is evidence that some of his remains were taken back to Antioch and preserved.

St. Ignatius's feast day is now celebrated throughout the Roman Catholic Church on October 17.

Reading Comprehension

1. What practices did Ignatius encourage the Church in Antioch to practice during the time of persecutions?

2. What are two ways Ignatius continued to proclaim his faith while being transported to Rome for execution?

3. How did Ignatius's "Letter to the Smyrnaeans" teach that the bishops are symbols of unity and right teaching in the Church?

4. What day is the current feast day of St. Ignatius of Antioch?

Writing Task

Ignatius of Antioch wrote to the Church in Rome, imploring Christians there not to interfere with his death: "I write to all the churches and charge them all to know that I die willingly for God, if only you do not hinder. Suffer me to become the food of wild beasts, through whom I may attain to God" ("Letter to the Romans," chap. 4). Write two reasons why you think Ignatius would have made this request. Then look up his "Letter to the Romans" and write two of the reasons that he gave.

Explaining the Faith

Why can only men be priests?

Remember that *everyone* who is baptized is made a priest, a sharer in the royal priesthood of Christ. This is the common priesthood. However, the Sacrament of Holy Orders is reserved for men only. That means that only men may be ordained deacons, priests, and bishops.

The question of why the priesthood is reserved for men is an important one. On the surface, it may seem sexist, unfair, or outdated of the Church to hold steadfast to this teaching. However, if one digs a little deeper, it is clear that the male priesthood is essential and does not denigrate the dignity of women. Here are a few points necessary to understanding this teaching.

1. *Jesus chose only men as his Apostles.* Jesus could have picked women from among his disciples to be among the Twelve Apostles, but he did not. Some claim that Jesus was just bound by the societal norms of the time, in which women were treated inferiorly. However, many of Christ's words and actions were very countercultural, even his interactions with women. For example, he conversed with the Samaritan woman at the well, a public sinner, to whom even rabbis would not have spoken (see John 4:4–18). And he interacted with and forgave a sinful woman whom no one else would even have touched (see Luke 7:36–50). Furthermore, many religions of Jesus' time (although not Judaism) did, indeed, have priestesses, so it would not have been completely out of the ordinary for Jesus to choose a woman as an Apostle. Jesus did not even choose the greatest, most revered of his disciples, his mother, Mary, to the specific mission of the Apostles or call her to the ministerial priesthood.

2. *The priesthood is a participation in Christ's priesthood, and he is male.* A man's priesthood is not his own; instead, it is a share in Christ's eternal priesthood (see Chapter 6, Section 1, "Christ Is the High

Priest"). Christ was not genderless; he was a man. Men and women are created with equal dignity, but they are not the same. So too, if a priest is to be an *alter Christus*, he must share in the essential maleness of Christ, who laid down his life for his Bride, the Church. Ministerial priests share in Christ's priesthood, which includes his masculinity, both physically and spiritually.

3. *The ministerial priesthood will always be reserved for men.* The Apostles continued Christ's tradition of ordaining only men. And this tradition has continued unbroken to the present day. No one, not even the pope, can change what Christ did and taught. The Church does not say she *will not* ordain women but rather that she *can not*. She is bound by the actions and intentions of Jesus. The Church cannot change the essential matter of the Sacrament of Holy Orders or any sacrament. In an important 1994 apostolic letter to the Church, *Ordinatio Sacerdotalis*, Pope John Paul II definitively proclaimed, "I declare that the Church has no authority whatsoever to confer priestly ordination on women and that this judgment is to be definitively held by all the Church's faithful" (4).

4. *An all-male priesthood does not mean women are unequal to men.* The Church has always maintained that men and women are equal in dignity. However, many people confuse equality with sameness. It is possible to be equal in dignity but to have different functions. The greatest example of this is women's ability to bear a child. It is not discrimination against males that only women can be mothers; it is the way they were made. Similarly, priests are only male, not because the Church is discriminating against women, but rather because Christ himself was male and priests are an icon of him and his relationship to his Bride, the Church. And just as motherhood can only be received as an unmerited gift in that a woman cannot will herself to be a mother, so too, the ministerial priesthood is not a right, but rather an unmerited gift, a calling.

Further Research

Read the apostolic letter *Ordinatio Sacerdotalis*. Summarize its content in two to three well-written paragraphs.

Prayer
Prayer for Priests

Gracious and loving God, we thank you for the gift of our priests.

Through them, we experience your presence in the sacraments.

Help our priests to be strong in their vocation.

Set their souls on fire with love for your people.

Grant them the wisdom, understanding, and strength they need to follow in the footsteps of Jesus.

Inspire them with the vision of your Kingdom.

Give them the words they need to spread the Gospel.

Allow them to experience joy in their ministry.

Help them to become instruments of your divine grace.

We ask this through Jesus Christ, who lives and reigns as our Eternal Priest.

Amen.

THE CELEBRATION OF THE SACRAMENT OF HOLY ORDERS

Man Hears the Call to Priesthood in Belize

Mark Wendling was lying prostrate, surrounded by more than ten thousand people, his face pressed to the floor of St. Peter's Basilica in Rome. About to be ordained a priest by Pope John Paul II, he thought to himself, *How did it ever come to this? My life is way bigger than I ever imagined, or than it should be. I'm lying down in Rome in the Vatican getting ordained by the pope. This is Mark Wendling?*

The second of five children, Mark was born and raised in Ontario, Canada, within a family to whom the Catholic faith was important. Although he never explicitly thought about being a priest, Mark had the sense throughout his childhood that he would do anything for God.

By the time he reached college, his priorities began to be centered on his personal successes. As he encountered people of other religions and philosophies at the University of Toronto, Wendling also began to drift from practicing his Catholic faith. Although he never denied God's existence or abandoned his Catholic identity, he rarely attended Mass or prayed.

After graduating, Mark decided to do volunteer work for a year. He wound up as a volunteer teacher at a high school run by the Society of Our Lady of the Most Holy Trinity in Benque Viejo, Belize, in Central America. The experience changed the course of his life forever.

Wendling says that God paved the path for his faith conversion during his volunteer year in three ways. First, his service to the children he taught changed him. "Serving makes you automatically live according to God's image and likeness, because God is selfless," he says. Second, the priest who was the pastor at the mission witnessed to him a joy he had never before seen. And third, the other volunteer teachers showed him what it was like to have sincere friendships.

These experiences led to his returning to the Sacrament of Penance for the first time in six years. Mark decided to stay a second year as a volunteer. It was during this time that he heard the call to the priesthood. For the first time, he asked God in prayer whether or not he should consider being a priest. The very next day, a priest he did not know well asked him while he was at confession, "Have you ever thought about being a priest?" And that moment changed everything: "I was hit with joy, with something really exciting and beautiful." He says that after this confession, he went into the empty church, looked at the tabernacle, and said to the Lord, "I'll do this." He continues, "Then I said to the Lord, 'You have to do one thing: you have to make me happy.' And right then, I felt joy. I was just so happy. It was wonderful."

FOCUS QUESTION

How is the
SACRAMENT OF HOLY ORDERS PREPARED for
and **CELEBRATED**?

INTRODUCTION
The Call to the Priesthood

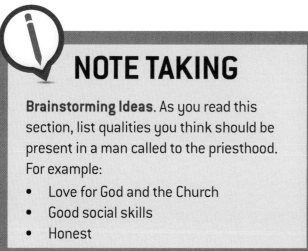

NOTE TAKING

Brainstorming Ideas. As you read this section, list qualities you think should be present in a man called to the priesthood. For example:

- Love for God and the Church
- Good social skills
- Honest

Like all vocations, the priesthood is a calling from God. The vocation to the priesthood is always at God's initiative, but a man has the freedom to say yes or no to this specific calling. Jesus said, "It was not you who chose me, but I who chose you" (Jn 15:16). Remember, God knows you better than you know yourself; specifically he knows what will make you happiest in this world and, more importantly, the path that will gain you eternal happiness with him in heaven.

Every Catholic man should at the very least be *open* to the vocation to the priesthood. A Catholic man should learn about what a priest's life is like and pray that if he is called to the priesthood, his heart will desire it. Women and those men not called to the priesthood should also pray for priestly vocations. God calls all different types of men from every background to be priests. Consider these stories of priestly discernment:

- *Fr. Robert Stec from the Diocese of Cleveland* says that during his senior year in high school "no less than twenty-five people suggested that I be a priest." This invitation by his classmates led Stec to attend a weekend at the local seminary for those who might be interested in the priesthood. He added, "I attended with the idea that I would disprove that I had a vocation, but in that weekend I knew that this is where I needed to be—to listen, to hear, and to understand God's call. I prayed, 'What is it, God, that you want me to do?' I listened and felt peacefulness in God's answer. Later, I kept being affirmed in this vocation choice."[1]

- *Fr. Peter Clark of the Diocese of Lansing, Michigan*, was a successful doctor before becoming a priest. He had gone through college, medical school, and residency, and he had his own private medical practice. He had dated and was even engaged at one point. Although he was very active in his Catholic faith, it took him years to finally consider the priesthood. Even-  tually, he sold his medical practice, met with the voca- tion director of his diocese, and went through the discern- ment process. He says, "For someone already heavily involved in a career, stepping out toward the priesthood involves sacrifice and achieving a distance from superfluous attachments. Prepare yourself to respond to the call. Do things that free you to move on with a clear conscience. Be patient. Consideration of the priesthood is a long-term project with highs and lows, clarity and obscurity, confidence and doubt. We are in this Kingdom of God for the long run, so the vocation process takes time."[2]

- *Fr. Aaron Qureshi of the Archdiocese of Washington* had a fulfilling life as a com-

puter program-  mer. He attended Mass regularly and prayed at certain moments, but his life felt disjointed in that he would have peace at Mass or Adoration but often feel spiritu- ally lazy the rest of the week. Fr. Qureshi says, "My fellow parishioners and my Catholic friends helped me piece together the puzzle. God was calling me to a life that was wholly devoted to him, a life that was integral and not fragmented, a life that was permeated by his presence day by day. I could not live that life in my world. And so I quit my perfect job, moved out of my perfect condominium, and turned my path towards seminary—and towards Perfection himself."[3]

For some men, the call to the priesthood may be present from early in life, manifesting itself as a nagging but joyful understanding that God is calling them to a unique way of life. Or it may be something that enters into a man's heart later on in life. A man who senses himself pulled toward a vocation to the priesthood should further discern this possibility. The first step on such a journey is always abandonment to God's will. Pope John Paul II offered this advice for men who feel called to the priesthood: "If such a call comes into your heart, do not silence it! Let it develop into the maturity of a vocation. . . . Respond to it through prayer and fidel- ity to the commandments! For 'the harvest is plentiful' and there is an enormous need for many to be reached by Christ's call, 'Follow me'" (Apostolic Letter to Youth of the World, March 31, 1985).

Some practical steps in discerning a call to the priesthood are listed in the feature "Practical Steps in Discerning a Vocation to the Priesthood."

Fostering Priestly Vocations Is Everyone's Responsibility

The priesthood is for the Church, which includes you. The vocation to the priesthood is an incredible good for the man called, but it is also a great gift to the Church as a whole. Promoting vocations to the priesthood is the responsibility of all baptized persons. Without priests, you would not have access to the sac- raments, especially the Sacrament of the Holy Eucha- rist. The Second Vatican Council clearly proclaimed, "The duty of fostering vocations falls on the whole Christian community, and they should discharge it principally by living full Christian lives" (*Optatam Totius*, 2).

The Church specifically says that families should be a place in which an openness to all vocations, especially that of the priesthood, is nurtured. Your friendships also should be encounters in which specific vocational states of life are discussed and encouraged. Do you have a friend or classmate who you think would be a good priest? In a nonpressuring manner, you should let him know. Some men never even think about this vocational path until someone mentions it to them. That said, a vocation is always deeply personal and should be respected as such.

At the very least, you should be praying that men called to the priesthood will be open and willing to say yes to this heroic vocation. The prayer in this chapter's review section is a good starting point.

Practical Steps in Discerning a Vocation to the Priesthood

Section 2 of the Introduction to this text offered a synopsis or general plan for discerning your vocation. However, if you think you are called to the priesthood, you may need to take more practical steps of discernment. The United States Conference of Catholic Bishops shared some suggestions for men who are considering a specific vocation to the priesthood. Even if you are not called to be a priest, you can pass these ideas on to someone who may be deliberating a vocation to the ministerial priesthood.[4]

1. Attend daily Mass.
2. Receive the Sacrament of Penance often.
3. Spend time in Adoration of the Blessed Sacrament.
4. Engage in daily prayer.
5. Participate in personal spiritual direction from a priest or another trained individual.
6. Attend discernment programs with other men discerning the priesthood, such as a weekend retreat at a seminary, vocation evenings, or a discussion group.
7. Develop a devotion to the Blessed Mother.
8. Get involved in some form of service within the Church.
9. Talk to a vocation director at a diocese or religious order.

For more information on priestly discernment, see "Discerning Men" on the US Bishops' website, www.usccb.org.

ASSIGNMENT

Do the following:

- Look up the vocations office of your diocese. Report on three initiatives they offer that are designed to encourage new candidates to the priesthood.

- Choose a religious community with priests. Report on how the community's efforts to encourage priest candidates differ from your diocese's efforts and how they are the same.

SECTION ASSESSMENT

NOTE TAKING

Use the brainstorming list you made to help you complete the following items.

1. Name the top three qualities you think should be present in a man called to the priesthood. Write two or three additional sentences explaining why you chose these.

COMPREHENSION

2. Why are vocations to the priesthood an important concern for all Catholics?

3. How should a man respond to a call to the priesthood, according to Pope John Paul II?

CRITICAL THINKING

4. How can the Church encourage more priestly vocations? List several practical suggestions.

Preparation for Holy Orders

MAIN IDEA
After being accepted into a priestly formation program, a man enters seminary, where he is formed humanly, spiritually, intellectually, and pastorally.

As a man continues to discern his call to the priesthood, he often does so in an unofficial manner, such as by talking to priests or **seminarians** or meeting with a vocation director. Foremost, he must be in a "prayerful dialogue with God and with the Church."[5] However, when he thinks he is ready to enter priestly formation, there is a more formal application process.

Applying for Candidacy to the Priesthood

The official process to apply for formation in the priesthood varies by diocese or religious community. Yet the following general steps usually occur. Once a man decides to make an official inquiry and/or application to be a candidate for priesthood, he undergoes a series of interviews with a priest to determine both his sense of calling and whether he meets some candidacy

> **seminarians** Men who attend a seminary or school focusing on theology and training and formation for the life of a priest.

NOTE TAKING

Connecting Categories and Examples. Make a three-column chart like the one here. In the second column, write an example for each area of priestly formation. In the third column, briefly explain why this area of priestly formation is important.

Area of priestly formation	Example	Why it is important
Human	Develop affability	Priest's personality must be a bridge between people and the Lord.
Spiritual		
Intellectual		
Pastoral		

requirements. Often this formal time of discernment is called the *aspirancy*, which suggests that the man is aspiring to know more about the priestly vocation. It usually takes place over four or five months and involves conversations between the man and a priest adviser.

The formal application process for candidacy also includes submitting a written application along with several letters of recommendation and school transcripts. The man may also be asked to write an autobiographical statement that expresses his sense of calling and complete a full psychological evaluation. If the man is applying for diocesan priesthood, the bishop will likely request a formal one-on-one interview with him at this time. In a religious order, several interviews may be required between the applicant and representatives of the community, including the religious superior.

To be accepted as a candidate for ordination, a person must be a mature male (generally between the ages of eighteen and forty) who has completed Christian initiation, willingly and knowingly wishes to be ordained, and has been accepted as a candidate by Church authorities.

An applicant for priestly formation must have evidence of personal balance, good moral character, love for the truth, and proper motivation. He should show a proper maturity for his age, a capacity for growth and conversion, an ability to live a celibate life, and a desire to be for others the likeness of Christ. He must pray daily, belong to a parish, attend Mass at least on Sundays, and participate regularly in the Sacrament of Penance. An aspirant should show an awareness of the Church's mission and a desire to promote it.[6]

Also, he must be free from both psychological and medical conditions that would inhibit him from exercising a full life of ministry and free from all canonical impediments and other grounds for disqualification on moral or legal grounds, such as certain prior criminal records or personal legal obligations.

Most importantly, the man should have a compelling desire to respond to Christ's call to have a closer relationship with him. In other words, he should have a great desire to be holy.

Formation for the Priesthood

Formation for the priesthood is not the same as job training or schooling; it is "first and foremost cooperation with the grace of God."[7] Pope John Paul II echoed the words of the Second Vatican Council on the importance of priestly formation in his apostolic exhortation *Pastores Dabo Vobis* (*I Will Give You Shepherds*), in which he outlined four crucial areas of formation: human, spiritual, intellectual, and pastoral.

Living in a seminary with other men in brotherhood helps a seminarian learn to share his life, grow his faith, and love others.

Human Formation

As "the basis of all priestly formation," human formation finds its foundation in Jesus Christ, who, while fully God, became a man. The priest's ministry—the proclamation of the Gospel, the celebration of sacraments, and leading within the Church—is all done through the relation of the priest to individual human beings. For this reason, the priest needs to be formed so that his personality is a bridge, not an obstacle, to other people meeting Jesus Christ through him. It is of special importance that the priest relate well with others. He must develop himself so that he is affable, hospitable, sincere, prudent, generous, encouraging, understanding, and forgiving. He must also grow in his ability to be celibate, live a life of simplicity, and be obedient to his superiors. Part of this growth comes from living at a seminary with other men in brotherhood. While learning how to love others, he must share with others the encompassing nature of love and how love involves the entire person.

Seminarians are expected to pray daily, belong to a parish, attend Mass at least on Sundays, and participate regularly in the Sacrament of Penance.

Spiritual Formation

If human formation is the starting point, then spiritual formation is the "center" of all priestly formation. Spiritual formation should be such that the candidate forms an intimate communion with Jesus Christ. Jesus himself said to his Apostles, "I no longer call you slaves. . . . I have called you friends, because I have told you everything I have heard from my Father" (Jn 15:15). Attention to spiritual formation includes cultivating a deep prayer life, "as a living and personal meeting with the Father through the only-begotten Son under the action of the Spirit, a dialogue that becomes a sharing in the filial conversation between Jesus and the Father" (*Pastores Dabo Vobis*, 47). This includes a

renewed dedication to the Eucharist, the highest form of Christian prayer. Part of spiritual formation teaches the candidate how to embrace, love, and live celibacy for its true motives—that is, to be able to use the gift of celibacy in order to share God's love with all people. (For more on priestly celibacy, see this Chapter's "Explaining the Faith.")

Seminarians typically dedicate six years of their life to prayer, study, and pastoral work.

Intellectual Formation

If you were asked to describe what a man does in his years of preparation for ordination, you might answer "go to school" or "study." These answers would relate to a third area of necessary formation: intellectual formation. A candidate does spend years studying theology and also philosophy, which leads to a deeper understanding of what it means to be human. Theology itself focuses on understanding Sacred Scripture and Sacred Tradition as handed down by the Magisterium. A candidate's intellectual formation also has a pastoral focus, as it will be the priest's job to help the laity understand theology and the truth of Christ's teaching, especially when that truth is contradicted by modern culture. Finally, a sound intellectual formation will help the priest evangelize—that is, share the Gospel of Christ in a clear manner with a pluralistic world.

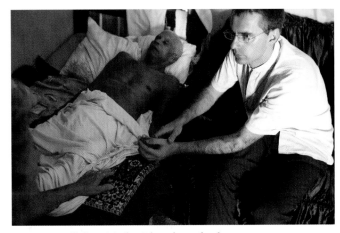

Priests are called to visit the sick and care for the poor.

Pastoral Formation

The fourth area of priestly formation outlined by Pope John Paul II is pastoral formation, which is the underlying goal of the entire scope of formation for candidates for the priesthood. Priests are formed in pastoral ministry so as to become shepherds of souls in imitation of Jesus Christ, the Good Shepherd. Candidates are taught how to be pastoral—that is, how to teach, sanctify, and lead their flock. "To be a true 'shepherd of souls' means standing with and for Christ in the community, the Christ who teaches and sanctifies and guides or leads the community."[8] Often pastoral formation involves practical experience in a parish prior to ordination; this allows candidates to engage concretely in many aspects of pastoral ministry: visiting the sick, caring for the poor, engaging in other charitable works, and helping to prepare for liturgical functions.

Agents and Setting for Priestly Formation

The bishop of the diocese and, in fact, the entire Church have primary responsibility in forming a man for the priesthood. However, a man's formation usually begins within his family and in his interactions with other role models, long before he enters seminary. Ultimately, it is the graces of Christ and the gifts of the Holy Spirit that illuminate the man's vocation.

The seminary is the primary setting for priestly formation. The entire formation program—encompassing the four areas of formation described previously—should be oriented "to the formation of true shepherds of souls after the model of our Lord Jesus Christ, teacher, priest and shepherd" (*Optatam Totius*, 4). If the man enters the seminary with a bachelor's degree including some courses in theology and philosophy, the seminary program of formation is usually four or five years in length, which sometimes includes

a supervised year of pastoral experience, usually in a parish. However, this timeframe varies among dioceses and religious communities.

Life in the Seminary

A seminary is essentially a house of prayer, study, and formation. Study takes up quite a bit of a seminarian's daily life; typically a seminarian takes twelve to fifteen hours of academic courses per semester, which translates into many hours of reading and studying. Courses may be taken in areas such as sacraments and liturgy, moral theology, systematic theology, Scripture, and language.

During the week, a seminarian's day usually begins with communal Morning Prayer from the Liturgy of the Hours followed by breakfast and morning classes. Afternoons may be less structured, with a chance for exercise and individual study. Seminarians gather together again for Evening Prayer from the Liturgy of

the Hours. Attendance and participation at daily Mass is a requirement.

Personal prayer is another integral part of the seminarian's day. Many seminarians are encouraged or required to spend an hour in private prayer each day. Seminarians are assigned a spiritual director to help them grow in their spiritual lives. A seminarian also meets with the seminary rector or another advisor in the seminary to discuss his progress toward ordination. There may be a weekly practicum exploring the various parts of the liturgy that includes workshops allowing candidates to hone their skills in writing and delivering homilies at Mass.

Some seminarians have "house jobs" within the seminary, such as serving food in the cafeteria, filing papers in the office, or cashiering in the bookstore. Many seminarians also have pastoral assignments within the community, such as teaching religious education classes to young people, making hospital visits, or working in a homeless shelter.

The seminarian's ongoing formation as priest and preparation for ordination and priesthood continues in the midst of this routine. Sometimes seminarians will spend summers, a semester, or even a year taking a break from academic studies to focus on pastoral skills. This time of "internship" allows the candidate to be mentored by a pastor, live in a rectory, and learn the daily and weekly rhythms of parish life. A seminarian takes a proximate step toward priesthood when he is ordained a deacon; this is when he makes a promise to live a life of obedience and celibacy for the Church. A transitional deacon usually spends six months to a year in this role before priestly ordination.

♥Lectio Divina:
A Prayer to Hear God's Call

The ancient practice of **lectio divina**—"holy reading"—involves focused meditation on the Scriptures. Choose one of the Scripture readings suggested below. Then follow the process of lectio divina as it is outlined. In your time of prayer, reflect on the call to priesthood or religious life. Focus on how God is calling you personally *today* to be in relationship with him.

SCRIPTURE SUGGESTIONS

- Jeremiah 1:4–9 ("Before you were born I dedicated you.")

- 1 Corinthians 12:4–11 ("There are different kinds of spiritual gifts but the same Spirit.")

- John 21:15–19 ("Feed my lambs. . . . Tend my sheep. . . . Follow me.")

PROCESS

Find a quiet place to pray. Ask the Holy Spirit to inspire your heart and mind with what he wants to tell you. Then follow these ancient steps:

> **lectio divina** A classical prayer practice that involves a reflective reading of the Bible. It means "holy reading."

1. *Lectio* (reading)—Read one of the passages to take in its literal meaning.

2. *Meditatio* (meditation)—Read the passage again very slowly, asking yourself, "What does this text say to *me*?" and "How does it apply to my life *today*?"

3. *Oratio* (prayer)—Allow your meditation to lead into a prayer to God. This can be a simple conversation with God.

4. *Contemplatio* (contemplation)—An encounter with the Lord should guide you to a transformation or change in your life. Read the Scripture passage once again. In this step, ask God what in your life needs to be transformed by his grace. What needs to happen so that you follow his will and not your own?

Close with another prayer in which you thank the Lord for this time of inspiration with him. Beg him to transform your life and heart so that you may live this Scripture in any ways in which you have been inspired by this prayer exercise.

A Seminarian Called to Something Higher

Brian Bergkamp grew up on a farm in rural Kansas, the third of seven children. According to his mother, his childhood and young adulthood were fairly typical of farm life, which included waking up at five o'clock in the morning to help his father milk cows.

As a child, Brian was described as "bright-eyed" and "talkative." Remarkably, he spoke about wanting to be a priest at a young age. The desire didn't go away; after a year of college, he applied to be a candidate for the priesthood in the Diocese of Wichita. He was accepted and entered Conception Seminary in Missouri. He was diligent in his studies and found peace in the prayer and rhythm of seminary life. "He was never about himself, always looking to do something for others. He was really an inspiration to us in the seminary and really a man that you want to model yourself after, a man of great faith," remembered a fellow seminarian who knew Brian during his time at Conception.

Next, Brian was assigned to Mount St. Mary's Seminary in Maryland, where he spent two more years in study and formation. During the summer before his third year at Mount St. Mary's, he volunteered at a soup kitchen in Wichita that serves more than two thousand people each day. Brian wrote at the time, "At this point in my life, I believe I will become much more than just a priest, that I am called to something higher, enabling me to reach out to thousands of Catholics."

This call to do "something higher" would happen unexpectedly on a Saturday morning that summer. On July 9, 2016, Brian was kayaking with some friends on the Arkansas River. The turbulent waters overturned the kayak of a friend, and she was thrown into the river without a life jacket. Brian bravely abandoned his own kayak to save her. He was successful; the woman was brought to safety. However, the rushing waters took hold of Brian, and he drowned.

Fr. Brendan Moss, O.S.B., Conception Seminary's rector, said, "In his life, and most especially in this moment, Brian was a true friend of Jesus. Like the Master, Brian laid down his life for another. He was a doer of the word and not a hearer only."

At his funeral, Wichita bishop Carl Kemme poignantly summarized Brian's life: "He may not have been a priest, but he lived and died a most priestly life."[9]

SECTION ASSESSMENT

NOTE TAKING

Use the chart you made to help you answer the following questions.

1. Why is human formation described as "the basis of all priestly formation"?
2. What is the primary focus of spiritual formation?
3. What is the focus of the study of theology in the process of intellectual formation?
4. How might a seminarian be formed pastorally?

COMPREHENSION

5. What are some qualities that should be developed in a seminarian?
6. How long does a seminary program typically last?
7. Why is a time of discernment for the priesthood known as *aspirancy*?

VOCABULARY

8. Who is a *religious superior*? What is his role in the candidate's application process to the seminary?

CRITICAL THINKING

9. How is formation for the priesthood different from "job training"? Explain.

SECTION 2
The Rite of Ordination

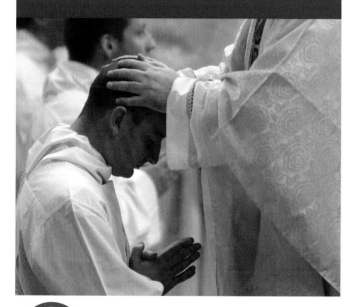

After years of preparation, those called to the priestly vocation are finally ordained. It is important to remember that only baptized men who have been called by God to this vocation can receive the Sacrament of Holy Orders. The *Catechism of the Catholic Church* makes it clear that Holy Orders is foremost a gift, not something "earned." This means that

> no one has a *right* to receive the Sacrament of Holy Orders. Indeed no one claims this office for himself; he is called to it by God. Anyone who thinks he recognizes the signs of God's call to the ordained ministry must humbly submit his desire to the authority of the Church, who has the responsibility and right to call someone to receive orders. Like every grace this sacrament can be *received* only as an unmerited gift. (CCC, 1578)

All three degrees of the Sacrament of Holy Orders for the bishop, priest, and deacon follow the same movement and take place within the Eucharistic liturgy. The rites of ordination are rich in symbolism and meaning

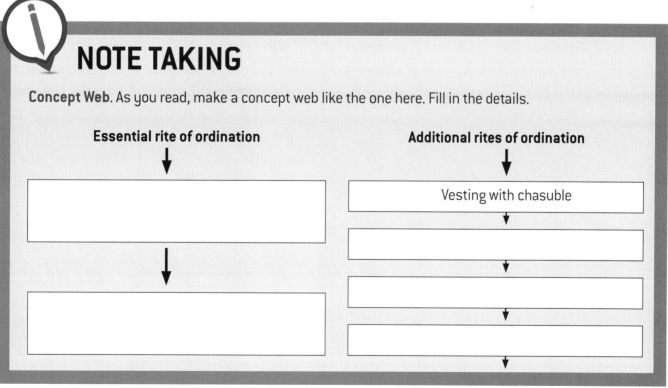

NOTE TAKING

Concept Web. As you read, make a concept web like the one here. Fill in the details.

Essential rite of ordination

↓

[ ]

↓

[ ]

Additional rites of ordination

↓

Vesting with chasuble

↓

[ ]

↓

[ ]

↓

[ ]

↓

After an ordination (held on the Saturday after Easter) at the Basilica of the Sacred Heart at the University of Notre Dame, the Congregation of Holy Cross welcomes its newly ordained priests.

regarding the nature of the episcopate, presbyterate, and diaconate.

Essential Rites of Holy Orders

Because he has the fullness of the priesthood, the minister for Holy Orders is always a bishop. For all three degrees, the essential rite of the sacrament is the bishop's imposition of hands on the head of the man being ordained while the bishop invokes the Holy Spirit as he recites a special consecratory prayer that asks God for the specific gifts related to the ministry for which the man is being ordained.

Sacred chrism is used in the ordination of priests and bishops. In priestly ordination, the man's hands are anointed with chrism; in the ordination of a bishop, chrism is poured on his head.

Ordinations are typically scheduled in the diocesan cathedral for either Saturdays or Sundays so as many people as possible can attend.

The Rite of Priestly Ordination

At the beginning of the Mass of ordination for the priesthood, the candidate wears an **alb** covered by a **stole** worn diagonally across his left shoulder to signify that he is a deacon and not yet a priest. He takes the first place in the opening procession ahead of the other priests who will concelebrate the liturgy. The initial rites of ordination begin after the Gospel. The bishop, wearing his miter (see "Special Items of a Bishop" later in this section), sits in his chair. The candidate is called forward, goes before the bishop, and makes a sign of reverence. A designated priest, often the rector of the seminary, testifies for the candidate to the bishop. The

> **alb** A liturgical vestment with origins in the celebration of Baptism that is a long white robe. Only clergy may wear a stole over the alb.
>
> **stole** A long narrow cloth that comes in the color of the liturgical season and is worn by the bishop, priest, or deacon. Stoles were originally worn by Jewish rabbis as a sign of their authority.

bishop accepts the candidate for ordination (this is called the election) and asks for the consent of all the people. He says,

> We rely on the help of the Lord God and our Savior Jesus Christ, and we choose this man, our brother, for priesthood in the presbyteral order.

All of the faithful in attendance give their consent by saying, "Thanks be to God." The bishop then offers his homily, in which he spells out the essential duties of the priesthood.

After the homily, the candidate stands before the bishop, who questions him about his resolution to fulfill the duties of the priesthood: to celebrate the sacraments as they have been handed down by Christ, to preach the Gospel and teach the Catholic faith, and to unite himself more closely to Jesus, the High Priest. The candidate answers, "I am" or "I am, with the help of God," to each question. Then the candidate goes to the bishop, kneels before him, places his joined hands between the hands of the bishop, and pledges his respect and obedience to the bishop.

The initial rites of ordination conclude with the candidate lying prostrate on the floor of the sanctuary as a sign of his unworthiness and need for God's help (see the image below). The bishop kneels as the **Litany of the Saints** is sung. The litany is sung in order to allow the whole Church—including the Church in heaven—to pray for the candidate. At the end of the litany, the bishop stands and prays:

> Hear us, Lord our God,
> and pour out upon this servant of yours
> the blessing of the Holy Spirit
> and the grace and power of the priesthood.
> In your sight we offer this man for ordination:
> support him with your unfailing love.
> We ask this through Christ, our Lord.
> Amen.

The candidate then rises from the floor, goes to the bishop, and kneels before him. The bishop lays

> **Litany of the Saints** A prayer made up of various petitions addressed to the saints. It was first prescribed by St. Gregory the Great in the sixth century.

his hands on the candidate's head in silence. Next, the other priests lay their hands on the candidate's head as well. The bishop then sings or recites the prayer of consecration, which concludes with these words:

Almighty Father,
grant to this servant of yours
the dignity of the priesthood.
Renew within him the Spirit of holiness.
As a co-worker with the order of bishops
may he be faithful to the ministry
that he receives from you, Lord God,
and be to others a model of right conduct.

May he be faithful in working with the order
    of bishops,
so that the words of the Gospel may reach the
    ends of the earth,
and the family of nations,
made one in Christ,
may become God's one, holy people.
We ask this through our Lord Jesus Christ,
    your Son,
who lives and reigns with you and the Holy
    Spirit,
one God, forever and ever.
Amen.

Other Rites of Priestly Ordination

Several additional rites follow the consecration of the new priest. These rites express and complete the mystery that is accomplished in ordination. The assisting priests prepare the stole of the newly ordained priest and vest him in a **chasuble**. After being ordained a

> **chasuble** The outer garment worn by the bishop or priest over the alb and stole. It is the same color as the stole and the liturgical season.

Newly ordained priests are vested with a stole and a chasuble.

deacon, the man had worn the stole over his left shoulder; as a priest, he wears it over both shoulders. The stole is worn by priests and bishops as a sign of their order and authority when they celebrate Mass and the other sacraments or when they expose the Blessed Sacrament. Administering the stole, the bishop may remind the priest of the comforting words of Jesus in calling disciples to himself:

Take my yoke upon you and learn from me, for I am meek and humble of heart; and you will find rest for yourselves. For my yoke is easy, and my burden light. (Mt 11:29–30)

As the new priest kneels before him, the bishop anoints the priest's palms with sacred chrism as a sign of the special anointing of the Holy Spirit.

The Mass continues, and a deacon assists the bishop in receiving the gifts of the people. The deacon prepares the bread on a paten and the wine and water in the chalice for the offering of the Eucharist and brings them to the bishop, who then presents them to the new priest, saying:

Accept from the holy people of God the gifts to be offered to him.

Know what you are doing, and imitate the mystery you celebrate: model your life on the mystery of the Lord's cross.

Before continuing with the Mass, the bishop stands and exchanges a sign of peace with the newly ordained priest. Then the Liturgy of the Eucharist proceeds; the newly ordained priest, all the priests present, and the bishop concelebrate the Mass together.

Holy Orders for Bishops and Deacons

As mentioned, the Rite of Ordination for the other two degrees of the sacrament follows the same movement as for priests. Recall, too, that the fullness of the Sacrament of Holy Orders occurs in the ordination of bishops. Nevertheless, there are only slight differences between the rites for the three degrees, mainly involving the secondary rites. The essential rite of the laying on of hands remains the same for the ordination of bishops and deacons. However, only the principal bishop celebrating the liturgy and other participating bishops—but not the concelebrating priests—lay hands on the head of the bishop-elect or the deacon candidate.

A bishop-elect is presented by one of the priests of the diocese, who asks for ordination on his behalf. The consecrating bishop asks the priest, "Have you a mandate from the Holy See?" When the priest answers in the affirmative, the bishop asks that the **apostolic letter** be read to the congregation. The apostolic letter is usually sent to the bishop-elect when the pope nominates him as bishop.

A bishop is not presented a paten and chalice like a newly ordained priest is; instead, he is given the Book of the Gospels as a sign of his apostolic mission to proclaim the Word of God. The new bishop is anointed with sacred chrism not on the hands like a priest but on the head as a sign of the coming of the Holy Spirit,

The Book of Gospels is laid over the head of a new bishop at his ordination.

who makes the bishop's ministry fruitful. The new bishop is also invested with a ring, a miter, and a crozier (see "Special Items of a Bishop" in this section).

At the ordination of a deacon, he is invested with a deacon's stole and a *dalmatic*, the white outer garment he wears at liturgy. Kneeling before the bishop, the newly ordained deacon receives the Book of the Gospels while the bishop says,

> Receive the Gospel of Christ,
> whose herald you now are.
> Believe what you read,
> teach what you believe,
> and practice what you teach.

The Sacrament of Holy Orders in all three degrees has eternal significance for both the men being ordained and for the whole Church. The rites of the sacrament reflect that significance. St. Paul addressed the ordained in his Second Letter to Timothy: "For this reason, I remind you to stir into flame the gift of God that you have through the imposition of my hands" (2 Tm 1:6).

> **apostolic letter** A document issued by the pope or Vatican for various appointments, approving religious congregations, designating basilicas, and the like.

Special Items of a BISHOP

If you have ever seen a bishop in an official setting, you may have noticed several unique items that make up his garb. These special items have deeply historical and symbolic meaning. His ring, miter, and crozier are bestowed during his episcopal ordination. Some other items also have important significance and an interesting history.

PONTIFICAL OR EPISCOPAL RING. Every bishop has a ring, which is symbolic of his being "wedded" to the Church, specifically his diocese. The ring may be engraved with his episcopal "coat of arms" or another symbol. In past times the ring was used to imprint the bishop's seal upon documents with hot wax. The only time a bishop does not wear his ring is on Good Friday, as a symbol of mourning for the Death of Christ.

PECTORAL CROSS. This special cross that a bishop always wears gets its name from being worn on the breast (Latin *pectus*). He usually has a simple, everyday one and another, more ornate one called a pontifical pectoral cross. Traditionally, a pontifical pectoral cross contained a relic of the actual Cross of Christ or of a saint. When a bishop is wearing only his clerical suit and collar, the pectoral cross is often put in a shirt pocket with the chain still visible. When he presides at liturgies, the cross hangs from a green and gold cord over his alb.

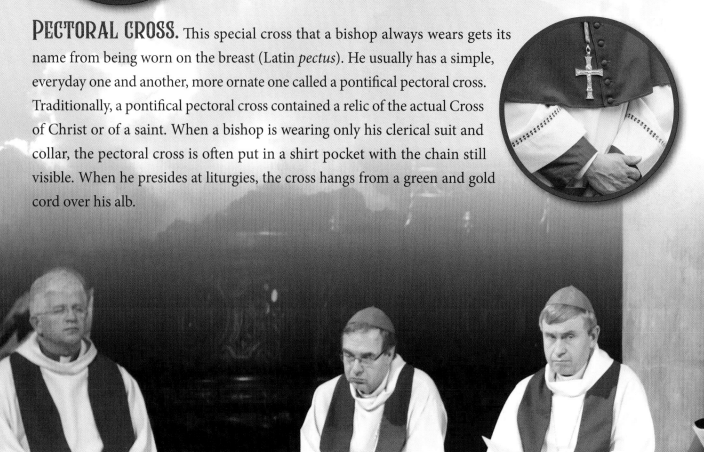

CROZIER. Also called the pastoral staff, this staff is shaped like a shepherd's crook. It signifies that a bishop is a model of Christ as the Good Shepherd and leads his flock after Christ's own heart. Shepherds used their crooks both to scare off the wolves that wanted to devour the sheep and to pull sheep back into the flock. Such is the duty of the bishop: to protect his flock and lead his people always back to the true Good Shepherd. The crozier can be made from precious metals or carved from wood.

MITER. This is a bishop's special headdress that he wears during the liturgy. The name comes from the Greek word *mitra*, which was a band of cloth tied around the head. Two fringed lappets or *infulae* (Latin for "bands") hang from the back of the miter. It is reminiscent of the headgear worn by the high priest in the Old Testament. Some say the origins of the miter go back to apostolic times. It was certainly in widespread use with bishops by the twelfth century. The miter points toward heaven and is meant to echo the laurels given to victorious athletes, like the "crown of righteousness" described by St. Paul (2 Tm 4:8). When the ordaining bishop places the miter on the head of the bishop being ordained, he prays, "Receive the miter, and may the splendor of holiness shine forth in you, so that when the chief shepherd appears, you may deserve to receive from him an unfading crown of glory." A bishop wears his miter while celebrating liturgy, though he removes it when he sings or leads the assembly in prayer, as in the Eucharistic Prayer.

PALLIUM. The pallium is reserved for metropolitan archbishops and the pope. It is a strip of white wool embroidered with six black crosses that is worn around the neck during liturgies. It symbolizes fidelity to Christ. Following a tradition reaching back to at least the tenth century, all pallia (plural of pallium) are made from lamb's wool sheared on the feast of St. Agnes. New pallia are kept near St. Peter's tomb in the Basilica of St. Peter in Rome. In the past, once a year on the feast of Sts. Peter and Paul, the pope blessed them and distributed them to the archbishops. In 2015, Pope Francis directed that the archbishop is to be invested with the pallium in his home diocese

SECTION ASSESSMENT

NOTE TAKING

Use the concept web you created to help you answer the following questions.

1. What is the essential rite of the Sacrament of Holy Orders?
2. Who is the minister of the Sacrament of Holy Orders?
3. What is the priestly stole a sign of?
4. What is the difference between the anointing of a priest with sacred chrism and the anointing of a bishop?

COMPREHENSION

5. Why does a candidate for the priesthood lie prostrate on the floor?
6. What are the symbolic meanings of the gifts presented to a bishop at ordination: the Book of the Gospels, ring, miter, and crozier?

VOCABULARY

7. Why is the *Litany of the Saints* sung at an ordination?
8. Name the wearers of an *alb* and a *dalmatic*.

REFLECTION

9. What is the best advice you could offer to a new priest on his ordination day?

SECTION 3
Effects of the Sacrament of Holy Orders

NOTE TAKING

Sentence Summaries. Write four or five sentences that summarize the content of this section. Use as many of the following words as you can in your sentences:

- indelible
- vows
- sacred power
- grace
- confers
- substitute

Recall from your previous study on the Sacrament of Matrimony and the other sacraments that all sacraments are *efficacious*, which means that they effect or accomplish what they represent. In other words, a sacrament is not merely fancy words and special actions; when a person receives any sacrament, something truly happens. Sacraments embody the reality that they represent; they achieve a real change in the recipient. This section outlines the effects of the Sacrament of Holy Orders.

An Indelible Character

Like Baptism and Confirmation, the Sacrament of Holy Orders gives the recipient an "indelible spiritual character" (*CCC*, 1582). This permanent seal means that once a man is ordained, he will always be marked as such. The diaconate, presbyterate, and episcopate each have a unique character, such that once a man is ordained a deacon, he can never be ordained a deacon again, and the same applies for priests and bishops.

This indelible mark conforms ordained men to Christ in a way that is unique. The one ordained receives Christ's "sacred power" (*Lumen Gentium*, 27). In the bishop and his priest designate, it is Christ himself who is acting in the celebration of the sacraments. Through the bishop or priest, it is Christ who offers the sacrifice of the Mass, Christ who baptizes, Christ who anoints the sick, Christ who witnesses marriages, and, through the bishop only, Christ who ordains.

It is important to stress that the priest is not a "substitute" for Christ; instead, Christ himself works in the person of the priest. Therefore, the way a priest or bishop acts does not affect Christ's presence in the sacraments. "Since it is ultimately Christ who acts and effects salvation through the ordained minister, the unworthiness of the latter does not prevent Christ from acting" (*CCC*, 1584). A bishop's or priest's sinfulness cannot impede the grace of the sacraments he celebrates.

An ancient icon depicts Christ as the High Priest.

A man who is validly ordained can, for serious reasons, be discharged from the functions and obligations linked to ordination, including celebrating the sacraments, but he can never again be a layman in the strict sense, because the character imprinted at ordination is truly permanent and forever.

The Grace of the Holy Spirit

In general, the grace of the Holy Spirit received by bishops, priests, and deacons from the Sacrament of Holy Orders is a connection to Christ as priest, teacher, and pastor. However, the graces differ according to each of the three degrees of ordination.

For the bishop, the gift of the Spirit is first of all the grace of strength to govern the Church, to defend it with prudence, and to show a preferential love for the poor, sick, and needy. This grace leads him to proclaim the Gospel to all, to be the model for his people, and to

identify himself with Christ, the redeemer at Eucharist, while offering his life on behalf of his flock.

Ordination confers on priests the grace to offer the sacrifice of the Mass, to forgive sins in the Sacrament of Penance, and to prepare people for their eternal destiny by preaching the Gospel. St. Paul described priests as "servants of Christ and stewards of the mysteries of God" (1 Cor 4:1). The priest's threefold mission and grace to teach, govern, and sanctify is received from the bishop, who holds these in fullness.

Deacons receive in sacramental ordination the graces of service in the liturgy, in the sharing of the Gospel, and in works of charity. St. Polycarp offered this counsel to deacons: "Let them be merciful, and zealous, and let them walk according to the truth of the Lord, who became servant of all" (*Lumen Gentium*, 29).

The Promises of the Priesthood

Related to the graces of the sacraments are the vows and promises of the priesthood. Priests who are part of a religious community such as the Benedictines or Franciscans take the vows of poverty, chastity, and obedience. Most took these vows before they were ordained. Diocesan priests make the promises of celibacy and obedience to their bishop as part of the Rite of Ordination. Although diocesan priests do not take a vow of poverty, they are expected to live simply.

All sacraments deepen the life of Christ within the person receiving it. The Sacrament of Holy Orders does so in a unique way. As Pope Pius XII said, "[The priest] is no longer supposed to live for himself; nor can he devote himself to the interests of just his own relatives, or friends or native land. . . . He must be aflame with charity toward everyone. Not even his thoughts, his will, his feelings belong to him, for they are rather those of Jesus Christ who is his life" (quoted in *Sacerdotii Nostri Primordia*, 6).

Three Modern
Saintly Ordained
Ministers

The graces of the Sacrament of Holy Orders not only help deacons, priests, and bishops to serve the Church but also aid them individually on the path to sainthood. Countless ordained ministers of the Church throughout her history have been canonized or are on the way to canonization. Note the variety in the paths and stories of the three ordained men described here.

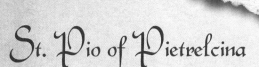

Padre Pio celebrating Mass

St. Pio of Pietrelcina

Born in a small town in Italy, Francesco Forgione, the man who was to be known widely as "Padre Pio," was devoted to God and the Church from a young age. He was said to have had direct communication with Jesus, Mary, and his guardian angel even when he was just a child. He entered the Capuchins, a Franciscan religious community, when he was fifteen years old and was ordained a priest in 1910 at the age of twenty-three.

A marking characteristic of Padre Pio's priesthood was his intense devotion to the Passion and sacrifice of Christ, especially during the celebration of the Eucharist. He would often go into long contemplative silences while celebrating Mass. One day when Padre Pio was praying in front of the crucifix after Mass, he received the *stigmata*, the physical wounds of Christ in his hands, feet, and side. They would remain on his body for more than fifty years, until he died. As with St. Francis of Assisi, his stigmata were a physical representation of his interior adherence to the suffering of Christ.

Padre Pio's deep devotion to Christ drew thousands of pilgrims to his monastery over the years. His normal day lasted almost nineteen hours and consisted of contemplative prayer, saying the Mass, and hearing innumerable confessions from those who came to visit. He died from his deteriorating health on September 23, 1968, just after making a confession and renewing his vows of poverty, chastity, and obedience. His stigmata faded away at his death. In 1971, Pope Paul VI, speaking to the superiors of the Capuchin order, said of Padre Pio: "What fame he had. How many followers from around the world. Why? Was it because he was a philosopher, a scholar, or because he had means at his disposal? No, it was because he said Mass humbly, heard confessions from morning until night and was a marked representative of the stigmata of Our Lord. He was truly a man of prayer and suffering."

Servant of God Emil Kapaun

A wounded soldier is helped by Fr. Emil Kapaun (far right)

Emil Kapaun was ordained a diocesan priest in 1940; four years later he joined the US Army as a chaplain. In 1950 he was sent to Korea during the Korean War. He bravely served the men fighting by comforting the dying, baptizing, and hearing confessions. Even amid the war, he was able to celebrate Mass on the battlefield by improvising an altar on the front part of an army vehicle.

During the Battle of Unsan, Fr. Kapaun stayed with the wounded men instead of escaping, and he was taken as a prisoner of war. He and the other prisoners had to walk sixty miles in the harsh cold to the prison camp; Fr. Kapaun carried wounded soldiers during the brutal march.

A prisoner for seven months, Fr. Kapaun lived in the prison camp heroically. He raised the morale among prisoners, nursed the sick, gave away his own food, and smuggled medicine for the severely ill. He would sneak into the prisoners' huts at night to pray with them.

Risking his life on Easter in 1951, he secretly celebrated Mass for the other prisoners with a missal he had kept hidden and a crucifix made from sticks. As Fr. Kapaun's own health worsened, he told his fellow soldiers, "I'm going to where I've always wanted to go. And when I get up there, I'll say a prayer for you." When he was being taken away to the place where he would die, he blessed the guards and prayed, "Forgive them, for they know not what they do."

Fr. Kapaun died of malnutrition and pneumonia on May 23, 1951. The United States Congress posthumously awarded him the Medal of Honor, even though he never even fired a gun in combat. Nicknamed the "Shepherd in Combat Boots," Fr. Emil Kapaun has been named "Servant of God," the first step to sainthood.

St. Óscar Romero

St. Óscar Romero of San Salvador was a living example of the grace of episcopal ordination. He was canonized by Pope Francis in Rome on October 14, 2018. Óscar Romero was consecrated archbishop in 1977 in the midst of social, political, and military turmoil in El Salvador that included coups, countercoups, and fraudulent elections. After he found himself saying Mass at the funeral of his friend, Fr. Rutilio Grande, a Jesuit priest who was assassinated as a result of his commitment to the poor and to the social teaching of the Church, Archbishop Romero strongly aligned himself with the poor and with those who were being mistreated. He began a series of weekly radio broadcasts in which he made recent violations of human rights known and called the Church to serve "the God of life rather than the idols of death."

On March 23, 1980, Archbishop Romero appealed directly to the military: "We are your people. The peasants you kill are your own brothers and sisters. When you hear the voice of man commanding you to kill, remember instead the voice of God." The next day while he was saying Mass in the chapel of a hospital where he lived, a single shot rang out from the rear of the chapel and pierced his heart. He died within minutes.

Archbishop Óscar Romero at Mass in San Salvador

ASSIGNMENT

Do the following:

- Research further one of the saintly ordained men profiled in this section, or choose and research another priest, deacon, or bishop who has been canonized or is a candidate for canonization.

- Make a paper poster or an electronic meme with symbols and facts about the man's life. Focus on how his ordination aided his path to sainthood.

SECTION ASSESSMENT

NOTE TAKING

Use the sentences you wrote to help you answer the following questions.

1. What is the "indelible spiritual character" a man receives in Holy Orders?
2. In general, what is the grace of the Holy Spirit for bishops, priests, and deacons given in the Sacrament of Holy Orders?
3. What is the gift of the Holy Spirit specifically for a bishop?
4. What graces does ordination confer on priests?

COMPREHENSION

5. Why can't the grace of the sacraments ever be impeded by the sins of the minister?
6. What are the two promises diocesan priests make to their bishop?
7. How did St. Paul describe priests?

CRITICAL THINKING

8. Explain why this statement is not true: "Through Holy Orders, a bishop or priest becomes a substitute for Christ."

Section Summaries

Focus Question

How is the Sacrament of Holy Orders prepared for and celebrated?

Complete one of the following:

 Research two Catholic seminaries in the United States. Summarize the application requirements for each.

Find out about the specific efforts of the Serra Club and the Knights of Columbus to increase vocations to the priesthood. Name three of their suggestions. Explain how you can personally enact one of the suggestions.

Investigate the meaning of sacred chrism. What is its origin? What is it made of? How should it be blessed? What are its uses and significance in the sacraments?

INTRODUCTION
The Call to the Priesthood

Like all vocations, the call to the priesthood is at God's initiative, but every baptized man should be open to hearing the call. God calls men from varying backgrounds. For some men, the call comes early in life; for others it may be something that enters later on in life. Because the priesthood is for the Church, it is everyone's responsibility to promote vocations to the priesthood. Everyone should pray that men who are called to the priesthood are open to the call.

 Name three ways you can personally help those around you hear the call to the priesthood.

SECTION 1
Preparation for Holy Orders

Answering and discerning God's call to the priesthood is a prayerful and purposeful process. There is a formal procedure for applying to priestly formation. Once accepted, a man spends much of his formation at a seminary. More than just studying or training for a job, priestly development involves human, spiritual, intellectual, and pastoral formation.

Research information on the seminary used by your diocese to train candidates for the priesthood. How does this seminary promote the four areas of a seminarian's formation: human, spiritual, intellectual, and pastoral?

SECTION 2

The Rite of Ordination

For each of the three degrees of the Sacrament of Holy Orders, the essential element of the Rite of Ordination is the laying on of hands accompanied by a special consecratory prayer. Several additional rites accompany the ordination of a new priest, including the administration of a new stole, a sign of order and authority. The rites and symbols of this sacrament illustrate the nature of the vocation to Holy Orders and the consequent calling of every deacon, priest, and bishop.

Read a recent Ordination Class Report listed under "Beliefs and Teachings/Vocations/Priesthood/Ordination Class" at the United States Conference of Catholic Bishops' website (www.usccb.org). Summarize three of its findings.

SECTION 3

Effects of the Sacrament of Holy Orders

The Sacrament of Holy Orders confers an indelible spiritual character upon the soul of the man receiving it. This seal conforms him in a distinctive way to the sacred power of Christ. Those ordained are given the graces to be united to Christ as priest, teacher, and pastor. Bishops receive the grace of strength to govern the Church in prudence and charity. Priests receive the graces to perform the sacraments. Deacons receive the graces of service in the liturgy, in the sharing of the Gospel, and in works of charity.

 Research and cite a scriptural example that shows that a bishop or priest should put service first in exercising his sacred power.

Chapter Assignments

Choose and complete at least one of the three assignments assessing your understanding of the material in this chapter.

1. Document Summary: Priestly Formation

The United States Conference of Catholic Bishops has an in-depth manual for priestly formation called *Program of Priestly Formation*. In the section on "The Formation of Candidates for Priesthood," the bishops explain in detail the four areas of formation for the priesthood.

- Find the *Program of Priestly Formation* on the United States Conference of Catholic Bishops' website, www.usccb.org.

- Pick one of the areas of formation: *human* (paragraphs 74–105); *spiritual* (paragraphs 106–135); *intellectual* (paragraphs 136–235); or *pastoral* (paragraphs 236–257).

- Read about the area of formation you chose, and summarize your reading in a two-page report.

2. Art Project: Images of Priesthood

Choose and create one of the following art projects in celebration of priesthood:

- Read Jesus' description of the Good Shepherd in John 10:1–30. Using any medium (e.g., painting, drawing, photography, etc.) create an art project that depicts this passage while also incorporating your own classic or contemporary image of the Good Shepherd.

- Research images that appear on the chalices of priests. Using these for prototypes, design two images of your own that could appear on a priest's chalice. Use any acceptable media for drawing.

- Design two media advertisements that might be used as part of your local diocesan vocations office to encourage young men to consider a priestly vocation. Possible ideas for media: a poster, an internet web feed, a screenshot that could be used on a website, or a social media platform. Use both images and words in your presentations.

3. One-on-One Interviews with Priests from Two Generations

Arrange to interview two priests (preferably in person, but by phone if necessary) from two different generations. Choose one priest who was ordained within the past ten years and one priest who has been ordained for over twenty years. Take written notes during the interviews or, with the priests' permission, make an audio or video recording of your discussion. Ask each priest to describe for you

- his call to the priesthood;

- his experience in the seminary; and

- his remembrance of his ordination.

Write a three-page report that compares the different experiences. As part of the report, include a short biography of each priest. *Optional*: Turn in the audio or video recording of the interview with your report.

Faithful Disciple

St. Philip Neri

Philip Neri was born in Florence, Italy, in 1515 at the height of the Renaissance, but he lived most of his life in Rome. There was always a lighter side to Philip; he had a colorful sense of humor as a child that carried into adulthood. One of four children, Philip was called *"Pippo buono"* for "good little Phil" by his family.

Philip was sent to live with a cousin in Rome at age eighteen. He spent about two years there studying theology and philosophy. Then one day he suddenly left his cousin's home and began to live as a type of hermit. Often he would wander the streets at night to find a place to pray. His favorite place was at the catacombs of San Sebastiano. Once, while praying in the catacombs, he had an experience in which it felt as though a globe of light entered his mouth and sank into his heart. This experience motivated him further to serve God. He went out into the streets and began to preach about God to anyone and everyone, from rich to poor.

St. Philip Neri

Philip's usual question to those he encountered was "Well, brothers, when shall we begin to do good?" He then showed them a way. For example, he would take his companions to visit the sick in hospitals or to pray in the Seven Churches of Rome (the four major basilicas and three of the minor basilicas). The total distance between these churches was about twelve miles. One of Philip's favorite days to make this pilgrimage was on Fat Tuesday, a day of partying before the start of Lent. He would arrange for music and a picnic for those who walked with him. He felt that the pilgrims would be too tired to drink to excess if they spent the day and evening with him.

At the age of thirty-four, Philip became convinced that his work would be even more effective if he became a priest. He was ordained on May 23, 1551. He lived at San Girolamo Church and spent most of his days hearing confessions. A steady stream of men and women would come to be counseled by him and receive the Sacrament of Penance. Philip made himself available to anyone, day or night. "They can chop wood on my back as long as they do not sin," he said.

Eventually a large room was built over the nave at San Girolamo so that Philip could have a place to receive visitors more easily. Several other priests joined Philip in his ministry in this *oratory* (a private chapel). These were the predecessors of a new religious congregation that St. Philip would found a few years later, the Priests of the Oratory.

Philip remained a teacher at heart. His lessons were personalized and often contained the subtle, sometimes silly humor he had always been known for. When one of his priests gave a well-received sermon, Philip told him to give the same sermon six weeks in a row so the people would think he only had one sermon. He always sought to attract attention on the streets. He was known for wearing outlandish clothing; once he even shaved half his beard. On one occasion, some visitors who had traveled a great distance to see him found him laughing as another priest read to him from a joke book.

Philip was never distracted or without time to pray. When asked how to pray, he said, simply, "Be humble and obedient and the Holy Spirit will teach you."

Philip Neri died in 1595 at the age of eighty. His feast day is May 26.

 # Reading Comprehension

1. Why did Philip suddenly leave his cousin's home?

2. What did Philip begin to do after he had an experience at prayer of a globe of light entering his body?

3. Why did Philip think Fat Tuesday was a good time to make a pilgrimage between the Seven Churches in Rome?

4. What is the name of the religious congregation founded by St. Philip Neri?

 # Writing Task

St. Philip Neri was known his entire life for his joyful and bright disposition. He once said, "Excessive sadness seldom springs from any other source than pride." Write one paragraph explaining what you think St. Philip Neri meant by these words.

Explaining the Faith

What are the reasons for priestly celibacy?

In the Latin Church, only men who have made a commitment to celibacy and who intend to remain celibate may be ordained priests and bishops. There are many reasons for this practice of the Church, but the key is that priestly celibacy is "for the sake of the kingdom of heaven" (Mt 19:12). Celibacy is not an end in itself; it points to something greater. Since priests stand *in persona Christi Capitis*, they are a witness of Christ's total self-gift to his Bride, the Church. By remaining celibate, priests are more fully conformed to Christ.

Called to give themselves with an "undivided heart to the Lord and to 'the affairs of the Lord,' [priests] give themselves entirely to God and to men" (*CCC*, 1579). Their celibacy frees them to live the law of self-giving for the People of God, the Church. While the presence of married priests in the early history of the Church and in the Eastern Churches today shows that celibacy is not demanded of priests by the nature of the Sacrament of Holy Orders, it is also clear that Christ recommended a commitment to celibacy for the sake of the Kingdom of Heaven by his own example (he did not marry) and in his own words: "Some are incapable of marriage because they were born so; some, because they were made so by others; some, because they have renounced marriage for the sake of the kingdom of heaven. Whoever can accept this ought to accept it" (Mt 19:12).

In his letters, St. Paul expressed that celibacy for the sake of the Kingdom was the preferred or superior state of life for those who were able to keep it. "Indeed, I wish everyone to be as I am, but each has a particular gift from God, one of one kind and one of another. Now to the unmarried and to widows, I say: It is a good thing for them to remain as they are, as I do" (1 Cor 7:7–8).

Celibacy for priests in the Catholic Church is a discipline, not a doctrine. While the practice of celibacy in the Latin Rite for priests dates from the time of Christ, it was not made mandatory for priests until the Second Lateran Council in 1139. The Second Vatican Council reconfirmed the Church's mandate of celibacy for the priesthood "provided that those who participate in the priesthood of Christ through the sacrament of Orders . . . humbly and fervently pray for it" and "exhorts all priests . . . that they magnanimously and wholeheartedly adhere to it" (*Presbyterorum Ordinis*, 16).

The following are some other reasons that celibacy is a wonderful gift for the ordained that enriches their ministry:

- It allows priests to more easily dedicate themselves to Christ and to the service of God. Celibacy frees a person from family obligations and therefore allows priests and bishops to give themselves totally to the Lord and to the Church. However, it would be shortsighted to say that priests should not be married just so they have more time to work for the Church. Remaining celibate does allow a man a certain freedom of availability for his people, but the call to celibacy should not be reduced to this: celibacy at its core is about an intimacy with Christ.

- By not marrying, a priest is a living sign of the heaven where there will be no marriage and Christ will be the Church's only spouse.

- Jesus spoke of the requirements of discipleship. Along with the willingness to give up one's life for his sake and the sake of the Gospel, forsaking the blessings of a spouse and a family is a dramatic step of acceptance of being a disciple. Jesus said, "And everyone who has given up houses or brothers or sisters or father or mother or children or lands for the sake of my name will receive a hundred times more, and will inherit eternal life" (Mt 19:29).

The Eastern Churches have practiced a different discipline regarding married clergy for many centuries. Married men can be ordained priests and deacons, while bishops are chosen solely from among celibate men. Nonetheless, priestly celibacy is still held in great honor in the Eastern Church, and many priests have freely chosen it. As in the Latin Church, a man who has already received the Sacrament of Holy Orders cannot then get married later.

You may know that there are some married priests in the Latin Church. These are rare exceptions for certain Anglican or Orthodox priests who have converted to Catholicism and wish to be priests in the Catholic Church. Those ordained to the permanent diaconate may also be married.

 # Further Research

Read paragraphs 1579 and 1580 of the *Catechism of the Catholic Church*. Answer the following question: What do you think it means to serve the Lord with "undivided heart"?

Prayer
Prayer for an Increase in Vocations to the Priesthood

Almighty and Eternal God, in your plan for our salvation you provide priests as shepherds for your people.

Inspire men to answer your call to become priests, because "the harvest is abundant but the laborers are few."

Grant your Church an increase of priests, and keep them faithful in their love and service to you and
the people entrusted to their care.

Through their faith and ministry may your light shine in the world and your kingdom be built among us.

Through Jesus Christ, our High Priest.

Amen.

THE
VOCATION
TO CONSECRATED LIFE

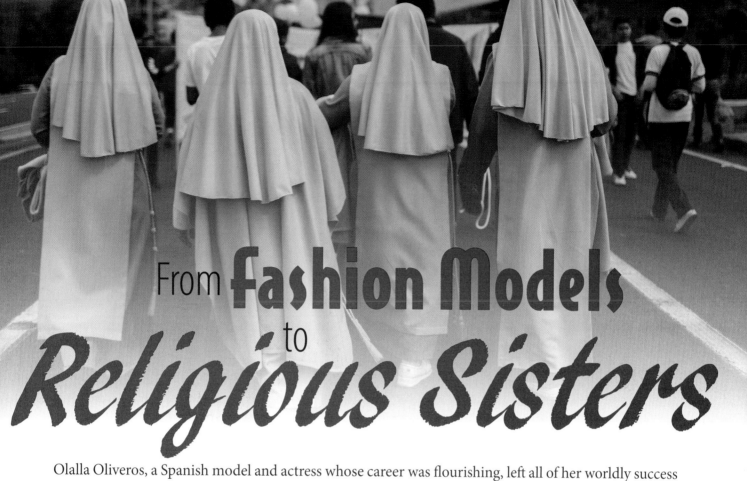

From **Fashion Models** to *Religious Sisters*

Olalla Oliveros, a Spanish model and actress whose career was flourishing, left all of her worldly success to enter the Order of St. Michael. She switched the designer clothes she had donned on billboards across Spain for a traditional blue habit, the clothing of religious sisters.

Her radical change was initially prompted by a visit to the shrine of Our Lady of Fatima in Portugal. There she had a powerful experience and could not stop imagining herself dressed as a sister. Even though she had just been offered a role in a movie, Oliveros realized that this was a call from the Lord to enter the religious life. She says, "The Lord is never wrong. He asked if I will follow him, and I could not refuse."[1] Her name is now Sr. Olalla del Sí de Maria, which means "Sr. Olalla of the Yes of Mary."

In 2005, famous Colombian model Amada Rosa Pérez also left the fast-paced world of modeling to become a religious sister. "Being a model means being a benchmark, someone whose beliefs are worthy of being imitated, and I grew tired of being a model of superficiality," Perez says. She continues,

> I grew tired of a world of lies, appearances, falsity, hypocrisy and deception, a society full of anti-values that exalts violence, adultery, drugs, alcohol, fighting, and a world that exalts riches, pleasure, sexual immorality and fraud. I want to be a model that promotes the true dignity of women and not their being used for commercial purposes.[2]

Though the majority of religious sisters have not previously been models, most come to the religious life following the direction of Christ himself: "For whoever wishes to save his life will lose it, but whoever loses his life for my sake and that of the gospel will save it" (Mk 8:35).

FOCUS QUESTION

Why do some people choose a **CONSECRATED LIFE**, taking public vows to observe the **EVANGELICAL COUNSELS** of **POVERTY, CHASTITY, AND OBEDIENCE?**

Chapter Overview

INTRODUCTION
Consecrated to Christ

MAIN IDEA
The vocation to the consecrated life is for those who dedicate and unite their lives more closely to Christ by taking vows of poverty, chastity, and obedience.

According to a common message ingrained in people today, the ultimate purpose in life is to have a good career, be independent, make money, own a home, and so forth—all of which can be good, of course. That some people—including successful models—leave all of that for a life of a poverty, chastity, and obedience goes completely against many people's understanding of success.

Yet you have to remember the crucial lesson from Chapter 1: God wants you to be happy, and since he knows you better than you know yourself, his path will always lead you to greater fulfillment than the path you set for yourself. Throughout the history of the Church, countless men and women have abandoned the comforts of their previous lives to embrace very different lives that may seem confusing to those on the outside but that unite them to God in a way that brings them the kind of happiness the fleeting things of this world could never offer.

This vocation is to the **consecrated life**. Every baptized person is actually consecrated to God, set apart

> **consecrated life** A permanent state of life recognized by the Church and chosen freely by men and women in response to Christ's call to perfection. It is characterized by profession of the evangelical counsels of poverty, chastity, and obedience.

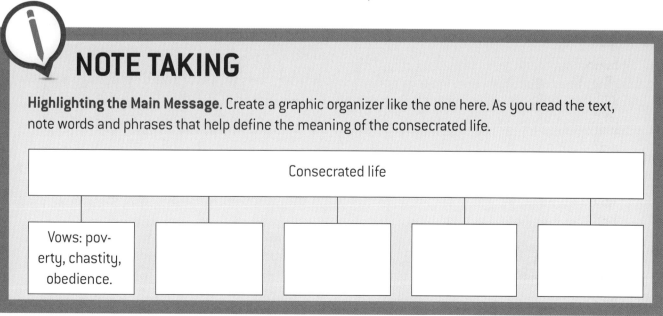

NOTE TAKING

Highlighting the Main Message. Create a graphic organizer like the one here. As you read the text, note words and phrases that help define the meaning of the consecrated life.

Consecrated life				
Vows: poverty, chastity, obedience.				

for the holy purpose of union with him. However, those who choose to embrace the vocation to the consecrated life through a profession of **vows** live out this holy purpose in a more intimate and unique manner.

There are various forms of the consecrated life, which you will learn more about in this chapter, but all are defined and marked (in most cases) by the public profession of the evangelical counsels of poverty, chastity and obedience (see Section 2). The *Catechism of the Catholic Church* explains, "Already dedicated to him through Baptism, the person who surrenders himself to the God he loves above all else thereby consecrates himself more intimately to God's service and to the good of the Church" (*CCC*, 931). Those called to the consecrated life vow to Christ that they will live their lives simply and dedicated exclusively to him.

Consecrated Life Is an Eschatological Sign

One of the essential characteristics of the consecrated life is the call to celibacy, "for the sake of the Kingdom" (*CCC*, 915). In making this commitment, those who enter the consecrated life do not reject the good of marriage; in fact, they value marriage very highly. Recall that marriage (and especially the sexual act) is a sign that points to heaven. The complete self-gift shared between the husband and wife images both the inner life of the Trinity and the union of Christ and his Church. In this way, marriage is a sign that points to everyone's ultimate vocation to eternal life in heaven, in which all who merit it will be united with Christ in a mystical nuptial union.

St. Gertrude of Nivelles (Belgium) practiced what is known as "nuptial mysticism," seeing herself as the bride of Christ.

Those called to celibacy in the consecrated life choose to "skip" the earthly sign of marriage and *live what the sign points to*: that is, intimate, total union with Christ. You may have heard **religious sisters** described as "brides of Christ." This is a very apt title, in that they live the heavenly marriage with Christ as their bridegroom. This is why the consecrated life is called an **eschatological sign**. Pope John Paul II

vows Acts of devotion in which a person dedicates himself or herself to God or promises God some good work. A vow is "a deliberate and free promise made to God concerning a possible and better good which must be fulfilled by reason of the virtue of religion" (*CCC*, Glossary). Religious women and men typically take vows of poverty, chastity, and obedience.
religious sisters Members of a religious order or congregation of women devoted to active service and/or contemplation. Members typically take vows of poverty, chastity and obedience.
eschatological sign Something that points to eternal life.

explained the eschatological nature of the consecrated life in his apostolic exhortation on the consecrated life, *Vita Consecrata (On the Consecrated Life)*: "The consecrated life proclaims and in a certain way anticipates the future age, when the fullness of the Kingdom of heaven, already present in its first fruits and in mystery, will be achieved, and when the children of the resurrection will take neither wife nor husband, but will be like the angels of God (cf. Mt 22:30)" (*VC*, 32). Sr. Helena Burns, F.S.P., affirms that consecrated persons are "walking eschatological signs" whose presence should not intimidate others, but rather remind them of the eternal life to come.

God is the spouse of every soul, the spouse of my soul. . . . It's so great to remember that God is so close to us, so real that he calls some to be exclusively his. God can be enough for us, truly fill our needs and make us happy. He can be trusted with our entire lives. Oh, and [the religious sister] reminds me that this isn't all there is—we're all headed to the wedding feast of heaven![3]

Those who choose celibacy and the consecrated life witness to everyone that there is more than just the here-and-now of this life. In a sense, they live "heaven on earth." Thus, the consecrated state is an objectively

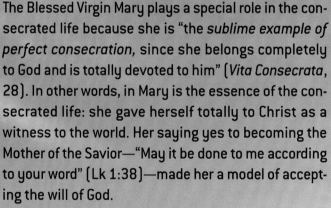

The Model of Mary: Consecration and Discipleship

The Blessed Virgin Mary plays a special role in the consecrated life because she is "the *sublime example of perfect consecration,* since she belongs completely to God and is totally devoted to him" (*Vita Consecrata,* 28). In other words, in Mary is the essence of the consecrated life: she gave herself totally to Christ as a witness to the world. Her saying yes to becoming the Mother of the Savior—"May it be done to me according to your word" (Lk 1:38)—made her a model of accepting the will of God.

Not only is Mary a model for the consecrated life but she is also an intercessor and example for all who want to follow Jesus, to be his disciples. She lived a quietly devoted life with Jesus and Joseph, and she was with Jesus at the critical moments of his public life. In this, "the Blessed Virgin teaches unconditional discipleship and diligent service" (*Vita Consecrata,* 28).

ASSIGNMENT

On the Cross, Jesus said to his beloved disciple, John, "Behold, your mother!" (Jn 19:27). In those words, Jesus gave his mother to all Christians. Thoughtfully complete the following items in your journal:

- Answer: In what ways can you allow Mary to be your mother?

- Compose a personal prayer in which you ask Mary to help you in your self-gift of discipleship to her Son, Jesus.

"higher" calling, in that those who live it are living what every person is ultimately called to. Looking to the example of the consecrated life should deepen and strengthen your own faith journey.

The consecrated life is also a living memorial of Jesus' own way of living and acting. The *Catechism of the Catholic Church* describes how the consecrated life shows everyone in the Church how to fully live out Christ's redemption: "In the Church . . . the consecrated life is seen as a special sign of the mystery of redemption. To follow and imitate Christ more nearly and to manifest more clearly his self-emptying is to be more deeply present to one's contemporaries, in the heart of Christ" (*CCC*, 932).

In their renunciation of many of the goods of the world (marriage, material possessions, etc.), those in the consecrated vocation show the world that Christ alone can indeed satisfy every longing of your heart. In their confidence in the promise of eternal life, they live a radical commitment to the reality that there is more to human existence than what can be seen in the physical world. As a "window" to what will come in heaven, they are a reminder to every person of humanity's eternal destiny.

SECTION ASSESSMENT

NOTE TAKING

Use the graphic organizer you completed to help you answer the following questions.

1. What distinguishes the vocation to the consecrated life from the consecration of all the baptized?
2. What does it mean to say that the consecrated life is an *eschatological sign*?
3. What does the consecrated life proclaim and anticipate?
4. How does the consecrated life show everyone in the Church how to fully live out Christ's redemption?

COMPREHENSION

5. Why are *religious sisters* sometimes described as "brides of Christ"?

CRITICAL THINKING

6. If the consecrated life does not reject the goodness of marriage, what is its relationship to marriage?

REFLECTION

7. How does witnessing the consecrated life factor into your own faith journey?

SECTION 1
Historical Development of the Consecrated Life

MAIN IDEA
The consecrated life has developed from individuals seeking a radical and solitary path of discipleship to more structured and diverse and often communal forms of consecrated life today.

The origins of the consecrated life are with Jesus himself, in that he was perfectly poor, both spiritually and materially; chaste; and obedient. Christ's entire life was consecrated, or set apart, to do the will of the Father. After his Ascension, the Apostles lived and acted in community, an early foundation for the religious life. The letters of St. Paul cite specific groupings in the early Church and clearly distinguished virgins and widows. There are references in second-century writings to women who consecrated their virginity to Christ.

Eremitic Life

A major development for the consecrated life emerged after the widespread persecution of Christians ended in the early fourth century. Before Constantine's Edict of Milan made Christianity a legal religion in the Roman Empire, all Christians lived with the strong possibility that they could be martyred for their faith. After Christianity became legal and the threat of martyrdom diminished, many Christians sought new ways to live a fervent faith and practice radical discipleship. Some, both men and women, left mainstream society

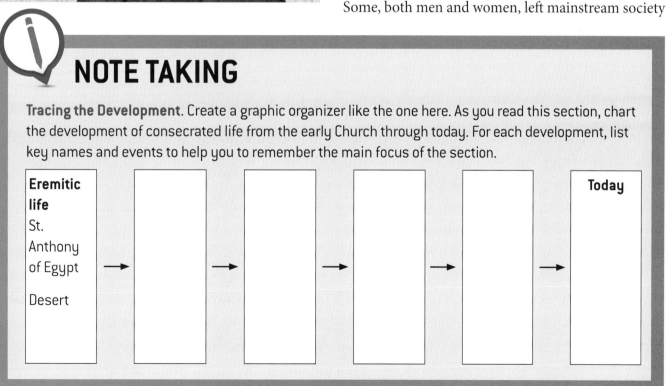

NOTE TAKING

Tracing the Development. Create a graphic organizer like the one here. As you read this section, chart the development of consecrated life from the early Church through today. For each development, list key names and events to help you to remember the main focus of the section.

Eremitic life St. Anthony of Egypt Desert	→		→		→		→		→		Today

and retreated into the desert, where they prayed and fasted in severe penance. Eventually, these individual **hermits** formed communities in which they lived an eremitic life. *Eremitic* is an ancient word referring to a hermit or religious recluse.

The most famous of these hermits was St. Anthony of Egypt (251–356). At the age of twenty, he inherited a large estate from his family. Soon afterward, he heard the Scripture call to "go, sell what you have and give to [the] poor" (Mt 19:21), and took it as intended for himself. He retreated to the desert, practiced *asceticism* (the renunciation of worldly pleasures), and became a model of ardent prayer and humility. Although he faced many temptations, St. Anthony persevered in his life of secluded devotion. Many others were inspired by St. Anthony and came to live near him, but not necessarily in direct community with him. His story was recorded by St. Athanasius, the bishop of Alexandria, and was read by a great number of men and women who wanted to live the life of a hermit.

A sermon by St. Ambrose (left) helped to convince St. Augustine (right) to convert to Christianity.

Rule of St. Augustine

Soon, out of the necessity for safety and to aid in the convenience of securing food and water, hermits began to live communally. Actual *monasteries* (residences for communities of men) and *convents* (residences for communities of women) began to form in the desert and across the Christian lands. In the late fourth century, an Egyptian man named Pachomius, a contemporary of St. Anthony, started a model for a common way of life, in which the consecrated persons prayed together and shared all goods in common. Around the same time, St. Basil established monasteries in what

is now Turkey. Many of these monks also engaged in teaching and other pastoral care.

Also, some bishops began encouraging their priests to live near the monks. The priests and monks would share common property, prayer, and meals and sometimes would even live at the monastery. These priests were called *canons*, which comes from a Greek word that means "rule" or "standard." One such bishop who gathered these canons together was St. Augustine, bishop of Hippo, a city in what is now Algeria. In about the year 400 he wrote what became known as the Rule of St. Augustine. All communities of bishops and priests who followed this rule would come to be known as "canons regular." St. Augustine wrote about such topics as poverty, obedience, detachment from the world, the duties of superiors and inferiors, prayer in common, fasting, care of the sick, and the appropriate times for silence.[4] This rule of monastic

> **hermits** Those who separate themselves from the world in prayer and penance in order to be devoted to the praise of God and the salvation of the world.

The *Rule* of *St. Benedict*

Although St. Benedict's famous rule was intended primarily for monks and nuns, many passages are still strikingly apropos for the laity in the modern world.

ASSIGNMENT

Read all of the following quotations from the Rule of St. Benedict. Choose one that stands out to you, and write a paragraph about how it applies to your life right now. Be as specific as possible.

- "Run while you have the light of life, lest the darkness of death overtake you." (Prologue)

- "The first degree of humility is obedience without delay." (Chapter 5)

- "One who never stops talking cannot avoid falling into sin." (Chapter 6)

- "The sleepy like to make excuses." (Chapter 22)

- "Idleness is the enemy of the soul." (Chapter 48)

- "Let all guests who arrive be received like Christ, for he is going to say, 'I came as a guest, and you received me' (Mt 25:35)." (Chapter 53)

---

life influenced the future of monasticism, and there are even religious orders today, including the Augustinians, that follow the Rule of St. Augustine.

Monasticism

Although monasteries and convents existed from the beginning of eremitic life, they flourished and became more structured with St. Benedict of Nursia (480–547), who is known as the "Father of Western Monasticism." St. Benedict founded an important monastery at Monte Cassino, Italy. He also helped his twin sister, St. Scholastica, form a convent nearby. The Rule of St. Benedict became the standard for monastic living for centuries to come, even into the twenty-first century. His rule promoted a more moderate life of

prayer, work, simplicity, hospitality, and obedience under one *abbot*, the name for a person who is the head of an abbey of monks. His famous phrase *ora et labora* means "prayer and work," the two occupations that were the cornerstone of his rule.

Because of their dedication to the study and preservation of Scripture and other sacred texts, Benedictine monasteries and convents in many ways helped preserve Christian history and culture over the ensuing years of political and societal disorder. The larger monasteries became important centers of their regions. They often had hospitals, schools, guesthouses, and farms associated with them. Other monastic orders, such as the Carthusians and the Cistercians (Trappists), that emerged later traced their roots to the Benedictines.

Mendicant Orders

Prior to the twelfth century, all consecrated persons primarily stayed near their monasteries or convents. If they ministered to the sick or taught others, it was generally done within close proximity to where they lived. In fact, one of the vows Benedictines took was of stability; it was a promise to remain in community at their chosen monastery. However, in the thirteenth century certain religious communities began to emerge that went out into the cities and towns to proclaim the Gospel and attend to the needs of the poor. They are known as *mendicant orders*. The word *mendicant* means "given to begging." Members of these orders were required to beg for their own needs like food and clothing.

St. Dominic de Guzmán and St. Francis of Assisi were two prominent founders of mendicant orders. In the face of a rampant heresy of the time that questioned the very nature of God and the human person, St. Dominic, a Castilian priest, responded to the call for bold, true preaching. In 1216, he formed the Order of Preachers (known as the Dominicans), a religious order that focused on preaching and teaching the ultimate truth of Christ and his Church. An influential Dominican from this period was St. Thomas Aquinas, one of the greatest theologians in the history of the Church.

Around this same time, St. Francis of

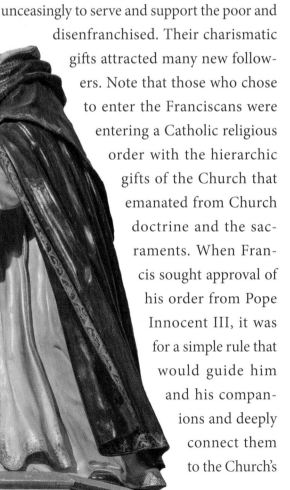

St. Francis of Assisi and St. Dominic de Guzmán were contemporaries in the thirteenth century.

Assisi, son of an Italian merchant, rejected the wealth and prestige of his youth and answered the call of God to "rebuild my Church," both literally, in that he rebuilt the chapel of San Damiano, and—more importantly—spiritually. He lived a life of complete poverty and detachment from the world and traveled around his native Italy preaching a return to God and obedience to his Church. He gained many companions, all of whom joined in his remarkable embrace of the Gospel. His Order of Friars Minor (one of the branches of which would come to be known as the Franciscans) was officially approved in 1209 by Pope Innocent III.

Men and women began to be drawn to these barefoot beggars who were enraptured by the joy of Christ. The Franciscans had unique charisms; the one that stands out is the charism of poverty. Franciscans lived lives in solidarity with the poor—including the extreme practice of begging—and they worked unceasingly to serve and support the poor and disenfranchised. Their charismatic gifts attracted many new followers. Note that those who chose to enter the Franciscans were entering a Catholic religious order with the hierarchic gifts of the Church that emanated from Church doctrine and the sacraments. When Francis sought approval of his order from Pope Innocent III, it was for a simple rule that would guide him and his companions and deeply connect them to the Church's larger mission of following Christ's "precepts of charity, humility, and self-denial" (*CCC*, 168 quoting *Lumen Gentium*, 5) while sowing the seeds of God's Kingdom on earth. The Franciscans enacted their unique charismatic gifts always in service of the Church.

The Dominicans and Franciscans, along with the other orders founded during this time, including the Carmelites and the Augustinians, still exist today in various forms and branches.

The Jesuits and Other Religious Orders Dedicated to Service

St. Ignatius of Loyola was a Spanish soldier who had a dramatic conversion to God while in recovery from battle wounds. He founded the Society of Jesus in 1540. Known as the Jesuits, this order became so widespread that, by the time of its founder's death in 1556, it had more than one thousand members and had established thirty-five schools. Out of his own religious experience, St. Ignatius created the Spiritual Exercises, a prayerful contemplation on the life of Christ that guides one

St. Ignatius of Loyola

to better discern and follow God's will in one's own life. The Spiritual Exercises form the foundation for the Jesuit way of life. The Jesuits established many missions, such as those to India and Japan spearheaded by St. Francis Xavier. The Jesuits were also known for their dedication to education, which continues today.

Over the centuries, many other religious orders and congregations have formed. Many of these new communities emphasized service to the poor and *catechesis*, the systematic teaching of the Catholic faith. In 1633, St. Vincent de Paul and his associate St. Louise de Marillac formed the first community of sisters who were not **cloistered**. Following a similar rule, St. Elizabeth Ann Seton (see the image in the Main Idea at the beginning of this Section) formed the first religious community of women in the United States in 1812. The schools they founded were the beginning of the parochial school system in America.

Consecrated Life Today

Consecrated life today is quite varied. The majority of consecrated men and women are part of religious orders or communities; these are the men and women who are considered part of the "religious life." They include professed **religious brothers** and sisters, as well as priests who are part of religious communities. Other names for religious sisters and brothers are **nuns** and **monks**; monks are sometimes also priests. It is important to note that while sometimes the titles "sister" and "nun" are used interchangeably, this is technically incorrect. A nun is a *type* of sister, specifically a sister who is cloistered, which means she never leaves her convent or monastery. If a sister is considered "active" (see Section 3), such as one who teaches or works in a hospital, she is not considered a nun.

> **cloistered** Term used to describe monks or nuns who strive for religious perfection within the confines of a monastery; comes from "cloister," the part of a monastery reserved only for the monks or nuns who reside in that monastery.
>
> **religious brothers** Men who take religious vows, usually vows of poverty, chastity, and obedience. A brother is not ordained to the priesthood.
>
> **nuns** Women religious living a cloistered, contemplative life in a monastery.
>
> **monks** Male members of a monastic or contemplative order.

For examples of contemporary religious communities, see "A Sampling of Religious Life Today."

Other Forms of Consecrated Life

Religious life is the most common form of consecrated life, but there are some consecrated lifestyles that do not require that a person be a fully professed member of a religious community.

One example is *consecrated virgins*. These are women who live a life of vowed perpetual virginity but remain laypeople and support themselves. They are consecrated by their local bishop to their diocese. The *Catechism of the Catholic Church* explains, "by this solemn rite (*Consecratio Virginum*), the virgin is 'constituted . . . a sacred person, a transcendent sign of the Church's love for Christ, and an eschatological image of this heavenly Bride of Christ and of the life to come'" (*CCC*, 923, quoting *Ordo Consecrationis Virginum*, *Praenotanda* 1). Consecrated virgins support the clergy through prayer and sacrifice. St. Agnes, St. Cecilia, St. Lucy, and St. Agatha are well-known virgin martyrs from the early centuries of Christianity. In many cases, today's consecrated virgins hold secular jobs in the world but maintain a special intimacy with Christ because of their consecration.

Secular institutes provide a form of consecrated life for single laypeople and diocesan priests. Members profess the evangelical counsels but do not take public vows and do not live in community. Secular institutes usually take on a special focus; for example, the Mission of Our Lady of Bethany, founded in 1948 in France, works and prays to bring God's love to the most rejected of society, including prostitutes and prisoners. Above all, those in secular institutes "share in the Church's task of evangelization, 'in the world and from within the world,' where their presence acts as 'leaven in the world'" (*CCC*, 929, quoting Pius XII,

Bishop William A. Wack, C.S.C., left, of the Diocese of Pensacola–Tallahassee, Florida, and Fr. Neil Wack, C.S.C., are pictured in St. Mary Cathedral after a Mass at which their niece Jennifer Sergio, center, became a consecrated virgin.

Provida Mater). There are more than thirty recognized secular institutes in the United States. Some are for men only or women only. Others have members who are laymen and laywomen and priests.

Also standing alongside the consecrated life are *societies of apostolic life*, whose members do not take public vows but engage in many good works for the Church. They "lead a life as brothers or sisters in common according to a particular manner of life, [and] strive for the perfection of charity through the observance of the constitutions" (*CCC*, 930). Sometimes members of societies of apostolic life profess the evangelical counsels, but they do not do so in a public way. A society of apostolic life needs the approval of the local bishop to operate within a diocese.

A SAMPLING of RELIGIOUS LIFE Today

The expressions of religious life today are quite varied. They all have a profession of the evangelical counsels and an eschatological witness as their basis, but they differ greatly in their **apostolates** and charisms. Below is a very small sampling of some of the religious communities thriving in the United States today.

RELIGIOUS SISTERS OF MERCY (R.S.M.)

The Religious Sisters of Mercy are dedicated to the spiritual and corporal works of mercy. They were founded by Ven. Catherine McAuley in Ireland in 1827. Catherine's original mission was to gather a group of lay social workers. The archbishop of Dublin asked her to form a religious community instead. Today, the Religious Sisters of Mercy serve the "poor, sick, and ignorant," primarily in the areas of health care and education. Because of the community's apostolate, many of the sisters are licensed medical physicians, such as family practice doctors, surgeons, and psychiatrists. This means that these sisters went through the intensity of medical school and residency while in their formation for religious life.

> **apostolates** From the word *apostle*; the activity of the Christian that works to extend the reign of Christ to the entire world (see CCC, Glossary). Apostolates include teaching, ministering to the sick, and many other tasks.

New York City mayor Bill DeBlasio (left) and Cardinal Timothy Dolan of New York meet with Friar Herald Brock after announcing a partnership to serve the homeless with the Franciscan Friars of Renewal.

FRANCISCAN FRIARS OF THE RENEWAL (C.F.R.)

This community of both religious brothers and religious priests (founded in 1987) tries to embrace the Gospel with the fervor of St. Francis of Assisi. The two main pillars of their apostolate are evangelization and working with the poor, especially the materially poor. They are often found in the most impoverished areas of cities. Some expressions of their apostolate are street evangelization, staffing missionary centers for the poor, young adult retreats, and parish missions. They serve primarily in urban areas such as the Bronx, New York, and Albuquerque, New Mexico, and even internationally in countries such as Nicaragua and Ireland.

SISTERS OF LIFE

Cardinal John O'Connor of the Archdiocese of New York founded the Sisters of Life in 1991 to help uphold the dignity of human life. In addition to the traditional evangelical counsels, the Sisters of Life take a fourth vow to protect and enhance the sacredness of human life. They pray for life and aim for a reverence and gratitude for the gift of every human being, made in the image and likeness of God. The sisters work in many areas, including serving pregnant women in need of a place to live and practical assistance, leading retreats for those who need spiritual healing after an abortion,

and acting as Respect Life coordinators for the Archdiocese of New York's Family Life Office.

DISCALCED CARMELITE NUNS (O.C.D.)

Following in the tradition of St. Teresa of Avila, there are several cloistered Carmelite convents for nuns in the United States and worldwide. Carmelite nuns live their lives in solitude, completely dedicated to prayer and union with Christ. Their prayer is not only for their own intimacy with God but also for the needs of the Church and all people. Often these nuns will have work within the cloister that supports their needs, such as gardening. Their days have a rhythm of liturgical prayer, personal prayer, work, and recreation.

The Discalced Carmelite nuns typically speak only in prayer.

POOR HANDMAIDS OF JESUS CHRIST (P.H.J.C.)

Founded in Derbach, Germany, in 1851 by St. Catherine Kasper, the Poor Handmaids of Jesus Christ came to the United States in the aftermath of the Civil War at the request of the bishop of Fort Wayne, Indiana, to minister to the many German-speaking immigrants in the region.

The Poor Handmaids were also called to Chicago, Illinois, to serve in a German orphanage. They ministered at the Angel Guardian Orphanage from 1868 until it closed in 1978. They also founded the congregation's first hospital in the United States, St. Joseph Hospital, in Fort Wayne in 1869.

Today the motherhouse of the Poor Handmaids of Jesus Christ is in Donaldson, Indiana, where the sisters sponsor several ministries, including a retirement center for seniors, a farm, a retreat center, and Ancilla College. The sisters also minister in education, spiritual, pastoral, and home care ministries throughout the Midwest.

DOMINICANS OF THE PROVINCE OF ST. JOSEPH (O.P.)

In the tradition of St. Dominic, the Dominicans of the Province of St. Joseph are religious priests (also known as "clerical brothers") and religious brothers (also known as "cooperator brothers") who follow the mission of the Dominicans for preaching and the salvation

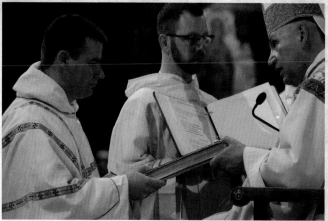

The ordination of religious priests of the Dominicans of the Province of St. Joseph

of souls. They dedicate themselves to study, prayer, and preaching in order to be effective instruments of the saving mission of Jesus. They serve as teachers, parish priests, hospital chaplains, itinerant preachers, and campus ministers. Although most of their priories are in the eastern part of the United States, they also serve internationally in such places as Nairobi, Kenya.

SECTION ASSESSMENT

NOTE TAKING

Use the graphic organizer you created to help you answer the following questions.

1. Which came first, the Rule of St. Augustine or the Rule of St. Benedict?

2. What is meant by the term "canons regular"?

3. How do you think St. Benedict's *ora et labora* changed monastic life?

4. What new aspect did mendicant orders bring to consecrated life?

5. St. Vincent de Paul and St. Louise de Marillac formed the first community of sisters that wasn't cloistered. What did that mean?

6. What is an example of a form of consecrated life today in which a person can remain a lay person and continue to support himself or herself?

continued on next page

continued from previous page

COMPREHENSION

Match the name of the saint with his or her description.

7. _____ St. Anthony of Egypt

8. _____ St. Augustine

9. _____ St. Benedict

10. _____ St. Dominic

11. _____ St. Francis of Assisi

12. _____ St. Ignatius of Loyola

13. _____ St. Vincent de Paul and St. Louise de Marillac

14. _____ St. Elizabeth Ann Seton

A. Founded the first religious community of women in the United States.

B. Founded one of the first mendicant orders, the Order of Friars Minor.

C. One of the most famous of the early hermits.

D. The "Father of Western Monasticism"; established a rule for monastic life that became the standard for centuries to come, even to today.

E. Founded one of the first mendicant orders, the Order of Preachers.

F. Founded the first community of sisters that was not cloistered.

G. Founded the Society of Jesus, known as the Jesuits.

H. As bishop, encouraged his priests to live in community; wrote one of the first rules for religious life.

CRITICAL THINKING

15. Why did some Christians seek an eremitic life after Roman persecution of Christians ended?

16. What is the difference between a nun and a sister?

SECTION 2
The Evangelical Counsels

It has already been noted that what defines the consecrated life is a public profession of the three evangelical counsels: poverty, chastity, and obedience. This section takes a deeper look at these three vows. The word *evangelical* comes from the Latin word *evangelium*, which means "gospel" or "good news." The origin of these counsels, or proposals for living, is with the Good News of Christ himself.

Jesus lived the perfection of poverty, chastity, and obedience. Therefore, when consecrated persons live these vows, in essence they are imitating Christ and showing the world the way to perfection. In leaving their ordinary lives behind and sharing a unique communion with Jesus, they are witnesses of his mission to the world. Pope John Paul II wrote, "By the profession of the evangelical counsels *the characteristic features of Jesus*—the chaste, poor and obedient one—*are made constantly 'visible' in the midst of the world* and the eyes of the faithful are directed towards the mystery of the Kingdom of God already at work in history, even as it awaits its full realization in heaven" (*Vita Consecrata*, 1).

NOTE TAKING

Concept Web. Create a concept web like the one here. In the larger circle, note some general characteristics of the evangelical counsels. In the smaller circles, name some particulars associated with each counsel.

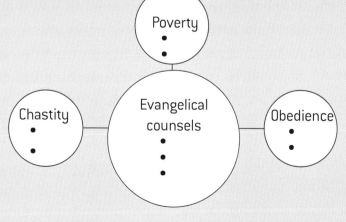

Dominican Sisters of Mary attend the national Christmas tree lighting in Washington, DC.

Therefore, the purpose of taking the evangelical counsels is to free a person from hindrances that would prevent the person from loving and worshipping God perfectly. They also allow one to be consecrated in a more total way to the service of God, to reproduce in oneself Jesus' way of life on earth, to be totally conformed to Christ, and to prolong in history the special presence of the Risen Lord (see *Vita Consecrata*, 19). For example, when Sr. Maria Veritas Marks, O.P., made her vows to observe the evangelical counsels, she felt joy in giving her whole life to Christ:

> I knew that the gift God was asking of me was not the academic career I would have chosen for myself but the dedication of my whole being, body, mind, and heart, to Him. Since God made and loves me, the vows by which He was inviting me to surrender the three greatest goods of human life—possessions, marriage and family, and self-determination—would not shackle but free me.[5]

It is important to note that the Church does not make the consecrated person celibate, poor, and obedient. Rather, the person *freely chooses* this way of life. This is not unlike marriage. The Church does not force a man and woman to be faithful to each other; rather, they freely choose faithfulness out of love for God, for their own good, and for the good of the other. The evangelical counsels are about more than just giving up some earthly goods; instead, they "are *a specific acceptance of the mystery of Christ, lived within the Church*" (*Vita Consecrata*, 16).

Most consecrated persons would say that it is precisely the evangelical counsels that are the impetus for their happiness and freedom within their vocation. Sr. Maria Veritas attested to this reality:

> I no longer have a closet-full of clothing and shoes, but I can now empty the contents of my room into three bags in half an hour and be wherever He needs me. I never have to wonder whether I'm dressed appropriately: in the habit, I'm as ready for a soccer game on the quad as for a meeting with the university's president. I don't get to choose when the wake-up bell will ring, and I don't get to choose where I'll be or what I'll be doing next year, but I do choose the exhilarating adventure of being fully available for Him.[6]

Finally, it is important to note that the three evangelical counsels are not just for those in consecrated life; in fact, they are proposed "to every disciple," but those who are consecrated live them in a "more intimate" manner (*CCC*, 915–916). (See "Practicing the Evangelical Counsels" later in this Section.) Indeed, it is this grace of intimacy with Christ in the consecrated life that "makes possible and even demands the total gift of self in the profession of the evangelical counsels" (*Vita Consecrata*, 16). More information on each of the counsels follows.

Poverty

You might hear the word *poverty* and perhaps think of the destitution of those in third-world countries or those who lack the basic necessities in your own community. Although these are true problems that need to be addressed, they are not exactly what poverty means in terms of the consecrated life.

The core of living a life of *holy poverty* is holding God as one's only treasure. Religious are to be poor, both in fact and in spirit. This means that they own nothing and that their hearts are emptied—or "impoverished"—so as to make room for complete dependence on God. Jesus said to the rich young man, "If you wish to be perfect, go, sell what you have and give to [the] poor, and you will have treasure in heaven. Then come, follow me" (Mt 19:21).

Like the other counsels, the embracing of poverty is a participation in the poverty of Christ. Jesus was literally poor and dependent upon others for all his physical needs. He was also spiritually poor, in that he was fully God, but "emptied himself" (Phil 2:7) and took the form of a human in the Incarnation. "For you know the gracious act of our Lord Jesus Christ, that for your sake he became poor although he was rich, so that by his poverty you might become rich" (2 Cor 8:9).

A typical room or "cell" of a Cistercian nun at the Cistercian Monastery of Ferreira in Spain is very plain.

Practically speaking, taking a vow of poverty means that those in the consecrated life do not own anything of their own. Even the clothes they wear belong to the community, not themselves. This does not mean that consecrated men and women live in destitution; rather, it indicates that they live simply, guided by their needs rather than their wants. For example, a religious sister may genuinely need a car in order to get to the school where she serves. She can use a car that belongs to the community for such purposes, but it is not her own vehicle.

The benefits of living this counsel are many:

Keeping her life simple helps eliminate distractions that could draw the woman religious away from God. A woman head over heels in love with God does not fix her attention on material things. . . . The vow of poverty invites the woman religious to focus her entire life on God and God's people. Because she is unencumbered with material possessions, she is able to go wherever she is needed. ("The Vowed Life," United States Conference of Catholic Bishops)

Poverty in religious life is always aimed at *freedom*. Detached from the pursuit of wealth and material things, those in religious life are free to pursue intimacy and radical self-gift with God.

Chastity

In the consecrated life, the virtue of chastity is lived out as committed celibacy. Recall that the celibacy of the consecrated person is an eschatological sign that skips the earthly sign of marriage and lives what the sign points to: the eternal heavenly marriage of Christ and his Church. In their spousal union with God, those in the consecrated life image the complete self-gift of the inner life of the Trinity.

In celibacy, the perfection of chastity, the consecrated person can be dedicated to God with an undivided love. As St. Paul wrote, "An unmarried woman or a virgin is anxious about the things of the Lord, so that she may be holy in both body and spirit" (1 Cor 7:34). Jesus was not married, so consecrated persons share in his perfection of chastity. Like all realities of the religious life, celibacy is not meant to be restrictive but liberating. Cardinal John O'Connor, the founder of the Sisters of Life, explained that

> the great gift of chastity, of celibacy, of vowed virginity, is a liberation, freeing you from looking merely at the externals; freeing you from the mere physical attractions or emotional attractions that you might experience; freeing you to see another person as made in the image and likeness of God; freeing you to love because in everyone, in every man, every woman, in every child, in every unborn infant, in every cancer-ridden patient in the hospital, in the most handsome man, in the most beautiful woman, your heart reaches out in love because always what you see is the image of God.[7]

In other words, chastity in consecrated life is not about self-absorption and selfishness. The practice of celibacy frees a religious woman or man to love others by serving them.

Obedience

Jesus said he came to do the will of the Father, and as a consecrated person is conformed more intimately to Christ's life, he or she can also say, "I do not seek my own will but the will of the one who sent me" (Jn 5:30). A consecrated person is ultimately obedient to God and his will, but he or she also vows obedience to the religious superior of his or her religious community. A consecrated person renounces his or her own will, and is ready with open hands to serve in the manner in which he or she is called.

St. Thomas Aquinas taught that obedience is the most difficult vow since humans value their liberty more than anything else. Yet the rewards of the vow of obedience are immense. St. Philip Neri wrote that "entire conformity to the divine will is truly a road on which we can't go wrong, and it is the only road that leads us to taste and enjoy the peace which sensual men know nothing of."[8] The obedience of one in the consecrated life is not ignorant or "blind"; rather, it is living in such a way as to show the liberating beauty of a dependence that is not servile (as a servant), but is filial (like a son or daughter). Such obedience requires real responsibility and trust (see *Vita Consecrata*, 21).

Many who take the vow of obedience as they enter the consecrated life find inspiration in the Virgin Mary, whose *fiat*, or yes, to the angel Gabriel's request that she be the Mother of God opened the way to the coming of Christ and the redemption of the world.

PRACTICING THE EVANGELICAL COUNSELS

Choose one way to enact each of the evangelical counsels in your life today. First, brainstorm two ideas for each counsel (note the suggestions). Write down your own ideas.

POVERTY

- Give away a material possession to someone who needs it more.
- Go without a physical comfort (e.g., listening to music, a dessert, etc.).

CHASTITY

- Avoid music, film, and other media with sexually explicit dialogue.
- Refrain from sexual innuendo, jokes, and gossip.

Obedience

- Follow and act on the advice of a parent, grandparent, or teacher.
- Make a good choice today that is out of the ordinary (e.g., talking to a classmate you have previously ignored).

Next, enact, one of your ideas for each counsel. Do all three ideas in the course of one day.

Finally, write a three-paragraph reflection on the experience. Tell what it was like to put the evangelical counsels into practice in your life.

SECTION ASSESSMENT

NOTE TAKING

Use the concept web you created to help you answer the following questions.

1. What is the purpose of vows to observe the evangelical counsels for those in the consecrated life?

2. How is the vow of poverty more than just a promise to give up basic physical necessities?

3. Who is a consecrated person obedient to?

COMPREHENSION

4. Why are the vows that religious take called the *evangelical counsels*?

5. Who has the perfection of all three counsels? Why?

CRITICAL THINKING

6. Why do you think many consecrated persons say the evangelical counsels are their impetus for happiness and freedom?

7. Many consecrated religious say that obedience is the most difficult vow of the evangelical counsels to keep. Why do you think they say this? Which vow would be most difficult for you? Explain.

SECTION 3
Other Characteristics of Consecrated Life

MAIN IDEA

The various religious communities—both active and contemplative orders—have elements in common, such as the importance of prayer, community life, and the steps of formation.

Religious communities can generally be categorized as either active or contemplative. The first duty for members of both types of religious communities is prayer and contemplation of the divine things, but there are differences between the two types of communities.

Active communities are those that have apostolates outside of the convent or monastery. Many religious act as teachers, nurses, writers, servants of the poor, and so forth. All apostolates must serve the Church's mission of evangelization, either directly or indirectly. For example, a religious brother who helps feed the hungry may not be preaching the Gospel in words, but through his service he is showing the love and mercy of Christ.

Contemplative communities are those whose *primary* work is prayer. These are often cloistered nuns or monks. Their vocation is to union with God through prayer and sacrifices for the rest of the world.

That said, many active religious communities also have an important contemplative dimension and vice versa. Some religious communities refer to themselves as "active-contemplative." Indeed, their activity and work arise from their prayerful relationship

NOTE TAKING

Identifying Details. Create a chart like the one here to keep track of some of the essential elements of the religious life.

Prayer	Community life	Formation
Liturgy of the Hours Mass	Communion with God	Stages Postulancy

A member of the Missionaries of Charity, the congregation founded by Mother Teresa, shares in fellowship with some of the people she serves.

with Christ. A good example of this is Missionaries of Charity, an active community founded by St. Teresa of Calcutta: the community's radical service to the poor emerges from their dedicated prayer life. The Cistercians of the Abbey of Gethsemani in Kentucky, a contemplative order, support themselves by the active work of producing and selling things such as nuts, fruitcakes, and jams.

Although the many communities of consecrated persons vary in other ways, there are elements common to all of them. This section examines some of these essential components of the consecrated life, with an emphasis on the religious life—that is, those consecrated persons who are members of a religious community.

The Primacy of Prayer

Prayer is the lifeblood of men and women in religious life. Most communities' days revolve around the Liturgy of the Hours and the Mass. There is also time for personal prayer. Many religious would say that they could never do the work they take on without a deep life of prayer. For example, the Missionaries of Charity are known for ministering to the most poor and vulnerable in the world. However, each sister or brother spends over five hours in prayer every day, which includes liturgical, communal, and personal prayer. This is no coincidence: prayer unifies the whole life and mission of the religious.

Specifically, the Missionaries of Charity are known for their devotion to a "Holy Hour," which is a full hour of prayer in front of the Blessed Sacrament. St. Teresa explained that "all my sisters of the Missionaries of Charity make a daily holy hour . . . because we find that through our daily holy hour our love for Jesus becomes more intimate, our love for each other more understanding, and our love for the poor more compassionate."

Community Life for the Religious

The vocation of all people is to enter into communion with God and others. Made in the image of God, all people are called to imitate the loving relationship of the Divine Persons in the Blessed Trinity. The consecrated religious person undertakes this human vocation in a profound way. The religious focuses not only on a deepened relationship with God, especially through prayer, but on forming loving, fraternal or sororal relationships with others in the community. Because his or her relationship with others is essential for the identity of a religious brother or sister, it is extremely rare for a religious to live alone apart from the community. The necessity for communal living within religious life finds its basis with the lives of the early disciples: "They devoted themselves to the teaching of the apostles and to the communal life, to the breaking of the bread and to the prayers. . . . All who believed were together and had all things in common; they would sell their property and possessions and divide them among all according to each one's need" (Acts 2:42, 44–45).

Religious community life is meant to be more than just membership in a club or an organization. In actuality, religious life is to be like family life. As would siblings in a natural family, religious share everyday tasks and events such as meals, chores, and recreation. They also share their personal joys, triumphs, struggles, and sorrows. Their life together is strengthened and nourished by their life of prayer, both communal and personal prayer.

Those in religious life truly keep everything in common—not just their material items but also their spiritual goods, talents, and inspirations. Pope John Paul II wrote, "In community life, the power of the Holy Spirit at work in one individual passes at the same time to all. Here not only does each enjoy his own gift, but makes it abound by sharing it with others; and each one enjoys the fruits of the other's gift as if they were his own" (*Vita Consecrata*, 42).

Even those rare persons who are called to be hermits and live away from others are still in community with the Communion of Saints. Through their life of prayer and sacrifice, they are in communion with Christ and with the whole Church.

Formation for Religious Life

There is some variance among religious communities in how they form their new members. After a man or woman has prayerfully discerned that he or she is called to the religious life, often with the help of a spiritual director and by researching and visiting different communities, he or she must apply and be accepted to the community. This often involves a written application and a series of interviews with the vocation director and perhaps the religious superior.

Once a man or woman is accepted to the congregation, these stages of formation are typical:

- *Postulancy.* The first stage is one in which the candidate lives with the community in one of its houses and participates in one of the apostolates the community is involved in. The candidate is called a *postulant*—that is, one who is beginning formation.

- *Novitiate.* After a period of about one year, the candidate progresses to a more intensive time of discernment that focuses on study of both theology and the community's history and charism. A *novice* begins to live the vowed life of the community. He or she may begin to be referred to as "brother" or "sister." He or she may also choose a new name at this time, usually the name of a saint. This period typically lasts for one to two years, with time set

A Day in the Religious Life

The days of active and contemplative religious are similar in some ways—both include daily Mass, prayer, and the Liturgy of the Hours—but they are different in others. Below is an example of a daily schedule from two different communities of women.

The Dominican Sisters of St. Cecilia in Nashville, Tennessee, are an active religious order with a strong spirit of contemplation. Their primary apostolate is teaching, including elementary school, high school, and college. The schedule of their day reflects this apostolate:

5:00 a.m.—Rise

5:30 a.m.—Meditation

6:00 a.m.—Lauds (from the Liturgy of the Hours)

6:15 a.m.—Mass

7:00 a.m.—Breakfast

8:00 a.m. to 5:00 p.m.—This varies by the stage of formation of a sister. For the sisters who are fully professed and work as teachers, this is when they are at their respective schools. For those who are still in their postulancy or novitiate (see "Formation for Religious Life" in this section), this is a time of academic study, spiritual direction, prayer, and house duties.

5:00 p.m.—Vespers (from the Liturgy of the Hours) and Rosary

5:30 p.m.—Dinner

6:30 p.m.—Recreation

7:30 p.m.—Spiritual reading

7:45 p.m.—Night Prayer and Compline (from the Liturgy of the Hours)

8:15 p.m.—Silence within the convent (This is when sisters spend time in personal prayer, study, or their teaching preparations.)

10:00 p.m.—Profound silence and bedtime

aside for solitude so that the novice can concentrate more on personal prayer.

- *Temporary profession.* At the end of the novitiate, the novice requests entrance into the community. She or he makes temporary vows with the full intention of remaining a permanent part of the community; these vows are renewed annually for up to nine years. This period usually lasts about three to five years, during which time he or she wears the full habit of the community and may be known as "junior professed."

- *Perpetual vows.* After several years, if the vowed religious continues to have a total desire to remain consecrated to God, he or she is invited to make a public, perpetual profession of religious consecration.

Formation programs vary from congregation to congregation, often depending on whether the community is an active or a contemplative community. Formation does not end with final vows. Throughout their lives, religious continue to form themselves to live more completely the counsels of poverty, chastity, and obedience. In doing so, the religious fulfills the mission of the consecrated life: to proclaim the coming of Christ by being faithful to his or her vows and thus cooperating with the Church's overall mission: to witness to Christ's redemption and second coming and to establish the eternal Kingdom of God.

The Carmelite Nuns of the Carmelite Monastery in Terre Haute, Indiana, are cloistered sisters who see prayer as their primary duty. "Through our life of prayer and contemplation, we lift up the needs of the Church and of the world, remaining with Christ deep within our soul as with an intimate friend."[9] They keep a spirit of silence throughout the day, only speaking when necessary to accomplish a task. Their meals are eaten in silence while listening to spiritual readings.

5:30 a.m.—Rise

6:00 a.m.—Angelus, Office of Readings

6:30 a.m.—Prayer in solitude

7:30 a.m.—Mass

8:30 a.m.—Lauds and Terce (from the Liturgy of the Hours)

9:00 a.m.—Breakfast

9:30 a.m. to 12:30 p.m.—Work within their monastery (such as answering mail, designing spiritual gifts that they sell, attending to guests, gardening, and performing other basic household duties)

12:30 p.m.—Mid-Day Prayer, Examination of Conscience

12:45 p.m.—Lunch

1:15 to 3:15 p.m.—Free time (often includes Mid-Afternoon Prayer, spiritual reading, and work time)

3:15 p.m.—Work, novitiate class, or study (depending upon level of formation)

4:15 p.m.—Tea break

4:30 p.m.—Vespers (from the Liturgy of the Hours)

5:00 p.m.—Prayer in solitude

6:00 p.m.—Dinner and cleanup

7:00 p.m.—Community recreation (talking is permitted at this time)

8:00 p.m.—Examination of Conscience and Compline (from the Liturgy of the Hours)

9:00 p.m.—The Great Silence (in speech and action) and solitude, which continues until the end of Morning Prayer the next day

11:00 p.m.—Bedtime

Religious Habits

Religious habits are the distinctive garb that many consecrated persons wear. Church law requires only that the garments be designed in a such a way as to witness to the evangelical counsels, so habits differ greatly from community to community.

Very often habits consist of a simple tunic under a long strip of fabric, called a scapular, draped front to back.

Monks or friars have hoods on their habits, and many sisters and most nuns have veils, which signify their role as "brides of Christ."

Many religious wear belts or ropes around their waists that symbolize being guarded in purity.

Some orders, such as the Dominicans, wear a rosary hanging from the belt.

Others have a rope with three knots, which indicate the three evangelical counsels.

Many habits include a simple crucifix or cross worn around the neck.

In women's communities that wear veils, it is common for those in the novitiate to wear a white veil, while fully professed sisters wear a black veil.

Sometimes the color of the habit gives an indication as to the order of the religious. For example, Carmelites typically wear brown, Benedictines generally wear black, and Dominicans usually wear white.

SECTION ASSESSMENT

NOTE TAKING

Use the flowchart you created to help you answer the following questions.

1. What are the three main ways prayer is manifested in a religious community?
2. Why is it rare for a consecrated religious to live alone?
3. What are some examples of apostolates?
4. What is typically the first stage of formation in religious life after a candidate is accepted?
5. Name two things that occur for a religious during the novitiate.

COMPREHENSION

6. Explain the difference between an active religious community and a contemplative religious community. How are they alike?
7. What is the purpose of religious habits?

REFLECTION

8. If you were choosing between an active and a contemplative religious community, which would you prefer? Why? What criteria would you use to make your final decision?
9. In the type of religious community you chose for yourself in the previous question, what type of apostolate would you feel called to and capable of? Explain.

Section Summaries

Focus Question

Why do some people choose a consecrated life, taking public vows to observe the evangelical counsels of poverty, chastity, and obedience?

Complete one of the following:

Research and record in writing the requirements for entrance into a religious community that interests you. In addition, write a two-paragraph summary that highlights the community's charism and apostolates. *Optional*: Format this information as a "Help Wanted" advertisement.

Using photos from this chapter and other photos from outside sources as references, sketch the religious habits of both a women's and a men's religious community. Fill in details using colored pencils.

Research and name both a secular institute and society of apostolic life. Answer: What is their mission? When were they founded? What is their nation of origin? What are the membership requirements? How many members do they have worldwide? Summarize the answers in a one-page essay.

INTRODUCTION

Consecrated to Christ

All Christians are consecrated to Christ in Baptism. Some, however, are called to make a deeper, more profound consecration to God through the public profession of vows of poverty, chastity, and obedience. One of the marking characteristics of the consecrated life is the embrace of celibacy for the sake of the Kingdom. Consecrated celibates skip the earthly sign of marriage and live what marriage points to: the eternal union of Christ with the Church in heaven. In their renunciation of the goods of this world, those in the consecrated life witness to the world to come.

Compose a checklist of five essential qualities that would make a person a good candidate for the consecrated life.

SECTION 1

Historical Development of the Consecrated Life

The development of the consecrated life began with the desert hermits, who wanted to live a radical life for Christ even after the threat of martyrdom diminished. Next, the consecrated life became more communal. It was greatly systematized with St. Benedict's monasticism. The development of the mendicant religious life followed, in which religious communities went out into the world to preach the Gospel rather than remaining at the monastery. Many other religious congregations formed over the ensuing centuries. Today, most consecrated life is in the form of religious communities, but there are also consecrated virgins, secular institutes, and societies of apostolic life.

 Pick a saint mentioned in this section, and research his or her specific contribution to the development of consecrated life. Write a two-paragraph summary of your findings.

SECTION 2

The Evangelical Counsels

The evangelical counsels are proposals from the Gospels that all baptized persons are called to embrace, but those who take consecrated vows live in a more profound, public manner. In Jesus is the perfection of the counsels: he is the ultimate poor, chaste, and obedient one. Holy poverty means that religious live out of their material needs, not wants. It also means that they are spiritually empty so as to rely totally on God. In the consecrated life, chastity is lived as committed celibacy. Those who take a vow of celibacy are a sign to the world of the Kingdom to come, in which there will be no marriage between men and women, because all will be mystically united to God. The vow of obedience means that all religious vow to do God's will and what their superiors ask of them.

Write a three-paragraph reflection on which evangelical counsel is most difficult to live out in the modern world. Give good support and examples for your choice. Include an example of a contemporary person who is living the counsel you chose well.

SECTION 3

Other Characteristics of Consecrated Life

Although religious communities vary in many ways, they also have many elements in common. There are two types of religious life: active and contemplative. Prayer is essential for the consecrated life; it is manifested through liturgical, communal, and personal prayer. Also vital is community life, in that every person is called to communion with God and with one another. The steps of formation for the religious life are postulancy, novitiate, temporary profession, and perpetual vows.

Do these two things: (1) name an active religious community within one hundred miles of where you live, and write one paragraph about its primary apostolate; and (2) name any contemplative religious community in the United States, and write one paragraph about its heritage or mission.

Chapter Assignments

Choose and complete at least one of the three assignments assessing your understanding of the material in this chapter.

 1. Classifying Religious Communities

Most religious communities specialize in a certain ministry that reflects their charism—for example, teaching, healing, praying, prophesying, or reconciling. Create and complete a chart that includes a sampling of sixteen religious communities within the Catholic Church, the ministries they specialize in, and the places in the world where they serve. For this exercise, include twelve religious communities for women and four religious communities of brothers for men. A chart sample follows:

Religious community	Charism	Apostolates	Locations
Daughters of St. Paul	The Pauline charism is to communicate the mystery of Christ to all peoples through their lives and through all the means of social communication.	• manage a bookstore • write books and articles • travel and meet people at schools, book fairs	The Daughters of St. Paul are an international community. The motherhouse is in Rome.
The Brothers of Holy Cross	The heart of the charism is to be educators in faith, supporting the development of the whole person in mind, body, and spirit.	• teachers and administrators in high schools and colleges • social services and rehabilitation for teens and adults	The Brothers of Holy Cross are an international community. The vocations office is located in Austin, Texas, at St. Edward's University.

 2. Sharing News about a Religious Vocation

The discernment of a religious vocation for a young man or young woman is accompanied by prayer, questioning, and finally a decision. At some point the person tells his or her family of the choice to further prepare for the priesthood or religious life. In most cases, the person's close family members have a sense of what he or she is leaning toward. Sometimes the decision catches some family members by surprise.

Imagine a situation in which a person your age who has been considering a religious vocation has just received news that he or she has been accepted into a preparation program for a religious community or a seminary. Now the person has gathered family members and close friends to tell them about this next step.

Write a dialogue of at least two pages in script form between the person and the characters listed below. Begin the script with the person's announcement of his or her plans. Continue with the dialogue, allowing every person to offer congratulations, ask questions, and share opinions (some supportive, some unsupportive). Include at least six of the following people in the script.

Characters

- The person with the vocation
- Mom
- Dad
- Twenty-year-old sister
- Fifteen-year-old brother
- Best friend
- A one-time romantic interest
- Grandma or grandpa
- Non-Catholic aunt or uncle

Add a postscript of two paragraphs describing how your own family would react if you told them you had a religious vocation.

 # 3. Religious Saint

Section 1 of this chapter, "Historical Development of the Consecrated Life," named many saints who were integral to the development of the consecrated life. However, there are countless more. For this assignment, pick a saint *not* mentioned in this chapter who founded a religious order or community, and write a three- to four-page report on the saint. Include as many of the following details in the report as possible:

- the name of the saint and the religious order he or she founded
- the years of the saints' life
- where the saint lived
- the family's influence on the saint's vocation
- some influential words or deeds of the saint
- the charisms of the saint's religious community
- the year the saint was canonized

Faithful Disciple

Bl. Irene Stefani

The day began early for Catholic pilgrims at the Mathari Mission Centre in Nyeri County, Kenya. Hundreds lined up at dawn near the chaplaincy of the center, where the relics of Sr. Irene Stefani had rested in a stone sarcophagus since they had been exhumed in 1995 to begin her cause for beatification. After confirmation that the remains had not been interfered with, hundreds of the faithful walked with the casket for several hours to Nyeri Town, where Mass would be celebrated at the St. Mary's Boys Secondary School.

Bl. Irene Stefani

With the approval of Pope Francis, Sr. Irene Stefani was beatified on Sunday, May 23, 2015, in the first beatification ceremony ever held on the continent of Africa. Archbishop Peter Kairo of Nyeri preached a homily of thanksgiving for Sr. Irene and exhorted the community to follow her example of selfless giving and loving of others.

Irene Stefani was born Aurelia Giacomina Mercedes in 1891 in Anfo, Italy. She was the fifth of twelve children. Her mother died when Aurelia was sixteen, so she cared for her younger siblings and instructed them in the Catholic catechism. She also helped her father run his small hotel business.

Aurelia wanted to become a missionary, but her father objected due to the needs at home. Finally, when she was twenty, he allowed her to join the congregation of the Consolata Missionary Sisters, a new order at that time that had been started by Bl. Joseph Allamano. Aurelia took the name Irene and trained as a nurse. In 1914, she made her final vows and then, with three other nuns, left Italy for Kenya.

At first, Sr. Irene supervised workers at a local coffee plantation and taught at a boys' school in Nyeri Town. She learned to speak the local language, Kikuyu. But when World War I broke out and spread into Africa, she joined the British Red Cross and traveled with them. She marched across savannas, rivers, and forests carrying supplies to the wounded. She and the other nurses were not trained to treat infections and contagious diseases. Many were exposed to diseases that would cost them their lives. Yet Sr. Irene continued to work with the ill. Around this time, several of the locals began to call Sr. Irene "Nyaatha," which means "a person of mercy."

After the war, Sr. Irene returned to Nyeri and worked in the Consolata Centre, training novices. In 1920, she was sent to a remote parish in the village of Gikondi. Sr. Irene mostly taught children and prepared adults for reception into the Church, but she left the village many times to minister to the sick. In 1930, a teacher she had worked with, Julius Ngari, who lived in the highlands, caught the contagious bubonic plague. Although the other sisters told Sr. Irene not to go to visit and care for him, she did so anyway. She caught the disease herself and died on October 30, 1930.

As the cause for Sr. Irene's beatification proceeded, a miracle due to her intercession was examined. The miracle occurred over a three-day period in January 1989 in Nipepe, Mozambique. Catholic catechists and students from the area were gathered for training when they were forced to take refuge in the church due to the proximity of fighting from a civil war. There were about 270 people, including many children. It was the hottest month of summer, and there was little water. The people prayed to Sr. Irene and, miraculously, there was enough water from the baptismal font for them to all drink and even bathe a baby who was born while they were captive. On their release, the people chanted, "It was Mama Irene who performed the miracle. Sr. Irene heard us and helped us."

Reading Comprehension

1. What was unique about Sr. Irene's beatification ceremony?

2. What was Sr. Irene's role with the Red Cross?

3. How did Sr. Irene contract bubonic plague?

4. Describe the miracle associated with Bl. Irene Stefani.

Writing Task

Research information on the Consolata Missionary Sisters. Write one paragraph summarizing their mission today.

Explaining the Faith

Don't men and women who take a vow of celibacy live lonely, unhappy lives?

No, not necessarily. Most men who become priests, monks, or brothers and most women who become nuns, sisters, or consecrated virgins live happy and fulfilling lives. A recent study by Msgr. Stephen Rossetti of nearly 2,500 priests from twenty-three dioceses discovered an extraordinarily high rate of happiness and satisfaction, among the highest rate of any profession.[10]

Remember, God gives the graces necessary for a person to live out his or her commitments in a fulfilling way. Also, built into the very nature of religious life is fraternal/sororal communion. Religious women and men are called to share in the lives of those they serve and of those with whom they live within community.

Certainly, some who promise lifelong celibacy may experience loneliness, but the same is true for some married people. Sexual intimacy is not essential for personal fulfillment and happiness; a relationship with God is what is ultimately necessary. The heart of celibacy is a truly loving relationship with the Lord, expressed in a self-gift to others in his name. Committed celibacy for the sake of Jesus Christ and his Kingdom brings consolation that cannot be appreciated by one who has not lived it. Living a life of committed celibacy gives one a sense of the gifts of the eternal life to come.

 ## Further Research

Read paragraph 1579 of the *Catechism of the Catholic Church*. What do you think this phrase means: "accepted with a joyous heart celibacy radiantly proclaims the Reign of God"?

Prayer
Prayer for Vocations to the Priesthood and Religious Life

O God, Father of all Mercies,

Provider of a bountiful harvest,

send your graces upon those

you have called to gather the fruits of your labor;

preserve and strengthen them in their lifelong service of you.

Open the hearts of your children

that they may discern your holy will;

inspire in them a love and desire to surrender themselves

to serving others in the name of your Son, Jesus Christ.

Teach all your faithful to follow their respective paths in life

guided by your Divine Word and Truth.

Through the intercession of the Most Blessed Virgin Mary,

all the angels and saints, humbly hear our prayers

and grant your Church's needs, through Christ, our Lord. Amen.

Epilogue: Looking to the Future

Your vocation exists in the *present* tense. In Baptism, you are given the grace to respond to God's call to become his son or daughter and to share his divine nature. That is something happening now—not just when you finish college, or start a family, or achieve success in a career, or become a priest, or enter religious life. Those mileposts may never come in God's plan for your life. But you have his grace to share in the intimacy of the loving relationship of the Divine Persons of the Blessed Trinity no matter what vocational path you follow.

Your ultimate vocation is to eternal life. This is a "supernatural" vocation because it is beyond the powers of any person to know or reach without God, and it begins now. It must take precedence over any other desires or wishes you have for your life. You must listen for this calling and discern how to best act on it. Whenever and wherever God gives you grace to recognize that he is with you and that he is calling you to eternity, you must be ready to subordinate all of your other goals to this call. When St. Joan of Arc was asked if she knew whether she was in God's grace, she replied, "If I am not, may it please God to put me in it; if I am, may it please God to keep me there." St. Joseph Cafasso said, "I have been made for heaven and heaven for me." The primary Christian task is to keep on the lookout for God's grace and to keep the focus of heaven always in mind.

Your Vocation to Life Everlasting

Single, married, priest, or religious, the goal for each person is to spend eternity in heaven. Everyone has some ideas of what heaven is like. St. Thérèse of Lisieux wrote, "God's gaze, his ravishing smile. This is my

St. Thérèse of Lisieux

heaven." The *Catechism of the Catholic Church* defines heaven as "the ultimate end and fulfillment of the deepest human longings, the state of supreme, definitive happiness" (*CCC*, 1024). Those souls in heaven will be in communion with the Holy Trinity, the Virgin Mary, the angels, and all the saints. To live in heaven is to be with Christ.

In practical terms, in heaven, time and space will have no effect on you. You will be reunited with family members and friends who have died before you in God's grace and friendship. You will never be burdened with sickness, disease, pain, or suffering again. You must make heaven your goal during this life. To do this you must live your life with your death, united with Christ, in mind. St. Thérèse said of her death, "I am not dying; I am entering life." Only through dying can you enter the fullness of God's Kingdom. That is heaven.

Reaching Heaven

The person who desires heaven will strive for holiness on earth. St. Thérèse wrote, "God would never inspire me with desires which cannot be realized; so in spite of my littleness, I can hope to be a saint." God has written this desire on your heart. He has chosen you to live with him in heaven. Jesus said, "You did not choose me, but I chose you. Go and bear much fruit" (Jn 15:16).

How does God want you to do this? The answer is love. Each vocation is a response to God's call to live the greatest commandment:

> "Hear, O Israel! The Lord our God is Lord alone! You shall love the Lord your God with all your heart, with all your soul, with all your mind, and with all your strength." The second is this: "You shall love your neighbor as yourself." There is no other commandment greater than these. (Mk 12:29–31)

Authentic *agape* love expresses itself in many forms: the love of a parent for a child who needs to be disciplined, the love of a friend sharing another friend's sorrow, the love and concern of a priest for a troubled parishioner, or the care of a religious sister for one of her students are just a few of countless examples. Ultimately, the love of every vocation is an echo of the self-giving love and communion found in the Divine Persons of the Blessed Trinity. When St. Thérèse discovered her vocation of love she was overcome with joy. She wrote in her autobiography, *The Story of a Soul*, "I cried, 'Jesus, my love. At last I have found my vocation. My vocation is love. In the heart of the Church, my mother. I will be love, and then I will be all things.'"

With God's grace you too have a vocation to live in the heart of the Church. You were made by the love of God and for a great and lasting love in heaven. In a letter in preparation for a 2018 Synod on Youth, Pope Francis implored, "Do not be afraid to listen to the Spirit who proposes bold choices; do not delay when your conscience asks you to take risks in following the Master."

Always be assured that God is with you in the process of discernment. God has set before you an invitation to follow him. The whole Church is sure of your ability to lovingly and prayerfully set forth your response to his call.

FINAL ASSIGNMENT

Your final assignment for this course is to write a five-hundred-word essay that you could use as part of one or more college applications with only minor revisions. In lieu of face-to-face interviews, many colleges ask prospective students to write an essay that introduces the "real you" and allows the admissions staff to get a glimpse of your personality, sense of humor, and motivations, as well as your dreams and goals for life.

For this essay, incorporate how the discernment you have begun regarding a life vocation (marriage, priesthood, consecrated life) fits into your plans.

Here are some tips for writing your essay:

- Pray before you begin writing. Ask for the inspiration of the Holy Spirit.

- Be genuine. Don't write something you think your teacher or an admissions officer wants to hear. Write something that describes the real you.

- Look deeper. Reflect on the heart of your life. Be soulful.

- Incorporate some of your uniqueness into your writing. Remember you are trying to communicate to the reader who you really are.

- Have fun. This isn't a typical term paper or theme. Let the writing flow.

Beliefs

Apostles' Creed

I believe in God,
the Father almighty,
Creator of heaven and earth,
and in Jesus Christ, his only Son, our Lord,
who was conceived by the Holy Spirit,
born of the Virgin Mary,
suffered under Pontius Pilate,
was crucified, died, and was buried;
he descended into hell;
on the third day he rose again from the dead;
he ascended into heaven,
and is seated at the right hand of God the
    Father Almighty;
from there he will come to judge the living and
    the dead.

I believe in the Holy Spirit,
the holy catholic Church,
the communion of saints,
the forgiveness of sins,
the resurrection of the body,
and life everlasting. Amen.

Nicene Creed

I believe in one God,
the Father almighty,
maker of heaven and earth,
of all things visible and invisible.

I believe in one Lord Jesus Christ,
the Only Begotten Son of God,
born of the Father before all ages.
God from God, Light from Light,
true God from true God,
begotten, not made, consubstantial with the
    Father;
through him all things were made.
For us men and for our salvation
he came down from heaven,
and by the Holy Spirit was incarnate of the
    Virgin Mary,
and became man.

For our sake he was crucified under Pontius
    Pilate,
he suffered death and was buried,
and rose again on the third day
in accordance with the Scriptures.
He ascended into heaven
and is seated at the right hand of the Father.
He will come again in glory
to judge the living and the dead
and his kingdom will have no end.

I believe in the Holy Spirit, the Lord, the giver
    of life,
who proceeds from the Father and the Son,
who with the Father and the Son is adored and
    glorified,
who has spoken through the prophets.

I believe in one, holy, catholic and apostolic
    Church.

I confess one baptism for the forgiveness of sins

and I look forward to the resurrection of the dead

and the life of the world to come. Amen.

Next Steps for Discerning Your Vocation

While you are not ready to make a commitment to a permanent vocation of marriage, Holy Orders, or consecrated religious life, you should be conducting an ongoing discernment process of your Christian vocation while imagining yourself in one of the permanent primary vocations.

This section provides more information and lists several resources relating to the following areas:

- Four habits of discernment
- Catholic colleges and universities in the United States
- Committed service efforts
- Teen-focused retreats
- Religious vocations guides
- Catholic seminaries in the United States
- Marriage preparation

Four Habits of Discernment

The process of discernment, especially the intensive discerning of a primary vocation, requires habits of prayer and behavior. These habits are part of the Christian life, and you can always go deeper in each one. As you become immersed in the habits, be aware of signs and graces that God sends to let you know his will for you.

1. Keep God and the call to holiness at the center of discernment. Remind yourself that you are not on your own. God has a plan for you that is driven purely by love. It is good to talk to other people when making important decisions, but at some point you will need time to be alone with your thoughts and with God. Invite God into your decision-making process.

Questions to think about:

- How do I see God's love for me?
- In what ways do I need to grow in trust?
- In what ways has God's plan in my life already led me to be holy?
- How do I see God in the everyday circumstances of my life?

2. Be available and open. It is important to have an attitude of openness and availability to what God might be telling you. Most people don't actually hear a voice when God speaks. However, God will use other people, experiences, and especially prayer to guide you. If you struggle with how to pray, don't worry. Begin with the sacraments, particularly the Eucharist. Strive for attentiveness in Mass instead of tuning out. The prayers you have memorized are a great beginning. Use them perhaps in making a visit to your parish church or in Eucharistic Adoration to put yourself in a prayerful mentality. Allow yourself time after you have quieted your heart to be in silent prayer, both talking and listening to God.

Questions to think about:

- How often do I pray?
- What kinds of thoughts, feelings (especially love, joy, and peace—or a lack thereof), and memories might God be stirring within me to help me make my decision?
- What Scripture story or saint's life comes to mind that might enlighten my decision? Find the passage or story and prayerfully read it.
- Is my heart open to whatever God is calling me to?

3. Consider what God has already given you. Self-knowledge is one of the fruits of a prayerful life. You have been given certain gifts and abilities to complement God's plan. Though he knows them already, God wants to hear what your desires are and what you feel in your heart. Be confident that God will not work against the good gifts he has given you: talents, skills, things you value, and the movements of your heart.

Questions to think about:

- What have I learned from significant relationships in my life?

- What spiritual and practical abilities or talents has God given me so far?

- Are there abilities I have that I have not explored, or that I have not used well?

- Do I sense a degree of potential satisfaction, hope, or joy when I consider a certain vocation?

4. Clear away obstacles, and beware deception. Sin and noise are two obstacles to discernment. Only when you are free from sin can you give a complete yes to God. Receiving the Sacrament of Penance and frequently examining your conscience is the best way to free yourself from attachment to sin. Attachment to your phone, constant activities, and idle conversation are not evil in themselves, but without moderation they can create spiritual static and dull your sensitivities. St. Teresa of Calcutta reminds you that the fruit of silence is prayer. Another obstacle you will face is deception from the world and from Satan, which can pull you away from following God's will and must be resisted through grace and prayer.

Questions to think about:

- How often do I examine my conscience and celebrate the Sacrament of Penance? How could I do these more often if I need to? What sins do I need to bring to prayer to be free?

- Are there practical steps I can take to avoid the near occasion of sin?

- How can I create a quiet space in my daily schedule?

- How is the "voice of the world" in music, entertainment, and advertising affecting my spiritual life? Do these things bring me closer to God?

- How is the "voice of the devil" tempting me to doubt God or turn away from doing what is good?

Catholic Colleges and Universities in the United States

As you prepare for college, you might consider attending a Catholic college or university. There are more than two hundred Catholic colleges and universities in the United States. They have undergraduate enrollments of all sizes—from less than one thousand to more than twenty thousand students. They are also located in every region of the country in urban, suburban, and rural areas. Some Catholic universities also have renowned medical and law schools and offer several other professional and graduate degrees. Here are some other reasons for you to consider attending a Catholic college:

- *Community environment.* At a Catholic college you won't be treated like a number. You will meet new friends of many different racial, religious, and socioeconomic backgrounds. You will be supported by caring professors and staff.

- *Moral environment.* Don't be fooled: students at Catholic colleges are not perfect and make their share of immoral choices. However, the policies of the institutions themselves are geared to promote Christian morality (e.g., speaking out for the right to life for everyone, from the unborn to the aged and infirmed).

- *Global environment.* One of the marks of the Church is that it is catholic, or universal. The first universities were Catholic and connected to monasteries. There are Catholics and Catholic colleges worldwide, and many of the Catholic colleges in the United States have excellent study abroad programs. Also, courses are taught from a global perspective in which solidarity with the entire human race—especially the poor—is stressed.

- *Faith environment.* Whether it is a crucifix in a classroom, a priest or religious serving as a rector in a dorm, a required theology course, or the celebration of the sacraments on campus, a Catholic college offers the opportunity to continue to practice the faith you first learned in your family and will want to practice in your own life and family in the future.

Fr. Bernie O'Connor, O.S.F.S., a Catholic college president, wrote that receiving a good preparation for life is the number-one reason for a student to attend a Catholic college. He added, "We know what makes a successful marriage, we know what is required for a happy and productive career, we know what it takes to care for children, we know about the struggles of the elderly, the sick, the disabled, the forgotten."

The National Catholic College Admission Association provides information for prospective students and their families. The Cardinal Newman Society also provides several resources for choosing a Catholic college.

If you are not able to attend a Catholic college, most public colleges sponsor a Newman Club, named after Cardinal John Henry Newman, who was a priest in the Anglican Church before converting to Catholicism in the mid-nineteenth century at the age of forty-two. In the past, it was rare for Catholics to attend non-Catholic colleges. The first Newman Club, sponsored at the University of Pennsylvania in 1883, insisted that its members not become "clannish or narrow in a religious sense." This sensibility continues today, as Newman Clubs have an interfaith focus while including celebration of the sacraments, RCIA

classes, and catechetical studies more specifically for their Catholic members.

Committed Service Efforts

As part of a high-school curriculum or parish project, you may have committed yourself to hours and works of Christian service. Typical efforts usually involve either focused work in your own community or a project where you travel to an area in need and spend a week or two helping to do physical repairs on houses, schools, or churches. If you have not participated in a committed service effort up to this point in high school, it is a wise choice to begin to now.

St. Teresa of Calcutta offered this advice about service: "Just begin, one, one, one. Begin at home by saying something good to someone in your family. Begin by helping someone in need in your community, at work, or at school. Begin by making whatever you do something beautiful for God."

Catholic Charities USA is the largest private network of social service organizations in the United States working to support families, reduce poverty, and build communities. There are local chapters of Catholic Charities in each Catholic diocese. Explore the volunteer opportunities offered in your diocese through Catholic Charities. You may find a chance to volunteer in a food bank, as a senior citizen companion, as a mentor to a young student, or in providing relief services for a natural disaster in your area or even in another part of the country.

In the future, when you are of college age, there are several "summer immersion" volunteer opportunities that encourage participation in a focused area of service. These programs usually include time for community building, reflection and prayer, and education before, during, and after the actual experience. The programs may take place in the United States or in another country. For example, one Catholic college offered a program in which students work with local agencies in the poverty-stricken Appalachian region as well as another program in Ghana in which students train youth in computer skills.

After college, many Catholic new graduates choose to do a year of service prior to beginning their careers. Oftentimes, this year affords the opportunity to discern clearly a future path not only in career but also in vocation. For example, the largest Catholic volunteer agency is the Jesuit Volunteer Corp. Volunteers are assigned to various places and tasks, including working with the elderly, teaching in impoverished schools, and ministering to people with AIDS. The volunteers live in community with one another, making time for prayer and learning to model simple living. Many other religious orders—male and female—sponsor associate programs in which young adults can participate in an extended service program. A typical feature of these programs is daily and weekly prayer time, often led by the participants themselves.

Teen-Focused Retreats

You may have also been on one or more retreats while in high school. As the term indicates, the experience is meant to allow you to "retreat" from your daily cares, concerns, and responsibilities to take up a focused, faith-filled experience that includes many of the following elements: an opportunity for a deepening of prayer, a sense of belonging with fellow retreatants, interaction with older Catholics (usually the retreat leaders), informal celebrations of the sacraments, especially the Sacraments of Penance and Holy Eucharist, and an increased awareness of and desire to make an adult-level faith commitment.

Teens Encounter Christ is a Catholic spiritual movement that focuses on the Paschal Mystery. Founded in 1965 in Lansing, Michigan, following the Second Vatican Council, the retreat is meant to encourage older teens and young adults to come to know Christ in a personal way and to make a heartfelt decision to follow him. The retreat is usually held over three days and includes songs, music, witness talks, and celebration of the sacraments. It is available on a regular basis in most dioceses.

Another popular outreach program that you may consider attending as a participant, and perhaps later as a leader, is sponsored by National Evangelization Teams. NET is based in Saint Paul, Minnesota, but sends out teams of young adults (usually between eighteen and thirty years old) after a period of training to dioceses across the country. Once at their destination, the teams meet with a diocesan contact person and are told specifically how the diocese would like them to minister to their youth. Some dioceses have NET work in a Catholic high school for a week, visiting a different class each day. Others sponsor youth rallies. Many have retreats scheduled at several different parishes. Usually a team will stay in a diocese for two to five weeks. Sometimes team members stay at a rectory or parish center. Mostly they stay with host families.

Look for an opportunity to participate in a retreat sponsored by your parish, school, or other entity in your diocese. Use the time away to reflect on your high-school experience, your life with your family, and ways you will be able to take the lessons learned to a future vocation.

Religious Vocations Guides

The United States Conference of Catholic Bishops provides a wealth of information on ways to discern a religious vocation and ultimately contact a bishop or religious superior for more information. These resources can be explored at the following link: www.usccb.org/beliefs-and-teachings/vocations/index.cfm.

Note a special section for vocations to the consecrated life at www.usccb.org/beliefs-and-teachings/vocations/resources/resources-on-consecrated-life.cfm.

A good starting point for delving further into a religious vocation is your own diocesan website. Look for a tab labeled "Vocations."

Catholic Seminaries in the United States

Catholic seminaries are places where students prepare humanly, spiritually, intellectually, and pastorally for the priesthood. Seminaries prepare men for both the diocesan and religious order priesthood. There are more than seventy-five seminaries in the United States in twenty-five states.

If you are discerning the possibility of a vocation to the priesthood, explore the history and programs at several seminaries in the United States while simultaneously speaking with a parish priest and diocesan or religious community vocation director.

One link for Catholic seminaries in the United States websites is www.usccb.org/beliefs-and-teachings/vocations/priesthood/priestly-formation/seminaries-and-organizations.cfm.

Marriage Preparation

There are several parish and diocesan programs for marriage preparation that you can seek out once you have become engaged and are planning your wedding. Note the links to marriage preparation materials provided by the United States Conference of Catholic Bishops at www.usccb.org/issues-and-action/marriage-and-family/marriage/marriage-preparation/index.cfm.

Prayers for Making Good Choices

Prayer for the Road Ahead

My Lord God, I have no idea where I am going. I do not see the road ahead of me. I cannot know for certain where it will end. Nor do I really know myself, and the fact that I think that I am following your will does not mean that I am actually doing so. But I believe that the desire to please you does in fact please you. And I hope I have that desire in all that I am doing. I hope that I will never do anything apart from that desire. And I know that if I do this, you will lead me by the right road, though I may know nothing about it. Therefore will I trust you always, though I may seem to be lost and in the shadow of death. I will not fear, for you are ever with me, and you will never leave me to face my perils alone.

—Thomas Merton

- Create an image or a chart that represents the main theme of these words.

Prayer to Know Your Vocation

Lord, my God and my loving Father, you have made me to know you, to love you, to serve you, and thereby to find and to fulfill my deepest longings. I know that you are in all things, and that every path can lead me to you.

But of them all, there is one especially by which you want me to come to you. Since I will do what you want of me, I pray you, send your Holy Spirit to me: into my mind, to show me what you want of me; into my heart, to give me the determination to do it, and to do it with all my love, with all my mind, and with all of my strength right to the end. Jesus, I trust in you. Amen.

—United States Conference of Catholic Bishops

- Add a final paragraph to this prayer, personalizing it with choices you are considering for your own vocation.

Prayer for a Good Death

Good Lord,
give me the grace so to spend my life,
that when the day of my death shall come,
though I may feel pain in my body,
I may feel comfort in soul;
and with faithful hope in thy mercy,
in due love towards thee
and charity towards the world,
I may, through thy grace,
part hence into thy glory.
—St. Thomas More

- Write a prayer for your own good death that focuses on how you plan to spend your life doing God's will.

GLOSSARY

adultery Marital infidelity, or sexual relations between a married person and someone other than his or her spouse. Adultery is a sin against the Sixth Commandment (see *CCC*, Glossary).

alb A liturgical vestment with origins in the celebration of Baptism that is a long white robe. Only clergy may wear a stole over the alb.

altar of holocausts In the Old Testament, a small mound of stones upon which the flesh of sacrificed animals could be burned. The word *holocaust* means "sacrifice."

annulment A declaration by the Church that a sacramental marriage was invalid, that it never existed validly from the beginning; also called a *declaration of nullity*.

apostolates From the word *apostle*; the activity of the Christian that works to extend the reign of Christ to the entire world (see *CCC*, Glossary). Apostolates include teaching, ministering to the sick, and many other tasks.

apostolic letter A document issued by the pope or Vatican for various appointments, approving religious congregations, designating basilicas, and the like.

apostolic succession The handing on of the Apostles' preaching and authority directly from the Apostles to the bishops through the laying on of hands. Apostolic succession continues to this day.

beatific vision "The contemplation of God in heavenly glory, a gift of God which is a constitutive element of the happiness (or *beatitude*) of heaven" (*CCC*, Glossary).

Benediction The rite in which Jesus, in the Blessed Sacrament contained in a monstrance, is exposed to the Adoration of the faithful.

calumny A false statement that "harms the reputation of others and gives occasion for false judgments concerning them" (*CCC*, 2477).

canonization "The solemn declaration by the Pope that a deceased member of the faithful may be proposed as a model and intercessor to the Christian faithful and venerated as a saint on the basis of the fact that the person lived a life of heroic virtue or remained faithful to God through martyrdom" (*CCC*, Glossary).

celibacy "The state or condition of those who have chosen to remain unmarried for the sake of the kingdom of heaven in order to give themselves entirely to God and to the service of his people" (*CCC*, Glossary).

charism "A specific gift or grace of the Holy Spirit which directly or indirectly benefits the Church, given in order to help a person live out the Christian life, or to serve the common good in building up the Church" (*CCC*, Glossary).

chastity The moral virtue which provides for the successful integration of sexuality within one's whole identity, leading to the inner unity of the physical and spiritual being (see *CCC*, 2337).

chasuble The outer garment worn by the bishop or priest over the alb and stole. It is the same color as the stole and the liturgical season.

civil divorce The dissolution of a marriage contract by the legal system. It does not free a person from a valid marriage.

cloistered Term used to describe monks or nuns who strive for religious perfection within the confines of a monastery; comes from "cloister," the part of a monastery reserved only for the monks or nuns who reside in that monastery.

cohabitation The occasion of an unmarried man and unmarried woman living together in the same home and having a sexual relationship.

collegiality The participation of each of the worldwide bishops, with the pope as their head, in a "college" that takes responsibility for both their local diocesan churches and also the Church as a whole.

common law marriage The occasion of a man and woman living together for a prolonged time and holding themselves to be married but having not been formally married in the Church or through the legal system.

common priesthood The priesthood of the faithful. Christ has made the Church a "kingdom of priests" who share in his priesthood through the Sacraments of Baptism and Confirmation.

communion of Persons A complete giving-of-self, shown perfectly in the life of the Divine Persons of the Blessed Trinity.

complementarity A way to describe two realities that belong together, producing a whole that neither is nor can be alone.

concupiscence The tendency or inclination toward sin every person experiences as a result of Original Sin.

consecrated life A permanent state of life recognized by the Church and chosen freely by men and women in response to Christ's call to perfection. It is characterized by profession of the evangelical counsels of poverty, chastity, and obedience.

consent In the context of marriage, a free and unconstrained act of the will in which spouses promise to give themselves to each other in marriage.

continence Refraining from use of the sexual faculties and any sexual act through self-control, which is a fruit of the Holy Spirit, and is granted a person through the aid of prayer.

contraception Various methods of preventing pregnancy that are intended to alter or prevent the body's natural state of fertility. Examples include condoms, "the pill" (artificial hormones that render women infertile as long as they are taken), and the intrauterine device. Use of contraceptions are intrinsically evil and against the teachings of the Church. Some products marketed and sold as contraception, such as Depo-Provera, really function as abortifacients.

convalidation Making an invalid marriage valid in the Church through new expression of the spouses' consent; sometimes referred to as the blessing of a marriage. The word *convalidation* derives from a Latin word for "firm up" or "strengthen."

covenant "A solemn agreement between human beings or between God and a human being involving mutual commitments or guarantees" (*CCC*, Glossary).

de facto union The occasion of an unmarried couple living together, usually for an extended amount of time.

Deposit of Faith The body of saving truths and the core beliefs of Catholicism that are contained in Sacred Scripture and Sacred Tradition and faithfully preserved and handed on by the Magisterium. The Deposit of Faith contains the fullness of God's Revelation.

detraction Disclosure of another's faults and sins, without an objectively valid reason, to persons who did not know about them, thus causing unjust injury to that person's reputation (see *CCC*, 2477).

direct abortion The direct or deliberate and intentional killing of unborn life by means of medical or surgical procedures.

direct sterilization A direct or deliberate medical or surgical procedure that leaves a person unable to reproduce.

discernment The process of discovering what God wants of you in a given situation.

disciple A person "who accepted Jesus' message to follow him. . . . Jesus associated his disciples with his own life, revealed the mystery of the Kingdom of God to [them], and gave them a share in his mission, his joy, and his sufferings" (*CCC*, Glossary).

disposition An interior and exterior attitude that reflects openness to receiving the graces of a sacrament.

Divine Economy The name for the divine plan of salvation. "The ultimate end of the whole divine economy is the entry of God's creatures into the perfect unity of the Blessed Trinity" (*CCC*, 260).

domestic church *Ecclesia domestica*, a name for the family that signifies a miniature Church.

Eastern Churches "Churches of the East in union with Rome (the Latin Church), but not of Roman rite, with their own liturgical, theological, and administrative traditions," such as those of the Byzantine, Coptic, and Syriac rites (*CCC*, Glossary).

ecumenical council An assembly of representatives from the entire Church for consultation on Church matters. There have been twenty-one ecumenical councils. The first was the First Council of Nicaea (325). The most recent was the Second Vatican Council (1962–1965).

efficacious Effecting or accomplishing that which a thing represents.

epiclesis The prayer, said in every sacrament, petitioning God to send down the sanctifying power of the Holy Spirit (see *CCC*, Glossary).

eschatological sign Something that points to eternal life.

evangelical counsels "In general, the teachings of the New Law proposed by Jesus to his disciples which lead to the perfection of Christian life. . . . The public profession of the evangelical counsels of poverty, chastity, and obedience is a constitutive element of state of consecrated life in the Church" (*CCC*, Glossary).

evangelize To proclaim "Christ and his Gospel (Greek *evangelion*) by word and the testimony of life, in fulfillment of Christ's command" (*CCC*, Glossary).

express dispensation A permission granted by the Church releasing a person from following a canonical requirement, such as a certain impediment to a valid marriage.

fecundity Fruitfulness. In relation to marriage, fecundity refers to procreation and education of children as one of the promises of marriage.

fidelity Faithfulness. In relation to marriage, fidelity refers to one of the promises of marriage. Both spouses "give of themselves definitely and totally to one another. They are no longer two; from now on they form one flesh. The covenant they freely contracted imposes on the spouses the obligation to preserve it as unique and indissoluble" (*CCC*, 2364).

fornication "Sexual intercourse between an unmarried man and unmarried woman. Fornication is a serious violation of the Sixth Commandment of God" (*CCC*, Glossary).

free will The capacity to choose among alternatives. Free will is "the power, rooted in reason and will . . . to perform deliberate actions on one's own responsibility" (*CCC*, 1731). True freedom is at the service of what is good and true.

fruits of the Holy Spirit "The perfections that the Holy Spirit forms in us as the 'first fruits' of eternal glory. The tradition of the Church identifies twelve fruits of the Holy Spirit: charity, joy, peace, patience, kindness, goodness, generosity, gentleness, faithfulness, modesty, self-control, and chastity" (*CCC*, Glossary).

hermits Those who separate themselves from the world in prayer and penance in order to be devoted to the praise of God and the salvation of the world.

holiness The state of being set apart for God.

Holy Family The family of Jesus, Mary, and Joseph in which Jesus was raised and lived until he began his public ministry.

impediments External circumstances or facts that make a person ineligible for entering into a sacramental or legal marriage.

in vitro fertilization The achievement of pregnancy without sexual intercourse through collecting eggs from a mother and fertilizing them with sperm outside of the womb.

indissolubility Permanence. In relation to marriage, indissolubility means that a marriage cannot be dissolved either by the withdrawal of consent of the married partners or by civil authorities.

individualism The philosophy that places the private interests of each person above the common good of society. It is often practiced by sacrificing social values and norms to the personal desires of individuals.

infallibility "The gift of the Holy Spirit to the Church whereby the pastors of the Church, the pope and bishops in union with him, can definitively proclaim a doctrine of faith or morals for the belief of the faithful. This gift is related to the inability of the whole body of the faithful to err in matters of faith and morals" (*CCC*, Glossary).

infertility The inability on the part of a male or female to achieve pregnancy.

laity All the baptized faithful except those who have received the Sacrament of Holy Orders or who have taken solemn vows in consecrated life.

Latin Church The vast majority of the Roman Catholic Church which uses the Latin Rite liturgies and has its own distinctive canon law.

law of self-giving The principle that encapsulates one's call to communion and self-donation with another. It means that you can discover your true self only through a sincere gift of self (cf. *Gaudium et Spes*, 24).

lay ecclesial movements Associations of laypersons who come together with a common purpose and way of life.

lectio divina A classical prayer practice that involves a reflective reading of the Bible. It means "holy reading."

Litany of the Saints A prayer made up of various petitions addressed to the saints. It was first prescribed by St. Gregory the Great in the sixth century.

Liturgy of the Hours The official daily prayer of the Church, also called the Divine Office. It is a set of prayers for certain times of the day that carries out St. Paul's command to "pray without ceasing" (1 Thes 5:17).

Magisterium The official teaching authority of the Church. Jesus bestowed the right and power to teach in his name on Peter and the Apostles and their successors—that is, the pope and the college of bishops. The authority of the Magisterium extends to specific precepts of the natural law because following these precepts is necessary for salvation.

ministerial priesthood The priesthood of Christ, consisting of priests and bishops, received in the Sacrament of Holy Orders. Its purpose is to serve the common priesthood by building up and guiding the Church in the name of Christ.

monks Male members of a monastic or contemplative order.

Mosaic Law The laws, beginning with the Ten Commandments, that God gave to Moses for the Israelites. It includes rules for ritual religious observance as well as rules for everyday life.

Natural Family Planning (NFP) A method approved by the Church for naturally planning and spacing the birth of children in marriage that honors the unitive and procreative purposes of the sexual act.

nuns Women religious living a cloistered, contemplative life in a monastery.

nuptial blessing "Prayers for the blessing of a couple being married, especially of the bride," after the couple have given their consent to be married (*CCC*, Glossary).

Original Sin The personal sin of the first two people, called Adam and Eve, which in an analogous way describes the fallen state of human nature into which all generations are born. Adam and Eve transmitted Original Sin to their human descendants. Christ Jesus came to save the world from Original Sin and all personal sin.

Paschal Mystery Christ's work of redemption accomplished through his Passion, Death, Resurrection, and Ascension. It is celebrated and made present in the liturgy of the Church (see *CCC*, Glossary).

permanent deacons Ordained deacons who will permanently remain deacons.

personalism A philosophical movement that emphasizes the meaning and value of human persons and their relationality to each other and God.

primacy The authority of the bishop of Rome—the pope—over the entire universal Church.

primary vocation (state of life) The specific path God has for someone on his path to holiness. Primary vocations are marked by vows and/or a sacrament. The traditionally recognized primary vocations are marriage, priesthood, and the consecrated life.

procreation The cooperation of a married couple with God to bring about new life through sexual intercourse.

rectory The house in which a pastor and other parish priests live.

redemption A word that literally means "ransom"; the act of Christ in which he paid the price of his own sacrificial Death on the Cross to ransom, or set free, the world from the slavery of sin.

religious brothers Men who take religious vows, usually vows of poverty, chastity, and obedience. A brother is not ordained to the priesthood.

religious sisters Members of a religious order or congregation of women devoted to active service and/or contemplation. Members typically take vows of poverty, chastity and obedience.

religious superior The head or leader of a religious community charged with cultivating in the members of the community obedience to God's will, the Church, and the rules of the community.

sacrament "An efficacious sign of grace, instituted by Christ and entrusted to the Church, by which divine life is" given to those who receive it, "through the work of the Holy Spirit" (*CCC*, 1131).

saint "The 'holy one' who leads a life in union with God through the grace of Christ and receives the reward of eternal life. The Church is called the communion of saints, of the holy ones" (*CCC*, Glossary).

seminarians Men who attend a seminary or school focusing on theology and training and formation for the life of a priest.

sperm or egg donation The giving of sperm or eggs from a donor to a person who is not a sexual partner for the purpose of achieving pregnancy.

stole A long narrow cloth that comes in the color of the liturgical season and is worn by the bishop, priest, or deacon. Stoles were originally worn by Jewish rabbis as a sign of their authority.

surrogacy A prearranged legal contract in which a woman carries another person or person's child.

the Fall The disobedience of Adam and Eve, which introduced sin, death, and their effects into the world.

transitional deacons Ordained deacons who are only deacons temporarily as a step to becoming priests.

unilateral divorce A divorce in which one spouse contracts the divorce without the consent of the other spouse.

universal call to holiness The call to all Christians, no matter their state of life, to be sanctified. It is based on Jesus' words in the Sermon on the Mount: "So be perfect, just as your heavenly Father is perfect" (Mt 5:48).

vocation The calling or destiny one has in this life and hereafter.

vows Acts of devotion in which a person dedicates himself or herself to God or promises God some good work. A vow is "a deliberate and free promise made to God concerning a possible and better good which must be fulfilled by reason of the virtue of religion" (*CCC*, Glossary). Religious women and men typically take vows of poverty, chastity, and obedience.

Notes

Introduction: Calling You to Commitment

1. John Paul II, quoted in "World Youth Day—Frequently Asked Questions," United States Conference of Catholic Bishops website, http://www.usccb.org/about/world-youth-day/faqs.cfm.

2. Sherry Weddell, *Forming Intentional Disciples: The Path to Knowing and Following Jesus* (Huntington, IN: Our Sunday Visitor, 2012), 33.

1. Your Call to Holiness

1. Knights of Columbus and In Defense of Christians, *Genocide against Christians in the Middle East*, March 9, 2016, http://stopthechristiangenocide.org/scg/en/resources/Genocide-report.pdf, 10.

2. Joyce Coronel, "Tortured Priest Will Speak in Phoenix, Raise Support for Persecuted Christians," *The Catholic Sun*, April 22, 2016, http://www.catholicsun.org/2016/04/22/fr-bazi.

3. Matt Hadro, "House Backs Genocide Label for Christians under ISIS," Catholic News Agency, March 14, 2016, http://www.catholicnewsagency.com/news/house-backs-genocide-label-for-christians-under-isis-96950.

4. Benedict XVI, Message to the Second World Congress of Ecclesial Movements and New Communities, Vatican City: Libreria Editrice Vaticana, May 22, 2006, https://w2.vatican.va/content/benedict-xvi/en/messages/pont-messages/2006/documents/hf_ben-xvi_mes_20060522_ecclesial-movements.html.

5. Robert Barron, "The God Who Is Love," *Word on Fire* website, June 19, 2011, http://www.wordonfire.org/resources/homily/the-god-who-is-love/932.

6. Mike Schmitz, "Discerning Your Vocation," University of Minnesota Duluth Newman Center website, May 1, 2015, http://bulldogcatholic.org/discerning-your-vocation.

7. John Paul II, Message for the 37th World Day of Prayer for Vocations, Vatican City: Libreria Editrice Vaticana, May 14, 2000, https://w2.vatican.va/content/john-paul-ii/en/messages/vocations/documents/hf_jp-ii_mes_30091999_xxxvii-voc-2000.html.

2. The Vocation to Marriage

1. K. V. Turley, "Saints Are Still Being Made," *Crisis Magazine*, October 6, 2015, http://www.crisismagazine.com/2015/saints-are-still-being-made.

2. United States Conference of Catholic Bishops, "What Makes Marriage Work," For Your Marriage website, accessed May 18, 2016, http://www.foryourmarriage.org/everymarriage/what-makes-marriage-work.

3. United States Conference of Catholic Bishops, "What Are the Social Benefits of Marriage?" For Your Marriage website, accessed May 18, 2016, http://www.foryourmarriage.org/blogs/social-benefits-marriage.

4. "About" page, Theology of the Body Institute website, accessed May 25, 2016, http://tobinstitute.org/about.

5. Edith Stein, "Letter to Sister Callista Kopf," in *Self Portrait in Letters 1916–1942* (Washington, DC: ICS Publications, 1993), 99, quoted in Prudence Allen, "Man-Woman Complementary: The Catholic Inspiration," *Logos* 9, no. 3 (Summer 2006): 93.

6. Anne Hendershott and Nicholas Dunn, "The 'Hook-Up' Culture on Catholic Campuses: A Review of the Literature," *Studies in Catholic Higher Education* (June 2011), https://cardinalnewmansociety.org/hook-culture-catholic-campuses-review-literature.

3. The Celebration of the Sacrament of Matrimony

1. "Diriment Impediments in General," *Code of Canon Law* (Vatican City: Libreria Editrice Vaticana,

1983), bk. 4, pt. 1, title 7, chap. 2, http://www.vatican.va/archive/ENG1104/_P3X.HTM.

4. The Christian Family in God's Plan

1. John Paul II, Homily in Perth, Australia, November 30, 1986, https://w2.vatican.va/content/john-paul-ii/en/homilies/1986/documents/hf_jp-ii_hom_19861130_perth-australia.html.

2. Jeffery Fraser, "For Children without Parents, Risks Abound," *OCD Developments* 26, no. 1 (May 2012), https://www.ocd.pitt.edu/For-Children-without-Parents-Risks-Abound/249/default.aspx.

3. Mercedes Arzú Wilson, "The Practice of Natural Family Planning versus the Use of Artificial Birth Control: Family, Sexual, and Moral Issues," *Catholic Social Science Review* 7 (2002): 185–211.

4. Christopher West, *Theology of the Body Explained* (Boston: Pauline Press, 2003), 103.

5. Eliza Cook and Rachel Dunifon, "Do Family Meals Really Make a Difference?," Parenting in Context series (Ithaca, NY: Cornell University College of Human Ecology, 2012), http://www.human.cornell.edu/pam/outreach/upload/Family-Mealtimes-2.pdf.

6. National Conference of Catholic Bishops, *To Teach as Jesus Did: A Pastoral Message on Catholic Education* (Washington, DC: USCCB, 1972), 101.

7. Karen Mahoney, "Family Enjoys Triple Dose of Divinity," Archdiocese of Milwaukee *Catholic Herald*, April 12, 2012, http://catholicherald.org/news/local/family-enjoys-triple-dose-of-divinity.

5. Challenges to Marriage and Family Life

1. Elizabeth Scalia, "A Single Phrase Helped Save My Marriage," *Aleteia*, September 24, 2016, http://aleteia.org/2016/09/24/a-single-a-phrase-helped-save-my-marriage.

2. Centers for Disease Control, "Unmarried Childbearing," National Center for Health Statistics website, accessed October 16, 2019, https://www.cdc.gov/nchs/fastats/unmarried-childbearing.htm.

3. Cindy Wooten, "Too Many Couples Do Not Understand Marriage Is for Life, Pope Says," Catholic News Service, June 17, 2016, http://www.catholicnews.com/services/englishnews/2016/too-many-couples-do-not-understand-marriage-is-for-life-pope-says.cfm.

4. These points were made by Archbishop Charles J. Chaput in a pastoral letter "Of Human Life: On the Truth and Meaning of Married Love," July 22, 1998, https://www.ewtn.com/library/BISHOPS/CHAPUTHV.HTM.

5. Linda Waite and Maggie Gallagher, *The Case for Marriage* (New York: Doubleday, 2001), 148–49.

6. Mark M. Gray, "Divorce Still Less Likely Among Catholics," *Nineteen Sixty Four* (blog), September 23, 2016, http://nineteensixty-four.blogspot.com/2013/09/divorce-still-less-likely-among.html.

7. Francis, *The Name of God Is Mercy* (New York: Random House, 2016), 62.

8. United States Conference of Catholic Bishops, "Made for Each Other" (Washington, DC: USCCB, 2010), audiovisual file, http://www.marriageuniqueforareason.org/sexual-difference-video.

9. Alysse ElHage, "For Kids, Parental Cohabitation and Marriage Are Not Interchangeable," Institute for Family Studies blog, May 7, 2015, http://family-studies.org/for-kids-parental-cohabitation-and-marriage-are-not-interchangeable.

10. United States Conference of Catholic Bishops, *Marriage Preparation and Cohabiting Couples* (Washington, DC: United States Catholic Conference, 1999), http://www.usccb.org/issues-and-action/marriage-and-family/marriage/marriage-preparation/cohabiting.cfm.

11. Bishops of Pennsylvania, "Living Together: Questions and Answers Regarding Cohabitation and the Church's Moral Teaching," September 1999, reproduced on Catholic News Agency website, http://www.catholicnewsagency.com/resources/life-and-family/marriage/cohabitation-and-churchs-teaching.

12. Bishops of Pennsylvania, "Living Together: Questions and Answers Regarding Cohabitation and the Church's Moral Teaching."

6. The Vocation to Holy Orders

1. Tertullian, *De praescriptione haereticorum* [*The Prescription against Heretics*], chap. 21.

2. Wilton Gregory, "Teach, Govern and Sanctify the Lord's People," *The Georgia Bulletin*, October 1, 2009, https://georgiabulletin.org/commentary/2009/10/teach-govern-sanctify-lords-people.

3. Fulton Sheen, *The Priest Is Not His Own* (New York: McGraw-Hill, 1963), 78.

4. Mike Amodei, "The Parish Priest in the Year of the Priest," *Engaging Faith* (blog), June 24, 2009, https://www.avemariapress.com/engagingfaith/2009/06/parish-priest-in-year-of-priest.

5. Stephen J. Rossetti, *The Joy of Priesthood* (Notre Dame, IN: Ave Maria Press, 2005), 26.

6. Rossetti, *The Joy of Priesthood*, 26.

7. The Celebration of the Sacrament of Holy Orders

1. Kathleen Glavich, *Called to Love* (Notre Dame, IN: Ave Maria Press, 2000), 33.

2. Catholic Diocese of Lansing Department of Vocations, "Priest Discernment Stories," accessed January 26, 2019, http://www.dioceseoflansing.org/vocations/priest-discernment-stories.

3. Archdiocese of Washington Office of Priest Vocations, "Vocation Stories," accessed January 26, 2019, http://www.dcpriest.org/meet-us/stories-and-videos/702-vocation-stories-702.

4. United States Conference of Catholic Bishops, "An Understanding of 'Discernment,'" accessed October 17, 2019, http://www.usccb.org/beliefs-and-teachings/vocations/upload/vocations-understanding-discernment.pdf.

5. United States Conference of Catholic Bishops, *Program of Priestly Formation*, 5th ed. (Washington, DC: USCCB, 2006), para. 33, http://www.usccb.org/upload/program-priestly-formation-fifth-edition.pdf.

6. United States Conference of Catholic Bishops, *Program of Priestly Formation*, para. 37.

7. United States Conference of Catholic Bishops, *Program of Priestly Formation*, para. 68.

8. United States Conference of Catholic Bishops, *Program of Priestly Formation*, para. 238.

9. Tom Hoopes, "Seminarian Who Drowned While Saving Kayaker 'Lived and Died a Priestly Life,'" *National Catholic Register*, September 15, 2016, http://www.ncregister.com/daily-news/a-most-priestly-life.

8. The Vocation to Consecrated Life

1. Pat Archbold, "Beautiful Model Gives Up Flourishing Career to Become Nun," *National Catholic Register* blog, June 11, 2014, http://www.ncregister.com/blog/pat-archbold/beautiful-model-gives-up-flourishing-career-to-become-nun.

2. Catholic News Agency, "Former Colombian Model Shares Conversion Story," May 25, 2010, http://www.catholicnewsagency.com/news/former-colombian-model-shares-conversion-story.

3. Helena Burns, "What Is It Like Being Married to Jesus?" *The Berkley Forum*, November 5, 2014, https://berkleycenter.georgetown.edu/forum/what-is-it-like-being-married-to-jesus.

4. *The Catholic Encyclopedia*, 2nd ed., s.v. "Rule of St. Augustine," by Jean Besse, accessed September 6, 2017, http://www.newadvent.org/cathen/02079b.htm.

5. Christina Capecchi, "From Harvard to the Convent: I Am the Bride of Christ" Sister-Story, accessed January 24, 2019, https://www.sisterstory.org/story/community-education/harvard-convent-i-am-bride-christ.

6. Capecchi, "From Harvard to the Convent: I Am the Bride of Christ."

7. "Chastity: Love without Limits," Sisters of Life, accessed June 13, 2019, https://www.sistersoflife.org/vocations/chastity-love-without-limits.

8. Timothy M. Dolan, *Priests for the Third Millennium* (Huntington, IN: Our Sunday Visitor, 2009).

9. "Teresian Charism," Carmelite Monastery, accessed September 6, 2017, http://heartsawake.org/spirituality/teresian-charism.

10. Stephen J. Rossetti, *Why Priests Are Happy* (Notre Dame, IN: Ave Maria Press, 2011).

SUBJECT INDEX

sperm donation, 157
Spiritual Exercises, 315
spiritual fecundity, 157
St. Paul's Outreach (SPO), 13
Stec, Robert, Fr., 269
Stephen, St., 253, 257
sterilization, 155, 170
stoles, 282
storge, 75
Strand, Jerry and Bernadette, 168
success, 21
surrogacy, 157

T

Teens Encounter Christ, 351
temporal affairs, 45–46
temporary profession, 331, 336
Teresa of Avila, St., 318
Teresa of Calcutta, St., 166, 328, 349, 350
Theology of the Body, 82
Thérèse of Lisieux, St., 35–36, 56, 344–345
Thomas Aquinas, St., 231, 314, 325
titular bishops, 240
Trinity, 29, 33, 50–51, 73–74, 93, 145

U

unilateral divorce, 190
United States Conference of Catholic Bishops, 195–196, 199, 271, 351
unity, in the sexual act, 83–85, 153, 157
universal call to holiness, 33, 56
universities, 13, 349–350

V

vertical dimensions, 7, 15
Vincent de Paul, St., 315
vocations
    vs. careers, 7–8, 15
    complementarity of, 46
    defined, 4, 38–39
    family life as a source of, 166–168, 172, 270–271
    guides, 351–352

and the law of self-giving, 51–53, 57
lived in the church, 39–40
lived through discipleship, 40
to the priesthood, 269–271, 295
primary, 4, 57
"supernatural," 344
Vocations Week, planning, 53
volunteer service, 350–351
vows, 308

W

Wendling, Mark, Fr., 267
will, of God, 41
women
    as deaconesses, 252
    equality of, 264
    nuns, 315. *See also* consecrated life
Woolos, St., 125
World Youth Days, 1, 4, 32

Z

Zarama, Luis, Bishop, 235
Zélie Martin, St., 133

PRIMARY SOURCE INDEX

SCRIPTURE INDEX

OLD TESTAMENT

PHOTO CREDITS